Alfred de Musset
Five Plays

The Moods of Marianne
Fantasio, Lorenzaccio,
Don't Play With Love, Caprice

After Molière and Corneille, Alfred de Musset (1810–57) is the
most frequently performed playwright at the Comédie-Française.
An infant prodigy of French romanticism and much inspired by
Shakespeare and Schiller, he wrote the first modern dramas in
the French language. This anthology brings together the best of
Musset theatre, which is also some of the best of French theatre
of the nineteenth century. The translations in this edition, by
Michael Sadler, Brian Singleton and Donald Watson, are all
previously unpublished and include *Don't Play With Love*,
revived in 1993 on BBC Radio Three. Selected and introduced
by Claude Schumacher, Reader in French Theatre Studies at
Glasgow University, this is the first substantial collection of
Musset's work to be made available in English translation.

ALFRED DE MUSSET

Five Plays

The Moods of Marianne
translated by Donald Watson

Fantasio
translated by Brian Singleton

Lorenzaccio
translated by Donald Watson

Don't Play With Love
translated by Michael Sadler

Caprice
translated by Donald Watson

edited and introduced by Claude Schumacher

Methuen Drama

METHUEN WORLD CLASSICS

This edition was first published in Great Britain in 1995
by Methuen Drama
Methuen Publishing Ltd
215 Vauxhall Bridge Road
London SW1V 1EJ

www.methuen.co.uk

Methuen Publishing Ltd reg. number 3543167

The front cover self-portrait by Alfred de Musset reproduced courtesy of the
Bibliothèque Nationale de France, Paris

ISBN 0 413 69240 X

A CIP catalogue record for this book is available at the British Library

Typeset by Wilmaset Ltd, Birkenhead, Wirral
Transferred to digital printing 2002

Contents

Chronology

1810   11 December, birth of Louis Charles Alfred de
Musset, in Paris. [His elder brother Paul – who
was Alfred's closest friend and who became after
the poet's death his 'literary agent', editor and
biographer – was born in 1804.]

1819–27 Excellent student at the Collège Henry-IV in
Paris; shows keen interest in music and drawing.

1828   Beginning of a busy social, amorous and literary
life. In October, publication of a free translation
of Thomas De Quincey's *Confessions of an
English Opium-Eater* (1822), under the title
L'Anglais mangeur d'opium. Befriends the poets
Prosper Mérimée, Alfred de Vigny, the painter
Eugène Delacroix, and is introduced by the critic
Charles-Augustin Sainte-Beuve into the literary
coterie known as the 'cénacle' presided by
Charles Nodier and Victor Hugo.

1829   Public readings of his poetry at the cénacle.
December, publication of his first verse drama,
Les Marrons du feu.

1830   The Théâtre des Nouveautés accepts his short
drama inspired by Walter Scott, *La Quittance du
diable* (The Devil's Receipt), but the play is
never performed nor published in Musset's
lifetime (first publication in *La Revue blanche*,
May 1914). 1 December, first of two disastrous
performances of *La Nuit vénitienne* (The
Venetian Night) at the Théâtre de l'Odéon,

Paris. Musset vows never to write for the stage
again (see 'Early Stage History'). October 1830 to
June 1831, theatre and literary critic for the daily
Le Temps.

1832   December, publications of two verse plays, *La
Coupe et les Lèvres* (Twixt Cup and Lip) and *A
quoi rêvent les jeunes filles* (Such Stuff as Young
Girls Dream On) and of a dramatic
'improvisation', *Namouna*, subtitled 'an oriental
tale' under the general title of *Un spectacle dans
un fauteuil* (Armchair Theatre), clearly showing
that the plays were written without any
concessions to stage conventions.

1833   15 March, beginning of Musset's long
collaboration with the literary journal *La Revue
des Deux Mondes (RDM)*. 1 April, publication of
André del Sarto. 2 April, Musset signs a contract
with Buloz, *RDM*'s director, giving the journal
the exclusivity of all his writings. Until 1852,
when Musset all but gives up literary creation,
the *RDM* publishes his plays, poems, essays,
short stories, criticism . . . 15 May, publication
of *Les Caprices de Marianne* (The Moods of
Marianne). June, meets George Sand. 29 July,
Musset and George Sand become lovers. August–
December, writing of *Fantasio* and *Lorenzaccio*.

1834   1 January, publication of *Fantasio*. February,
during his stay in Venice with George Sand,
Musset falls desperately ill. At first his mistress
nurses him with devotion, but soon she starts an
affair with the poet's physician, Pietro Pagello.
29 March, Musset, alone, returns to Paris.
Passionate correspondence between the lovers. 1
July, publication of *On ne badine pas avec
l'amour* (Don't Play With Love). 23 August,
publication of two further (prose) volumes of *Un
spectacle dans un fauteuil*, comprising *Lorenzaccio*

and *Les Caprices de Marianne* (Vol. 1), and
*Fantasio, On ne badine pas avec l'amour, André
del Sarto* and *La Nuit vénitienne* (Vol. 2).

1835   1 August, publication of *La Quenouille de
Barberine* (Barberine's Spindle). 1 November,
publication of *Le Chandelier* (The Candlestick, or
Hidden Fires).

1836   1 January, publication of one of Musset's major
works, his autobiographical novel, *La Confession
d'un enfant du siècle* (A Modern Man's
Confession). 1 July, publication of *Il ne faut jurer
de rien* (Don't Swear on Anything).

1837   15 June, publication of *Un caprice* (Caprice).

1838   1 November and 1 December, publication of two
important reviews in *RDM*, putting forward a
theory of 'modern tragedy'.

1839   By the age of twenty-nine, Musset has written all
his major works. Although he added a few
poems, short stories and two or three minor
plays, the quality of his later work never attained
the soaring beauty achieved in most of Musset's
writing during the four short years from 1833 to
1837. His health deteriorated steadily, due
principally to his heavy drinking.

1845   24 April, the 'ageing' poet joins the establishment:
he is made Chevalier de la Légion d'honneur. 1
November, publication of *Il faut qu'une porte soit
ouverte ou fermée* (You Can't Have It Both Ways or
A Door Must Be Open or Shut).

1847–53 Musset's theatre is, at last, performed, but the
innovative playwright is forced a) to 'revise' his
plays structurally, and b) to tone down his
'unacceptable amoralism' in order to bring them
into line with the taste and prejudices of his
audience. It must be said that the 'ageing' poet
willingly censored his youthful work.

1849   22 February, first performance of *Louison*, a comedy in verse, recently written *for* the stage (first published in 1853).

1850   22 October–6 November, publication of a new play, *Carmosine*.

1851   1 November, publication of Musset's last play, *Bettine*.

1852   12 February, Musset is elected member of the Académie française, the ultimate 'Establishment' accolade for a French writer. 27 May, Musset's official reception at the Académie française.

1853   23 July, publication of the *Collected Plays* by Charpentier, in the 'bowdlerized stage versions' for the plays performed during Musset's lifetime.

1857   2 May, Musset dies in Paris. His last words: 'Dormir! . . . enfin je vais dormir.' ('To sleep! . . . at last I'm going to sleep.')

Early Stage History

1830   1 December, *La Nuit vénitienne* is performed at the Théâtre de l'Odéon. The play is booed and laughed off the stage after the second performance. Musset is determined never to write for the theatre again, but to let his imagination invent with total freedom when writing plays inspired by Shakespeare and Schiller, and to reject the straitjacket of French neoclassical rules.

1837   8 December, a Russian translation of *Un caprice* is performed with great success at the Alexandrevski Theatre of St Petersburg.

1843   4 December. *Un caprice* is again performed successfully in St Petersburg, at the Michel Theatre, in the original French, with Madame Allan in the role of Madame de Léry.

1847   27 November, Madame Allan plays the part she created in Russia at the Comédie-Française, under the direction of Buloz (Musset's publisher at the *Revue des Deux Mondes*). *Un caprice* is a great success in Paris and Buloz schedules further creations of Musset's plays.

1848   This is Musset's triumphant year! 7 April, *Il faut qu'une porte soit ouverte ou fermée*, at the Comédie-Française (then known as the Théâtre de la République).
22 June, *Il ne faut jurer de rien*, at the Comédie-Française (Théâtre de la République).

10 August, *Le Chandelier*, at the Théâtre
Historique, Paris.
21 November, *André del Sarto*, at the Comédie-
Française.

1849   22 February, *Louison*, at the Comédie-Française.
23 February [*sic*], *L'Habit vert*, farce written in
collaboration with Émile Augier, at the Théâtre
des Variétés.
30 May, *On ne saurait penser à tout*, at the
Comédie-Française.

1850   29 June, *Le Chandelier*, at the Comédie-Française
(censorship having been restored in late July, the
show was forced to close on 30 September).

1851   14 June, *Les Caprices de Marianne*, at the
Comédie-Française.
21 October, *André del Sarto*, at the Théâtre de
l'Odéon.
30 October, *Bettine*, at the Théâtre du Gymnase.

After Musset's death, theatre directors lost interest in his
work, despite his brother's desperate efforts to have his
plays performed. The Comédie-Française performed *On ne
badine pas avec l'amour* in 1861 (18 November) and
Fantasio in 1866 (18 August), in heavily edited versions
due to Paul de Musset. Although the idea of staging
Lorenzaccio was foremost in Paul's mind (he had also
concocted a stage version of the masterpiece), it had to
wait another 100 years before it would be produced in the
spirit it had been conceived. Its first performance was a
travesty: Sarah Bernhardt, then already fifty-two years old,
fancied herself in yet another breeches part (of a virile
adolescent!) and asked Armand d'Artois to write an
adaptation for her. The play was premièred at Sarah
Bernhardt's own theatre, the Théâtre de la Renaissance,
on 3 December 1896, '*Lorenzaccio* or Lorenza surrounded
by the shadows of Musset's characters'. Sixteen years
later, in 1912, then aged sixty-eight, she revived the play!

Unfortunately the great star inaugurated a theatrical 'tradition' and other, less famous, actresses were tempted by the part. Even the first production at the Comédie-Française, in 1927, had an actress, the 'sweet' and 'chubby' Marie-Thérèse Peirat impersonating the regicide of whom she 'had neither the voice nor the physique'. The first actor to interpret Lorenzo at the Comédie-Française was Claude Rich in 1976, but the most memorable Lorenzaccio to date remains Gérard Philipe (1922–59) who played the part over one hundred times at the Théâtre National Populaire, under the direction of Jean Vilar, between 1952 and his untimely death in 1959.

Introduction

'I should like to be Shakespeare or Schiller,' wrote Alfred de Musset to a school friend, in 1827, a few months before his seventeenth birthday – adding, 'that is why I do nothing.'

Musset? Who is Musset? Is his name recognized outside France? How is it pronounced, anyway? (*Mys'* – with equal stress on both syllables; the 'de' to be used only in conjunction with his first name, or in the polite form 'Monsieur de Musset'.)

The nineteenth century was the century of the theatre: for the first time in Western history a large, popular, 'uneducated' section of the population could afford to go to the theatre and theatre directors, like today's television bosses, catered for the perceived taste of the populace with an over production of melodramas, vaudeville, farces . . . And never had there been so many 'affluent' members of the bourgeoisie, high and low, whose only public entertainment was the theatre and the opera. Never were there so many new plays presented on Parisian stages; never were there so many revivals. But, despite the wealth of theatrical activity in France throughout the nineteenth century, hardly any play of enduring literary or theatrical value was written at the time. Alexandre Dumas *fils' The Lady of the Camellias* (1852) still has some dubious appeal and Edmond Rostand's boisterous *Cyrano de Bergerac* (1897) is revived at irregular intervals, even outside France. Both plays have a very strong central character, the expensive prostitute Marguerite Gautier and the long-nosed Cyrano, and as star vehicles they are extremely tempting. The most famous performances in recent years are screen adaptations: Isabelle Huppert as Marguerite (1980), Gérard Depardieu as Cyrano (1990). Yet the most universally performed of all nineteenth-century

French plays is Alfred Jarry's 'scandalous' *Ubu roi* (1896) now regarded by theatre historians as well as directors and actors as one of the cornerstones of modern theatre. *Ubu* is still youthful, suffused with anarchic energy and inspirational to enterprising and innovative directors who see theatre as the art of the living actor. These three plays belong to the world repertoire and are generally recognized as 'landmarks' of Western theatre; although only *Ubu* had a lasting effect on dramatic writing and theatrical presentation. Three plays . . . not much of a harvest for the city which was, for decades, hailed as the undisputed world capital of culture . . . These three plays do not place their authors into the Pantheon of great playwrights, and only Jarry is of lasting importance.

Why then, in this theatrical wasteland, do Musset's towering achievements attract nothing more than a footnote in Anglo-American histories of the theatre, if he is not altogether ignored?

As this volume abundantly shows, Musset wrote plays that can be placed alongside those of the greatest world dramatists. His peers, in France, are Corneille, Molière and Racine in the seventeenth century, Marivaux and Beaumarchais in the eighteenth, and he stands alone in the nineteenth. If he does not equal Shakespeare (who does?), he compares most favourably with Schiller. The reason for the critical neglect outside France must be found in the poor reception his plays received during his lifetime and also, I suspect, because of his 'quintessential Frenchness' which leads theatre people and spectators to think that the literary quality of the original will be irremediably lost in translation and that the same Frenchness is synonymous with lack of theatrical quality. It is our hope that the new translations offered here will help to destroy such prejudices and that, before long, English-speaking audiences will be able to find out *in the theatre* as well as in these pages why the French revive Musset's plays more and more often, in ever more lavish and theatrically more exciting productions.

On 28 July 1830, Alfred and his brother, Paul de Musset, rejoiced at the fall of the Bourbon dynasty at the end of three days of rebellion (the 'Trois Glorieuses'), but they were soon disenchanted by the accession of Louis-Philippe, the 'bourgeois king', who killed all romantic ideals and institutionalized the reign of selfish bourgeois values exemplified by money-grabbing bankers and industrialists. Later that year, on 1 December 1830, just ten days before his twentieth birthday, Musset's first play, *La Nuit vénitienne*, was produced at the Théâtre de l'Odéon, the most prestigious Parisian theatre after the Comédie-Française. The play was misunderstood by all sections of the public: even the Romantics started to boo and whistle almost the moment the curtain went up. The disaster seems to have been inevitable, and the débâcle turned into farce when the juvenile lead covered her white dress in green paint after leaning against a balustrade, for the greatest joy of a hostile public. As for Jarry with *Ubu roi* or, more recently, Beckett with *Waiting for Godot*, Musset was charged with having written a hoax and, moreover, a play that 'is not theatre'. After such a failure, Musset was determined to ignore the tyrannical stage conventions inherited from seventeenth-century neoclassical theatre (the rules of decorum and verisimilitude, and the so-called 'three unities'), and to give his imagination free rein in writing his 'armchair theatre', his *'spectacle dans un fauteuil'*. (With the exception of *Caprice* the plays of our anthology were published as *Un spectacle dans un fauteuil*.)

All the plays in our selection were completed during the short period between 1833 and 1837. Musset did not attempt to have them performed and there is no record of any French theatre director showing any interest, although *Un caprice* was staged in St Petersburg, in a Russian translation, less than six months after its original publication. It will be ten years, almost to the day, before the same play will be staged in France, thanks to the appointment of Musset's publisher, Buloz, as director of the Comédie-Française. Following the very successful initial run of *Un caprice* (incidentally Musset himself considered that this one-acter was his only 'stageable' play without prior revisions), nine more plays were staged in the space of four years (see 'Early Stage History').

Musset is the first 'modern' playwright in the French theatre in that he places himself and his individual idiosyncrasies in the middle of the dramatic fiction and as the main – and often only – subject of the play. His love life is, in many respects, the main if not the only source of his inspiration. In this autobiographical novel, *La Confession d'un enfant du siècle*, he describes how he felt cruelly betrayed by his first mistress and how, after that initial act of betrayal, he was unable to trust any woman, however deeply he was in love with her. Towering over all other love affairs was his passion for the feminist novelist, George Sand (1804–76), whom he first met in June 1833 and with whom he had a passionate and tempestuous, yet short-lived, affair. Sand's independent and domineering temperament allied to Musset's romantic long-ings and self-doubt could only result in disaster. Warning signs were visible from the start of the love affair. In August 1833, during one of George's and Alfred's very first outings together, Sand witnessed a terrifying incident. While rock climbing in the forest of Fontainebleau, Musset fell to the ground (without hurting himself) and howled some kind of 'inhuman howl'. When the poet came to his senses in George's arms, he told her that he had heard someone singing an obscene song: it was a tramp of a ghost, dishevelled and his clothes in tatters. At first the apparition was running away from him, but when it turned round to face him, Musset recognized 'him': it was his 'double', old, drunk and miserable. The incident was never forgotten. Towards the end of 1833, the couple left for Venice, on a kind of honeymoon, which soon turned into a drama and almost a tragedy. On arrival in Italy, Sand fell ill and Musset, insouciant and selfish as ever, led the rakish life of a carefree dandy. But no sooner was the lady's health restored than the young man was struck by some fever which almost killed him. George Sand nursed him back to health with great devotion, but – in the process – she fell in love with Musset's physician, the youthful Doctor Pagello. The affair lingered on, with violent episodes, for some eighteen months, during which time Musset wrote *Fantasio, Don't Play With Love* and his masterpiece, *Lorenzaccio*.

The Plays

The Moods of Marianne (1833)

Les Caprices de Marianne, the play which opens our collection, dramatizes the split personality of the playwright in his dealings with women and his contacts with society. Cœlio loves the beautiful Marianne, wife to Claudio, a ridiculous, old and pompous magistrate. Cœlio is too shy to court the lady himself, but his best friend, Octave – who happens to be Marianne's cousin – will play the go-between. Cœlio trusts Octave implicitly, as one trusts one's alter ego. Indeed, Cœlio and Octave represent the two contradictory and warring facets of their creator: Octave who leads a life of debauchery is cynical, ironical, blasé, world-wise and world-weary whereas Cœlio, the love-sick youth, is melancholy, sincere and longing for purity. The same pure/impure dichotomy is present in Marianne. On her first entrance Marianne is shown as *pure*: the ideal, puritanical, virginal bride appears to Cœlio as virtue incarnate. But when Octave's robust campaign of seduction breaches her defences, she throws all modesty to the wind. And as she falls victim to a terrible misunderstanding which proves fatal to her true lover, she destroys all hopes of happiness for herself and Octave. In his first important play, Musset demonstrates masterfully how human beings can be the slaves of passion and how modern tragedy operates: his characters find in themselves the weapons of their own destruction. They are the puppets of their own impulses, not the victims of gods or some external fatality as was the case in classical drama.

In a letter dated 10 May 1834, after his return to Paris, Musset wrote to Sand: 'You often told me that there are two men in me: Octave and Cœlio. When I met you, I had the feeling that the former was dying away, but the latter, in his infancy, could only weep and cry like a child.' The dual male character – the gay and rakish Octave and the moody and sombre Cœlio – and the emerging female character are victim of a hypocritical society from which all forms of spontaneity are banished. As long as Marianne is without personality and behaves like a provincial automaton, she is safe. But, in the course of the play, the boys challenge her to act freely and, in doing so, they destroy her peace of mind. On her first apparition, as the curtain opens, she is the typical provincial stuck-up woman, satisfied to be the young wife of an old pillar of society. But as the action progresses, she learns to assert herself and refuses to be treated as a commodity of men. Her revolt, as Camille's in *Don't Play With Love*, has deathly consequences, but the blame ultimately rests with society, not with these young women – not even with the young men who force them into rash action as they too are entrapped by life denying conventions.

The heroines of lighter comedies, Madame de Léry in *Caprice*, Cécile in *Il ne faut jurer de rien*, the Marquise in *Il faut qu'une porte soit ouverte ou fermée* will be luckier. Asserting their freedom and their dignity against the amorous/sexual machinations of prowling males, they succeed in attaining their desired aims and on their terms. 'Such women,' writes Simon Jeune, 'give Musset strong credentials as feminist playwright.' (Pléiade, p. 907)

'Marianne' Bowdlerized or the Senseless Caprices of Censorship
Musset's contemporaries were not ready to stage or to watch his plays and when they eventually decided to put them into rehearsals, they required major alterations, in form as well as in content, thus diminishing to a great extent Musset's originality, in order to satisfy the more prudish and hypocritical theatre-goers. In all his 'stage adaptations' Musset was forced a) to cut down the number of locations, even if it contradicted the logic of the action; b) to shorten the dramatic time, even if it made nonsense of psychological verisimilitude; c) to tone down or to cut lines and situations

perceived as sexually too explicit; d) to excise any political or religious references deemed offensive, subversive or just critical . . . The irony is that, with the exception of *Un caprice*, the plays which were so drastically mangled were staged *after* the Republican uprising of February 1848 which resulted in theatre censorship being abolished and *before* 22 July 1850 when it was restored.

A lengthier analysis would be required to study all the implications of the enforced changes that were introduced to the plays before they could be allowed to be staged.

The play which suffered most drastically from Musset's own 'revisions' was *Les Caprices de Marianne*. There are two main reasons for this: *Marianne* was (with *Lorenzaccio*) Musset's most modern play, in content and in form, and the *written* text of the stage version had to be approved by the censor before the theatre could start rehearsals. Musset's first attempt at satisfying the authorities did not succeed: the play was still judged to be 'shocking', 'crude', 'improper', 'inadmissible'. The version finally accepted by the guardians of bourgeois morality and the watchdogs of theatrical orthodoxy betrays, structurally, the same uneasiness as Corneille's *Le Cid* (ironic when one recalls that the youthful Musset was battling against the shackles of neoclassicism). Its single setting ('*a square in front of Claudio's house*') and its adoption of a continuous time span with strict 'liaison de scènes'[1] relies on an improbable succession of chance encounters, whereas in the original each scene is dramaturgically essential, at the time and place it occurs, in order to map out the personal progress of the various characters, to increase the suspense of the action and to procure the highest possible emotional impact. In the revision the characters themselves become rather shallow and psychologically unconvincing: Marianne who, in the original version, is a truly tragic young

---

[1] i.e. each scene is linked to the preceding one in space and time by the presence of at least one actor or by visual or aural contact between simultaneously entering and exiting characters (e.g., *Marianne*, Act I, Scenes 10–11).

woman, confronted after years of a puritanical life by a deep feeling of love, unable to cope rationally with an irrational and overwhelming impulse, is translated into some silly goose, an empty-headed 'gal', scarcely aware of the impact of her actions, of her fatal 'caprices' and her sudden changes of mood. Hermia, Cœlio's mother, whose own tragic youth foreshadows both her son's and Marianne's fate, is relegated to the role of an incidental character whose presence is far from necessary. Her lack of stature in the 'stage version' robs the play of a strong 'adult' relationship between mother and son, and belittles Cœlio's own stature as a tragic character. Even more damaging is Octave's pervading presence (imposed by the unity of place). Never is the awkwardness of the new structure more obvious than in the final scenes when Octave is unable to prevent Cœlio's murder although everything is happening 'on the spot'.

Further alterations were rendered necessary by political, social and religious considerations. The foolish, yet murderous Claudio is no longer a judge, but the cuckolded husband is turned into a 'podestat' (the title refers not only to an obsolete Renaissance judiciary position, but it is also foreign); the bawd Ciuta, a gutsy and malevolent creature reminiscent of La Celestina, who has a hand in the fatal dénouement, is lamely replaced by a pale male servant, Pippo, who is nothing but a dramaturgical convenience. Finally, the removal of the recurrent verbal references to religious services (mass, vespers) and the absence of the ringing bells punctuating Marianne's entrances and exits rob the play of a powerful ideological, dramaturgical and theatrical framework.

Sad to say, with the rare exception of Théophile Gautier, most critics and spectators, applauded the author's self-mutilation! There were even those who thought that the play was still too licentious and that it should never be allowed on the stage, however tame the text had become.

After Musset's death his brother Paul spent the rest of his life promoting the playwright's work, offering to rewrite or to adapt any play in order to make it acceptable to the censors and to timorous theatre directors. But with little success.

Considering that no one at the time was ready to confront the more radical solutions which Alfred de Musset had put in practice in the writing of his plays, it is hardly a cause for regret.

Fantasio (1833)

The action is set in an imaginary Munich, in some feudal past, where a bourgeois prince rules over a sleepy population. The plot was inspired by a contemporary event: on 9 August 1832, Louis-Philippe's daughter, the princess Louise, was married off to the newly enthroned king of Belgium, Léopold I. She did not love him, but post-Napoleonic European politics required a show of international harmony and the girl had to be sacrificed. Musset's heroine, Elsbeth, is to marry a ridiculous Italian prince, the ruler of Mantua, and the population of Munich is celebrating. Among the revellers emerges a paradoxical character, Fantasio – whose true identity will remain a mystery. Fantasio, like Octave, is a cynical, nihilistic young man who, none the less, is in search of something that would give his life some meaning. His ironist's outlook helps him to understand intuitively the intimate tragedy which is Elsbeth's lot. But what can he – a nobody – do to help a princess? Nothing, unless chance comes to his (and her) rescue. And it does: on the eve of the projected marriage, the court fool dies. Quick as a flash, Fantasio dons his costume and steps into the role, forcing his way into the palace. In disguise, the dissolute young man is all wisdom and generosity. He lectures the princess on the importance of self-esteem and urges her not to marry the loathsome prince, even if her suitor threatens war. As Elsbeth hesitates, not wanting to cause her father or her subjects any grief, the fool accomplishes a foolish action by fishing the prince's wig off his head during his official entry into Munich. The prince declares war; Fantasio is imprisoned, but Elsbeth sets him free . . . A bleak reality is recast into a happier and more moral fiction.

In *Fantasio*, Musset plays with theatrical conventions as,

almost a century later, Pirandello will extend the theatrical boundaries with *Six Characters in Search of an Author*. Fantasio plays a role-within-a-role, he assumes the mask of the fool in full view of the audience and thus, paradoxically, becomes more real, more truly himself under the clown's disguise. Fantasio-the-fool is more lucid, more generous, wiser than Fantasio-the-man. 'Protected by the mask and his role-playing, the "hero" reveals himself, finds his unity and harmony within himself in order to achieve something worthwhile. Under the ironic mask, irony expresses itself freely and the man frees himself from his ironic attitude . . .' (Henri Lefebvre, *Musset*, Paris: L'Arche, 1970, p. 67)

Lorenzaccio (1834)

Lorenzaccio is not only Musset's masterpiece, it is the one French play of the nineteenth century which can be placed alongside the highest artistic achievements of mankind and sets Musset among the greatest playwrights, Shakespeare included. Yet this most romantic of romantic dramas has played no role in the development of French theatre. *Lorenzaccio* was not written *for* the stage, but *against* it (see Anne Ubersfeld, *Le Drame romantique*, Paris: Belin, 1993, pp. 155–9). More precisely, it was written against the academic French theatrical conventions of the time which were still enslaved to the dramaturgical rules inherited from the seventeenth century. *Lorenzaccio* is a vast fresco of fifteenth-century Florence, mixing freely a depiction of public life, of court intrigue with intimate scenes and moments of deep personal introspection. Musset abolishes the notion of time (as a measurable and continuous quantity) and treats space as infinitely fragmented. Despite its title – and despite the centrality of Lorenzo's role – this is not a monodrama, as too many megalomaniac actors (starting with Sarah Bernhardt) were fond to believe.

Florence, 1537. The reign of Duke Alexander is tyrannical and the Duke, himself a habitual murderer and rapist, condones all the crimes of his sycophantic and debauched courtiers. Among them, Lorenzo, the Duke's cousin, is the worst, pimping for his master day and night, and always pandering to his worst desires. But Lorenzo wears a mask: he has secretly sworn to kill the Duke in order to rid Florence of its pestilence. A republican party, led by Philip Strozzi, is galvanizing the opposition. But, unfortunately, this opposition is divided and when Lorenzo eventually kills the Duke, the republicans do not seize their chance and their revolt (and Lorenzo's heroism) comes to nothing. The pope and the emperor impose a puppet prince, Como de' Medici, another of Alexander's cousins. Lorenzo flees to Venice where he is knifed in the back and his body thrown in the lagoon . . .

Lorenzaccio is a highly complex play and Lorenzo is a highly complex character. In fact, nothing and no one in this tragedy is what it (he, she) appears to be. All characters are deceptive, either better or worse than we first think and their actions are constantly open to question. On his first appearance, Lorenzo wears the mask of debauchery and gives the impression of moral and physical cowardice. He is the antithesis of a tragic hero. In Florence duplicity rules supreme and Lorenzo must hide his true face which, he hopes, is one of courage, nobility and virtue. But there is a danger that a mask that has been worn for too long can become more real than the reality it is supposed to hide, and that the man gets swallowed up by his assumed effigy. This tension between reality and dream, between crime and virtue is the theatrical driving force of the play. The failure of Lorenzo is not a personal failure, but the failure of an entire political system which has corruption as its founding principle; it is the failure of society to recognize the hero in its midst; the failure of the blind to see the light of grandeur and of purity.

Like *Hamlet*, to which *Lorenzaccio* is constantly compared, Musset's play raises so many pertinent questions about man's place in society, about right and wrong, about reality and illusion, about the nature of theatre and its relationship to life, that it will go on fascinating readers, directors, actors and spectators for as long as such fundamental questions will fascinate mankind.

Don't Play With Love (1834)

Again love divides divided characters; again a simple
intrigue which should lead to a simple country wedding ends
in disaster. Perdican, having happily concluded his Parisian
studies, at the university and in ladies' boudoirs, returns
home to marry his beautiful cousin Camille whose education
was perfected in a nineteenth-century 'finishing school', i.e.
in a convent. The two 'children' are reunited in the family
castle, as they come of age, to be married. The community
expects nothing else. But as Perdican and Camille meet, the
girl plays the prude *and* the coquette, and gives him the cold
shoulder. No treatment could enflame the boy's youthful
ardour more. To win her, he thinks, he must awaken her
jealousy, and he 'trifles' with Rosette, a simple but sincere
peasant girl, whom he promises to marry. The stratagem
works wonders: Camille confesses her own passion for
Perdican. But it is too late. The unhappy Rosette, cruelly
betrayed, dies as she overhears her tormentors' love duet.
Camille returns to her convent and Perdican's future happiness is rather compromised . . .

This action which starts like a pastoral comedy but ends in
tragedy contains, like *Marianne*, a wealth of farcical ele-
ments. Two pompous and ignorant priests quarrel, like
spoilt brats, over drink and food and slander each other to
get the better seat at the dining table; a stupid and prudish
'nun' becomes the unwitting instrument of fate, hastening
the fatal outcome. The tragic destiny of the 'children' is seen
to be sealed by clown-like characters who have no understanding of humanity, let alone of the growing pains of
juvenile love. In Musset the grotesque and the sublime are
not only closely intermingled, but the sublime is often the
direct creation of the grotesque.

Caprice (1837)

The 'proverbe' which ends our selection is more closely
linked to contemporary life in Parisian society than Musset's
other plays. It depicts the very people who would read and,
eventually, see such comedies on the stage. Thanks to their

comic brilliance Musset's 'proverbes' (*Il ne faut jurer de rien* (1836), *Un caprice*, *Il faut qu'une porte soit ouverte ou fermée* (1845), *On ne saurait penser à tout* (1849)), inspired by high-society games in vogue before the Revolution and influenced by the 'comédies-proverbes' of Carmontelle, were performed with great success in 1847 and 1848 (even if the 1848 Revolution cut short a very promising run of *Il ne faut jurer de rien*).

Un caprice was Musset's first stage success and the play which is still most often performed. It is a dramatic proverb crafted to perfection: a simple action with real suspense, three attractive characters whose psychology and amorous gamesmanship are subtly analysed, a most witty and elegant dialogue. The metaphysical and existential considerations which pervade Musset's more ambitious works are here present in filigree only, but their discreet presence lends extra substance to this most enchanting play.

Mathilde has been married one year to Monsieur de Chavigny who is already cheating, or about to cheat on her. While he is playing the man-about-town, she is secretly knitting a little red purse for him. As she is about to hand it over, her husband produces a blue purse, which – she guesses – is a present from Madame de Blainville. Madame de Léry, Mathilde's friend, enters on cue to rescue her. She contrives a *tête-à-tête* between herself and Monsieur de Chavigny with whom she plays a game of love which the self-infatuated man fails to read correctly. During the flirtatious encounter a mysterious red purse is brought in by an elusive errand boy: Chavigny is convinced that Madame de Léry is offering herself to him and falls to his knees. It is in that position that he hears the truth and that he is taught his lesson. Happy ending all round: the husband's love for his wife is reaffirmed and instead of a 'cheap' mistress, Chavigny finds a true friend in Madame de Léry.

Conclusion

Our anthology brings together the best of Musset theatre,

which is also the best French theatre of the nineteenth century. The themes treated in his plays and the extraordinary freedom of creation with which these are presented make a neat summation impossible. Musset's ambition was to become Schiller or Shakespeare. He did better: he became Musset. Schiller, for obvious reasons, is rarely performed in France. Shakespeare, as everwhere in the Western world, remains the most successful playwright in France. But Musset is not far behind, proudly claiming third place at the Comédie-Française behind Molière and Corneille and achieving considerable success with the young generation of directors and actors who find in his plays a modernity and a complexity which is often lacking in contemporary writing.

This edition

The translations in this edition are all unpublished. Some were specially commissioned, others were known to me either because I had seen them performed or because I have directed them (*The Moods of Marianne*, at the University of Manchester; *Caprice*, for the Orange Street Theatre, Canterbury). As for *Don't Play With Love*, my commissioning the translation, the BBC's interest in the play (following their successful broadcast of Marivaux's *La Dispute*) and the French Institute's initiative to put on the play in English all happened almost simultaneously. But it is my wish that all the plays in this collection will soon find their way onto the English-speaking stage and into broadcasting media.

Our translations follow 'faithfully' the latest and most authoritative French edition: Alfred de Musset, *Théâtre complet*, édition établie par Simon Jeune, Paris: Nouvelle Revue Française, Bibliothèque de la Pléiade, Éditions Gallimard, 1990.

Further reading

Charles Affron, *A Stage for Poets: Studies in the Theatre of Hugo and Musset* (Princeton, N.J., 1971)

Cery Crossley, *Lorenzaccio* (London: Grant & Cutler, 1983)

Herbert S. Gochberg, *Stage of Dreams: The Dramatic Art of Musset* (Ghent, 1967)

Charlotte Haldane, *Alfred: The Passionate Life of Musset* (1960)

W. D. Howarth, *Sublime and Grotesque* (London: Harrap, 1975)

Cyril Francis Oliphant, *Alfred de Musset* (Edinburgh: Foreign Classics for English Readers, 1890)

Margaret A. Rees, *Alfred de Musset* (New York: Twayne's World Authors Series, No. 137, 1971)

David Sices, *Theatre of Solitude: The Drama of Musset* (University Press of New England, Hanover, New Hampshire, 1974)

Bibliography

Patricia Joan Seigel, *Alfred de Musset: A Reference Guide* (Boston, 1982)

Plays in English translation

Comedies, translated by S.S. Gwyn (London, 1890)

Love Is Not To Be Trifled With, translated by Eirene G. Owen (London: French's Acting Edition, 1947)

Seven Plays, translated by Peter Meyer, includes *Marianne*, *Fantasio*, *Camille and Perdican*, *The Candlestick*, *A Diversion*, *A Door Must Be Kept Open or Shut*, *Journey to Gotha* (1962)

Don't Fool With Love, with *The Candlestick* & *A Door Must Be Kept Open or Shut*, translated by D. Donnellan and P. Meyer (Bath: Absolute Press, 1993)

Fantasio and Other Plays, translated by P. Schmidt *et al.* (New York: Theatre Communication Group and London: Nick Hern Books, 1993)

The Moods of Marianne

Les Caprices de Marianne (15 May 1833)

translated by DONALD WATSON

2   The Moods of Marianne

Characters

Claudio, *a judge*
Marianne, *his wife*
Cœlio
Octave
Tibia, *Claudio's valet*
Ciuta, *an old woman*
Hermia, *Cœlio's mother*
Servants
Malvolio, *Hermia's steward*

Setting: Naples

Translator's note: In view of the deliberate setting back in time to sixteenth-century Italy and the constant Shakespearian echoes, it was considered desirable to stylize the language a little.

This translation was first performed by students of the Drama Department of Manchester University in January 1972 under the direction of Claude Schumacher.

Act One

Scene One

A street in front of **Claudio**'s *house.* **Marianne**, *holding a mass-book, is leaving her house when* **Ciuta** *intercepts her.*

Ciuta Fair lady, will you allow me a word?

Marianne What do you want with me?

Ciuta A young man from this town is mad with love of you. A whole month long he has vainly sought to tell you of his love. His name is Cœlio. He is of lordly birth and noble in his bearing.

Marianne Enough. Tell whoever sent you to save his time and spare his pains. And if he dare to bid me hark to such a tale again, I shall instruct my husband of it.

Exit.

Cœlio (*entering*) Well, Ciuta, what did she say?

Ciuta More proud and more devout than ever, she will, she says, if she is further troubled, instruct her husband of it.

Cœlio Ah! What a hopeless wretch am I! Now nought but death awaits me. Oh, cruellest of all women! . . . How, Ciuta, do you counsel me now? What ruse may I still try?

Ciuta My first counsel is to slip away at once. Look over there, her husband's coming!

Exeunt. Enter **Claudio** *and* **Tibia**.

Claudio Are you a faithful servant to me? My own devoted valet? Learn that I must have vengeance for an outrage.

Tibia You, sir!

Claudio My very self. Impudent guitars never cease their murmur beneath the windows of my spouse. But have patience! All is not done yet. – Withdraw a little over here and listen. There are some men who might overhear us. This evening you will seek out the cut-throat I told you of.

Tibia Why's that then?

Claudio I think Marianne has lovers.

Tibia You think so, sir?

Claudio Yes. Round my house there is a stench of lovers. No one goes past my door in the normal way. It rains guitars and bawds.

Tibia Can you prevent that your wife be serenaded?

Claudio No, but I can post a man behind the postern gate and rid myself of the first who tries to enter.

Tibia Fie, sir! Your wife does not have lovers . . . it were as if you said that I had mistresses.

Claudio Why should you not have them, Tibia? You are passing ugly, yet you have much wit.

Tibia That's right, I admit.

Claudio See, Tibia, you yourself admit I am right. There is no more room for doubt. My disgrace is public knowledge.

Tibia Why public?

Claudio It's public knowledge, I say.

Tibia Why, sir, throughout the town your wife is known as a dragon of virtue. She never sees a soul and never quits the house but to go to Mass.

Claudio Leave all to me. I am beside myself with rage, to think of all the presents she has had from me . . . Yes,

Tibia, at this very hour I am spinning a most frightful web. I feel I near must die of grief.

Tibia Oh, no, sir!

Claudio When I say a thing, do me the favour to believe it!

Exeunt.

Cœlio (*entering*) Unhappy the man who in the flower of youth submits to hopeless love! . . . Unhappy the man who yields to sweet and idle dreams before he knows where his chimera leads him, or even if his love can be requited! Softly reclining in his gentle bark he slips slowly further from the shore. Afar he glimpses plains that are enchanted, green pastures and the volatile mirage of his Eldorado. The winds draw him on in silence, and when reality awakes him he is as far from the longed-for goal as from the coast he has abandoned. He can no more pursue his quest than turn back to his homeland. (*The sound of musical instruments is heard.*) What is this masquerade? This must surely be Octave?

Enter **Octave**.

Octave How fares my gracious melancholy Sir?

Cœlio How mad you are, Octave! Your cheeks are afire, a foot deep in rouge! – Where did you find this apparel? Have you no shame, in broad daylight?

Octave How mad you are, Cœlio! Your cheeks are pallid, a foot deep in paste! Where did you find this broad black doublet? Have you no shame, in carnival time?

Cœlio What a life is yours! If *you* are not in wine, then it must be *me*.

Octave If *you* are not in love, then it must be *me*.

Cœlio More than ever, with the lovely Marianne.

Octave More than ever, with the Cypriot's fair grape.

Cœlio I was about to call at your house.

Octave I was about to call at my house too. How fares my house, I wonder? It's a whole week since I saw it.

Cœlio I have a favour to ask you.

Octave Speak, Cœlio, dear boy. Is it money you want? None left. Is it counsel you want? I am drunk. Is it my sword? Well, here's my Harlequin's bat. Speak, say on. I am at your service.

Cœlio How much longer can this endure? . . . A week away from home? . . . You will kill yourself, Octave.

Octave Never with my own fair hand, my friend. Never! I would rather die than end my days myself.

Cœlio And is this not a sort of suicide, the life you lead?

Octave Imagine a tightrope walker, in silver ankleboots, one fist round his balancing pole, posed halfway between Earth and Heaven. And down below, to left and right, tiny shrunken old gnomes, pale and wizened wraiths, agile old creditors, relatives and courtesans, a monstrous legion all clinging to his cloak, tugging at him from every side to pull him from his perch. A cavalcade of periphrastic phrases and pomp-encrusted words gallop around him, while a misty cloud of sinister omens dims his sight with the flapping of black wings. He pursues his airy course from east to west. If he looks down, his head will spin. If he looks up, his foot will slip. Faster than the wind he races on, and of all those outstretched hands around him, none will make him spill one drop from the joyful cup he holds high in his own. That, my dear friend, is my life. This is a faithful image of me.

Cœlio How happy you are to be mad!

Octave How mad you are not to be happy! Tell me now, Cœlio, what's wrong with you, what need you?

Cœlio A quiet spirit, that carefree ease which makes of life a mirror that offers a brief and fugitive image of all things. A debt, to me, is a subject for remorse. Love, which you others make into a sport, disrupts my life completely. You will never know, Octave, what it is to love as I love. My study remains empty. A month since, night and day, I roam around this house. How fatal is the charm I find, at moonrise, to lead my modest chorus of musicians beneath those little trees beside the square, myself to beat the measure, and then hear them extol the loveliness of Marianne! At her window she has never shown herself, never come to rest her charming head against the lattice.

Octave Who is this Marianne? Can it be my cousin?

Cœlio She it is, wife to old Claudio.

Octave I have never seen her. But she surely is my cousin. Claudio proves it. So confide your problems, Cœlio, in me.

Cœlio All the means I have employed to apprise her of my love have failed. Straight from her convent, she loves her husband and respects her duty. Her gate is barred to all the young men in the town. None may approach her.

Octave Phew! Is she pretty? – fool that I am! You love her, so no matter. What can we devise?

Cœlio Must I speak my mind? You will not laugh at me?

Octave Speak your mind and give me leave to laugh.

Cœlio Related as you are, you should have entry to the house.

Octave Do I have entry? I have no idea. Let us presume I do. But to speak honest with you, the august members of my family are not, like asparagus, a close-knit bunch. We rarely communicate except at times in writing. Marianne, however, knows my name. Should I intercede on your behalf?

Cœlio Twenty times I have attempted to approach her. And twenty times, as I drew near, I have felt my knees tremble. I was obliged to send old Ciuta to her. Each time I see her, my throat constricts. I suffocate, as if my heart had leapt to still my lips.

Octave I have known that too. So it is in forest glades, when a doe daintily steps over dry leaves and the hunter hears the heather brush against her anxious flanks like rustling taffeta: in spite of himself his hectic heart will beat. He lifts his weapon silently, but dares neither move nor breathe.

Cœlio Why am I like this? Is it not an old maxim among libertines that all women are alike? Why is it then that love is so rarely the same? It's true, Octave, I could never love this woman as you would love her. Nor as I could love another. So what is it all about? Two blue eyes, two scarlet lips, one white gown and two white hands. Why is it that what would make you fervent and full of joy, what would draw you like iron to a magnet, makes me sorrowful and lifeless? Who can say what gives rise to . gaiety and sorrow? Reality is naught but a shadow. What glorifies it? Call it folly or imagination. – Then beauty itself is mere fancy. Each man walks beneath a translucent veil that envelops him from head to foot. He thinks he sees woods and rivers: but this magic gauze blurs his vision and lends infinite tints and hues to universal Nature. Octave! Octave, come to my aid!

Octave I love your love, Cœlio. It bubbles through my brain like a flagon of wine from Syracuse. Give me your hand. I come to your aid, just wait a little. The fresh air fans my face and thoughts come back to me. I know this Marianne. She hates me heartily, though she has never seen me. A skimpy little doll, muttering Ave Marias without a stop.

Cœlio Do what you will, but deceive me not, I implore you. I am easy to deceive and know not how to parry a blow I would not strike myself.

Octave Why not climb over the wall?

Cœlio To what purpose if she will not love me?

Octave Why not write to her?

Cœlio She tears up my letters or sends them back.

Octave Why not love another? Come with me to Rosalind's.

Cœlio Marianne is the breath of life to me. One word from her lips can ruin or revive it. It would be easier for me to die for her than to live for someone else; I shall either win her or make an end. Ssh! She has just turned the corner of the street on her way home.

Octave Away with you! I'll accost her.

Cœlio Never think it! Not in that garb! Wipe your face! You look brain sick.

Octave That's quickly done . . . Intoxication and I, dear Cœlio, are far too close allies ever to come to blows. We always fulfil each other's wishes. Have no fear on that score. I am no student on vacation who imbibes so freely at a banquet that his head spins as he battles with his wine. It is in my character to be drunk, my way of life is to let myself go. And just now I would address the king himself as I shall speak to your fair beauty.

Cœlio My feelings are in turmoil. – No, do not speak to her.

Octave Why not?

Cœlio I cannot say why, but it seems to me you will deceive me.

Octave My hand upon it. I swear to you on my honour that, for all that in me lies, Marianne shall be yours, no other man's.

Exit **Cœlio**. *Enter* **Marianne**. **Octave** *accosts her.*

Octave Look not away, fair princess of beauty. Deign to turn your eyes upon the unworthiest of your slaves.

Marianne Who are you?

Octave My name is Octave, your husband's cousin.

Marianne Have you come to see him? Enter into the house, he will soon return.

Octave I have not come to see him, nor shall I enter the house, lest you chase me from it shortly, when I have said what brings me here.

Marianne Forbear to say it then and hinder me no further.

Octave Forbear I cannot, and beg you to be hindered long enough to hear it. Cruel Marianne! Your eyes have caused much sickness and your words are not fashioned to dispel it. What ill had Cœlio done you?

Marianne Whom do you speak of and what sickness have I caused?

Octave The most cruel of all, for it is sickness without hope of cure; the most terrible, for it is a sickness that nurtures itself and pushes the healing cup away, even from friendship's hand. A sickness that with poisons sweeter than ambrosia brings pallor to the lips, and dissolves the hardest heart, like Cleopatra's pearl, into a shower of tears. A sickness that all the spices, all the sciences of man are unable to assuage; that feeds its pain on an idle breeze, the perfume of a faded rose, a song's refrain, and draws eternal nourishment from the suffering that surrounds it, as a bee sucks honey from all the bushes in a garden.

Marianne And how is this sickness called?

Octave Let that man say it who is worthy to pronounce its name. May your nocturnal dreams, your green orange trees, and springtime teach you the word. May you seek it one fine evening and find it on your lips. If the sickness has no substance, then its name does not exist.

Marianne Is it so dangerous to utter, so terribly contagious that it alarms the tongue that pleads its cause?

Octave Is it so sweet to hear, cousin, that you demand it? You taught it to Cœlio.

Marianne   Then it is without my knowledge. For I know not the one or the other.

Octave   May you know them both together and never part them. That is my heart's desire.

Marianne   Truly?

Octave   Cœlio is the best of all my friends. If I wished to arouse your interest, I would tell you he is young and noble, handsome as the day, and I would not be lying. But I wish only to rouse your pity and I shall tell you that since the first day he saw you, he is sad as death.

Marianne   Is it my fault if he is sad?

Octave   Is it his fault if you are fair? He thinks of you alone. At every hour he prowls around this house. Have you never heard songs beneath your windows? Never at midnight lifted that blind or raised that curtain?

Marianne   This square belongs to everyone. Anyone may sing at nightfall.

Octave   Anyone may love you, too. Yet none may tell you so. How old are you, Marianne?

Marianne   A nice question! And if I were but nineteen, what difference would that make.

Octave   You still have five or six years to be loved, eight or ten for you yourself to love, and the rest to pray to God.

Marianne   Is that so? Well! To make the best of my time, I love your cousin Claudio, my husband!

Octave   My cousin and your husband, the two of them together, will never make but one village pedant. You have no love for Claudio.

Marianne   Nor for Cœlio. And you may tell him so.

Octave   Why?

Marianne   Why should I not love Claudio? He is my husband!

Octave   Why should you not love Cœlio? He is your lover!

Marianne   And will you tell me why I listen to you? Adieu, Signor Octave. This pleasantry has lasted long enough.

Exit.

Octave   By my faith I swear she has lovely eyes.

Exit.

Scene Two

Cœlio's *home.*

Hermia, *several* **Servants**, **Malvolio**.

Hermia   Arrange these flowers as I instructed you. Have the musicians been sent for?

Servant   Yes, Madame. They will be here at supper time.

Hermia   These closed shutters are too gloomy. Let in the light, but keep out the sun's rays. – More flowers around the bed. Is it a good supper? Shall we have our handsome neighbour, the Countess Pergoli? What time did my son go out?

Malvolio   To go out, he should first have come in. He slept from home last night.

Hermia   You know not what you say. – He supped out last night with me and brought me back home. Has that picture I purchased this morning been taken to the study?

Malvolio   During his father's lifetime, it would not have been like this. Anyone would think our mistress was eighteen years old, waiting upon her paramour.

Hermia But during his mother's lifetime, so it is,
Malvolio. Who charged you to supervise his conduct?
Take care that Cœlio meets no malevolent looks on his
return, nor hears you snarl like a stable dog safeguarding
his bone, or else by Heaven not one of you will spend the
night beneath his roof.

Malvolio I am no snarler, nor is my face an evil omen.
You asked me what time my master left. I tell you he
never came home. Since his head was turned by love, we
barely see him four times a week.

Hermia Why are Cœlio's books all covered in dust? Why
is the furniture not in its place? Why in my son's house, if
I want something done, do I have to see to everything
myself? It behoves you well to raise your brows over what
concerns you not, when your work is only half done and
the duties you are charged with fall to others to fulfil.
Leave me, and hold your tongue. (*Enter* **Cœlio**.) Well, my
dear boy, what pleasures shall be yours today?

The **Servants** *withdraw.*

Cœlio Yours, Mother.

He sits down.

Hermia What! Our pleasures shared, but not our pains?
Unjust division, Cœlio. Keep your secrets from me, child,
but not those which devour your heart and make you
insensible to everything around you.

Cœlio I have no secrets, and if I had, please God they
were of such a kind would make of me a statue.

Hermia When you were ten or twelve years old, all your
sorrows, all your woes were in relation to me. Upon the
look in my eyes, indulgent or severe, hung the sadness or
the joy in yours. From your small fair head the finest of
threads led to your mother's heart. Now, my son, I am
more like an older sister to you, perhaps unable to relieve
your cares, but not to share them with you.

Cœlio And you, Mother, were so beautiful, too! Beneath the silver hair that lays a shadow on your noble brow, beneath the long cloak that envelops you, one's eyes can still discern the majestic bearing of a queen and the gracious figure of Diana the Huntress. O, Mother! You invited love! From under your half-open windows came the murmur of guitars. And in bustling town-squares, in swirling festive crowds you once displayed the carefree pride of youth. But you have never been in love. A cousin of my father's died for love of you.

Hermia What memories you stir up!

Cœlio Ah! If they are not too sad for your heart to bear, if they do not provoke your tears, then recount me this adventure, Mother, tell me the whole story.

Hermia Your father had not yet met me at the time. Being connected to my family, he undertook to win approval for the young Orsini, who wished me for his bride, and as befitted his rank was welcomed by your grandsire and admitted to our circle. Orsini was an excellent match, yet I refused him. While pressing his friend's suit, your father had stifled the little love Orsini had kindled in my heart during two months of assiduous attentions. I never guessed the strength of his passion for me. When my answer was conveyed to him, he fell senseless into your father's arms. However, a lengthy absence, during which he set out on a voyage and enlarged his fortune, was said to have dispelled his grief. Your father switched his role and begged for himself what he had failed to obtain for Orsini. I loved him most sincerely and the esteem he had won from my parents allowed me no hesitation. That very day the marriage was decided, and a few weeks later the church received us. Orsini then returned, sought out your father and hurled reproaches at him. Accused him of betraying his trust and contriving the refusal he had suffered. Moreover, he added, if you wanted to destroy me, your wish will be fulfilled. Alarmed at these words, your father came in search of mine, begging him to hear him out and disabuse Orsini. – The time for that, alas, was past. The poor young man was found in his room, pierced through and through with several sword-thrusts.

Scene Three

Claudio's *garden.*

Enter **Claudio** *and* **Tibia**.

Claudio You are right and my wife is a treasure of perfect purity. What more can I say? A precious stone of virtue.

Tibia You think so, sir?

Claudio Can she prevent these serenades beneath her casement windows? The traces of impatience she may reveal at home spring from her character. Did you remark how her mother, when I plucked this chord, agreed with me at once?

Tibia In what respect?

Claudio In respect of these serenades beneath her casement windows!

Tibia It is no bad thing to sing. Myself, I am always humming.

Claudio But it is hard to sing well.

Tibia Hard for you and me. For, as nature failed to grant us voices, we have never trained them. Yet think how skilfully those actors in the playhouse come across.

Claudio Folk of that class spend their lives upon the boards.

Tibia How much do you think one gets paid a year?

Claudio Who? A Justice of the Peace?

Tibia No, a singer.

Claudio How should I know . . . A Justice receives a third of what my post is worth. And assessors half.

Tibia If I was a High Court judge here and my wife had lovers, I would sentence them myself.

Claudio To how many years in the galleys?

Tibia To be hanged by the neck. A death sentence is a wondrous thing to read aloud.

Claudio It is not the judge who reads it, it is the Clerk of the Court.

Tibia The Clerk of your Court has a pretty wife.

Claudio No. It's the President that has the pretty wife. I supped with them yester eve.

Tibia So has the Clerk! The cut-throat who will come this evening is lover to the wife of the Clerk of the Court.

Claudio What cut-throat?

Tibia The one you wanted.

Claudio There is no point his coming after what I told you just now.

Tibia In what regard?

Claudio In regard to my wife.

Tibia And here she comes in person.

Enter **Marianne**.

Marianne You know what happened to me while you were trotting about? I was accosted by your cousin.

Claudio Who can that be? Tell me his name.

Marianne Octave, who made me a declaration of love on behalf of his friend, Cœlio. Who is this? Know you this man? Accord me the favour that neither he nor Octave shall ever set foot in this house.

Claudio I do know him. He is the son of Hermia, our neighbour. How did you respond to this?

Marianne It is no matter what response I made. Do you understand what I say? Order your servants not to grant admission to this man, nor to his friend. I anticipate some nuisance from these importunate fellows, and I shall be well pleased to escape it.

Exit.

Claudio What think you of this adventure, Tibia? There is some trick about it.

Tibia You think so, sir?

Claudio Why would she not say how she answered? Such a declaration is impertinent, 'tis true, yet the reply deserves to be known. I suspect it is this Cœlio who is responsible for all those guitars.

Tibia To forbid your gates to these two men is the best way to keep them out.

Claudio Leave all that to me. – My mother-in-law shall be apprised of this discovery. I fancy my wife deceives me, and all this rigmarole is pure invention to put me off the scent and to trouble and confuse my mind.

Exeunt.

Act Two

Scene One

Enter **Octave** *and* **Ciuta**.

Octave He has given up, you say?

Ciuta Alas! The poor young man! He is more in love than ever, and he deceives himself with melancholy thoughts that feed on his desires. It would almost seem he mistrusts you. And me, and all that is about him.

Octave No, by Heaven, I will not give up. I am turning into another Marianne, but obduracy has its pleasures! If Cœlio does not win her, then I shall have lost my tongue.

Ciuta Will you then act against his will?

Octave Yes, to act in accord with mine, which is the elder. And so send our Master Claudio down to Hell, for I detest that judge from head to tail, despise him and abhor him.

Ciuta I will convey your answer, then I myself will cease to be concerned.

Octave I am like a man who holds the bank at faro for another and whose luck has turned against him. He would rather drown his best friend than give in. Anger at losing with someone else's money makes him a hundred times more furious than the thought of bringing ruin on himself.

Enter **Cœlio**.

Octave What's this then, Cœlio? You throw in your hand!

Cœlio What would you have me do?

Octave Do you mistrust me? What ails you? You are white as snow. – What's going on inside you?

Cœlio Forgive me, please forgive me! Do what you will. Go seek Marianne. Tell her that to let me down is to bring about my death. My life depends on the look in her eyes.

Exit.

Octave By Heaven, but this is strange!

Ciuta Be silent! Vespers are sounding. The garden gate has just opened and Marianne appears. – She is coming very slowly.

Exit **Ciuta**. *Enter* **Marianne**.

Octave You may sleep sound, fair Marianne. – Cœlio's heart is given to another. No more beneath your windows will he make his serenade.

Marianne What a shame! How great is my misfortune never to have shared a love like that! You see how chance rebuffs me, when I was just about to love him!

Octave Truly?

Marianne Yes, upon my soul. I swear I would have been his this evening. Or tomorrow morning. By Sunday at the latest. Who could fail to succeed with an ambassador like you? His passion for me seems to have been more like Chinese or Arabic that he should feel the need for an interpreter and be unable to express it for himself.

Octave Rail on! We have no more to fear from you.

Marianne Or perhaps this love of his was still but a poor babe at the breast, with you keeping him on leading-strings like a mindful nurse, only to let him fall, as you walked him through the town, head first.

Octave The mindful nurse was content just to make him drink a certain kind of milk that yours surely gave to you, and generously. You still have on your lips one drop of it, which colours every word you speak.

Marianne And what is the name of this magic milk?

Octave   Indifference. You know not how to love or hate.
You are like Bengal roses, Marianne, with neither thorn
nor fragrance.

Marianne   Well said. Did you prepare this simile in
advance? If you do not consign the rough draft of your
sermons to the flames, I beg you to give me this one that I
may teach it to my parrot.

Octave   Surely you find nothing in that to offend you? A
flower without fragrance is none the less fair. The very
opposite, those that are the fairest God has fashioned thus.
And the day when you, like some new species of a Galatea
have been fashioned into marble in the corner of some
church, what a charming statue you will make! A
confessional is bound to furnish you an honourable niche.

Marianne   My dear cousin, do you have no pity for the
destiny of women? Think but a little in what straits am I.
It is decreed by Fate that Cœlio should love me, or that he
should think he does. This Cœlio tells his friends as much.
And these friends in turn decree that on pain of death I
shall become his mistress. The youth of Naples deigns to
send me in your shape a worthy envoy instructed to
inform me that I must love the said Signor Cœlio within
the week. Reflect on that, I pray you. If I submit, what
shall be said of me? Is such a woman not utterly abject
who agrees point blank at the appointed hour to such a
proposition? Will she not be torn to pieces, pointed at in
scorn, and hear her name cited in the chorus of a
drinking-song? If conversely she refuses, is there a
monster can compare with her? Is there any statue colder
than she? And the man who addresses her, who dares to
detain her, mass-book in hand in a public place, has he
not every right to say to her, 'You are a Bengal rose, with
neither thorn nor fragrance'?

Octave   Come now, cousin! Calm yourself.

Marianne   Is it not laughable that there should be such
things as honest decency and keeping faith? Ridiculous

that a young girl should be reared with enough pride in her heart to set some value on it? Absurd that before her treasured blossom powders to dust and be cast upon the wind, its chalice should be laced with tears and bloom in fitful sunshine, half-opening to a gentle touch? All this is naught but a dream, is it not? A soap-bubble, ready to evaporate at the first sigh of some modish gallant?

Octave You misjudge us both, myself and Cœlio.

Marianne What after all is a woman? The occupation of a moment, a fragile cup that holds one drop of dew, first carried to the lips, then cast over the shoulder and discarded. A woman is a plaything! Why should a man not say on meeting one, 'There goes a night of pleasure'? And would he not be a schoolboy in such matters, a man who would lower his eyes before her and let her pass while he murmurs, 'There perhaps goes a lifetime of happiness.'

Exit.

Octave (*alone*) Tra la la, pom, pom! Derry down derry! – Strange little lady! (*At the tavern, calling.*) Hey there! Hallo! (*To a* **Waiter** *coming out of the inn.*) Bring me a bottle of vino, here, under the arbour.

Waiter What you will, Excellency. Do you wish for Lacrima Christi?

Octave Right, so be it. Get you gone awhile and search the streets around for Signor Cœlio, who wears a black cloak and a doublet even blacker. You will tell him one of his friends is here, drinking the tears of Christ and all alone. Then you will go to the main piazza and fetch me a certain Rosalind, who has red hair and is ever at her window.

Exit the **Waiter**.

I know not what sticks in my throat but I feel as sad as a cortege. (*Drinks.*) I might as well sup here: see how the light is fading. Ding! Dong! How gloomy are these vespers! Is it sleep that I need? It's as if I was turning to stone.

Enter **Claudio** *and* **Tibia**.

Octave   Cousin Claudio, you are a fine judge. Where are you bound so trottingly?

Claudio   What mean you by that, Signor Octave?

Octave   That you are a Justice of fine distinction.

Claudio   In expression or appearance?

Octave   In linguistic expression. Your wig bristles with eloquence and your legs make two charming parentheses.

Claudio   Let me remark, *en passant*, Signor Octave, that my door-knocker seems to have burnt your fingers.

Octave   How is that, most know-all of judges?

Claudio   In the act of knocking, most crafty of cousins.

Octave   And be so bold as to add, judge, full of respect for your knocker. Have it repainted by all means. I shall not fear to stain my fingers on it.

Claudio   And why is that, most clownish of cousins?

Octave   By never knocking, most caustic of judges.

Claudio   It has, however, happened before, since my wife has enjoined her household, the first time you do it again, to slam the door in your face.

Octave   Your spectacles are short-sighted, most gracious of judges: your compliment is wrongly addressed.

Claudio   My spectacles are perfectly sound, most specious of cousins: have you not made my wife a declaration of love?

Octave   On whose account, subtle magistrate?

Claudio On account, cousin, of your friend Cœlio. Alas, I have heard it all.

Octave Through which ear, incorruptible senator?

Claudio Through my wife's ear, swaggering sweetheart. She has told me everything.

Octave Absolutely everything, most idolized of husbands? Nothing left at all in that charming little ear?

Claudio Nothing but her answer, good tippler of the taproom, which I am charged to deliver.

Octave I am not charged to listen, dear taker of evidence.

Claudio Then it's my door will answer you in person, gay croupier of the gaming-house, if you ever wish to hear it.

Octave Of scant concern to me, sweet sentence of death. I can live happily without it.

Claudio May you be left in peace to do so, darling of the dice-box! May you prosper a thousandfold!

Octave Never fear, dear prison bolts and bars! I sleep peaceful as quarter sessions.

Exeunt **Claudio** *and* **Tibia**.

Octave (*alone*) That must be Cœlio approaching. Cœlio! Cœlio! What ails him now? (*Enter* **Cœlio**.) Do you know, my dear boy, the fine trick your princess has played on us? She has told her husband all!

Cœlio How do you know that?

Octave By the surest means of all. Claudio and I part this instant. Marianne will have her door slammed in our face, if we mean to importune her further.

Cœlio You saw her a while ago. What did she say to you?

Octave Nothing to prepare me for this welcome news. Yet nothing pleasant either. Look now, Cœlio, give this woman up. Hello there! Another glass!

Cœlio For whom?

Octave For you. Marianne is a prude. I scarcely know what she said to me this morning. I stood there like a dumb thing, with nothing to reply. Come! Never think of her again. Now, that's agreed. And may Heaven fall about my ears if ever I address her one word more. Courage, Cœlio, never think of her again.

Cœlio Goodbye, my dear friend.

Octave Where are you going?

Cœlio I have business in town tonight.

Octave You look as if you were off to drown yourself. Listen, Cœlio, what's on your mind? There are other Mariannes in the world. Let us sup together and to hell with this one.

Cœlio Goodbye, goodbye now. I cannot stay longer. I shall see you tomorrow, my friend.

Exit.

Octave Cœlio, listen! We'll find you a nice kind Marianne, gentle as a lamb, and above all one who doesn't go to vespers! Oh, those cursed bells! When will they stop calling me to my grave?

Waiter (*returning*) Sir, the red-haired demoiselle is not at her window, so she cannot accept your invitation.

Octave Devil take the whole universe! Has it been determined that today I shall sup alone? Night arrives post-haste. What in hell will become of me? All right then! This is for me. (*He drinks.*) At least I can immerse my sorrows in this wine, or this wine in my sorrows. Aha! Vespers are over. Here's Marianne on her way home.

Enter **Marianne**.

Marianne Still here, Signor Octave? And so soon at table? It is rather depressing, getting drunk alone.

Octave The whole world has abandoned me, so I am trying to see double, to keep myself company.

Marianne What's this? Not one of your friends, not one of your mistresses, to relieve you of the dread burden of loneliness?

Octave Must I admit it? I had sent for a certain Rosalind, who serves as my mistress, but she sups in town like a lady of quality.

Marianne Doubtless a dire misfortune. You must feel in your heart a frightful emptiness.

Octave An emptiness quite inexpressible, which I vainly try to communicate to this large goblet of wine. The vespers chimes have split my head ever since dinner.

Marianne Tell me, cousin, this wine you drink, is it fifteen sous the bottle?

Octave Do not price it so low. It is neither more nor less than the tears of Christ.

Marianne I am amazed you do not drink wine at fifteen sous. Drink some, I beg you.

Octave Tell me please why I should?

Marianne Taste it. I am sure it is no different from that one.

Octave As different as a lantern from the sun.

Marianne No, I tell you they are the same.

Octave May God forbid! You mock me!

Marianne You find there is a great difference?

Octave Most certainly.

Marianne I thought the same rule applied to women as to wine. Is not a woman too a precious vessel sealed like this crystal flagon? Does she not provoke intoxication of the senses or the soul according to her strength or value? And among women can one not find the tears of Christ and the plain wine of the people? What a poor wretch are you, then, that your lips should teach your heart a lesson? You would not drink the wine the common people drink, but the women they love, you love too. The generous spirit of inspiration in this golden flagon, this miraculous elixir that the lava of Vesuvius ferments beneath a blazing sun, will lead you weakly tottering into the arms of a courtesan. You would blush to drink rough wine, your gorge would rise. Oh yes! Your lips are fastidious. But your heart finds intoxication on the cheap. Goodnight, cousin. I hope this evening Rosalind comes to drive your cares away.

Octave A word, I beg you, lovely Marianne, and my answer will be brief. Do you know how long it takes to woo the bottle you see here, before it grants its favours? It is as you say filled with a celestial spirit, and the people's wine is as unlike this as a peasant to his lord. Yet observe how compliant this lass is. Without education, I suppose, and with no principles at all. See how good-natured she is. One word was enough to snatch her from her convent. Still powdered with dust, she escaped, to bring me fifteen minutes of oblivion, and then die. Her virginal crown, crimson with perfumed wax, at once flaked away and, I must needs confess it, she was near consumed entire upon my lips in the fervour of her first kiss.

Marianne Is she then worth more because of this? Are you so sure? If the secret of this golden fire were lost, would you not, like a perfect lover, go seek out the final drop even at the mouth of the volcano?

Octave She is worth neither more nor less. She knows she is good to drink and made to be drunk. God did not hide her source on some inaccessible mountain-top or in the recesses of some dark cavern, but suspended it in golden clusters on our shining hillsides. There she plies the harlot's trade, brushing the hand of a passer-by, displaying her plump little breasts in the sun's rays, while a whole host of courtier hornets and bees buzz round her from morn to night. The thirst-tormented traveller can lie down beneath her leaf-green bower. Never has she let him languish, never refused him those sweet tears with which her heart is full. Ah! Marianne, what a fatal gift is beauty, whose much-vaunted prudence is next of kin to avarice. Heaven has more compassion for her frailties than for her cruel rebuffs. Goodnight, cousin. May Cœlio forget you.

He goes back into the inn and **Marianne** *into her house.*

Scene Two

Another street.

Cœlio, Ciuta.

Ciuta Signor Cœlio, do not trust Octave. Did he not say the lovely Marianne had closed her door to him?

Cœlio Indeed he did . . . Why should I not trust him?

Ciuta Passing through this street just now, I saw him in conversation with her beneath a covered arbour.

Cœlio What is there so astonishing in that? He must have been spying out her movements and seized on some happy chance to speak to her of me.

Ciuta I mean that they talked in friendly style, like folk who have reached an understanding.

Cœlio Are you sure of that? Then I am the happiest of men. He must have pleaded my cause with passion.

Ciuta May Heaven favour you!

Exit.

Cœlio Oh, that I had been born to make my name in tournaments and battles! That I had been allowed to wear Marianne's colours and stain them with my blood. That I had had a rival to challenge, a whole army to contend with! That the sacrifice of my life could have been of service to her! I know how to do things, but I know not how to speak them. My tongue will not serve my heart, and I shall die without ever being understood, like a dumb man in a prison.

Exit.

Scene Three

At **Claudio's**.

Claudio, Marianne.

Claudio Do you imagine I am a dummy, or that I roam the earth just to scare away the crows?

Marianne Why this charming conjecture?

Claudio Do you imagine that an expert in criminal law does not know the value of words, that one makes play with his credulity as one would with some tumbling mountebank?

Marianne Who has upset you tonight?

Claudio Do you imagine I never heard your own protestation: if that man or his friend should call at my door, have it slammed in his face? And do you think I find it proper to see you, after sundown, conversing freely beneath an arbour with him?

Marianne You saw me beneath an arbour?

Claudio Yes, yes, with these very own eyes of mine, beneath the arbour of a tavern! A tavern arbour is hardly the place for a magistrate's wife to hold a conversation, and it's no good keeping your door shut if you set the ball rolling again out of doors with such immodesty.

Marianne Since when am I forbidden to chat with a relative of yours?

Claudio When one of my relations is one of your gallants, it is far better to refrain.

Marianne Octave! One of my gallants? Are you out of your mind? Never in his life has he paid court to anyone.

Claudio He was born dissolute. He haunts low dives to smoke tobacco.

Marianne All the more reason why he should not be, as you so delightfully put it, *one of my gallants*. But I enjoy a chat with Octave beneath the arbour of a tavern.

Claudio Watch well what you do. Do not let your wild folly force me to take extreme measures.

Marianne How far should I go to find out how extreme they will be? I am curious to know.

Claudio I would forbid you to see him or exchange one word with him, whether it be in my house, in the house of a third party or in any public place.

Marianne Aha! Is that so! There's something new! Octave is as much my relative as yours. I have the right to speak to him when I see fit, in a public place or wherever else. And in this house, if he please to come there.

Claudio Remember well the last phrase you just uttered. I have in mind for you a punishment that will be exemplary, if you go against my wishes.

Marianne Rest content that I shall follow my own, do with me what you will. I care not a fig for that.

Claudio Marianne, let us put an end to this. Either you admit the impropriety of lingering beneath an arbour, or you will reduce me to a violence abhorrent to my robe.

Exit.

Marianne (*alone*) Hallo! Who's there!

A **Servant** *enters.*

Marianne You see that young man down there, in the street, sitting at a table? Go tell him I must speak with him. Ask him kindly to come into the garden.

The **Servant** *goes to the tavern.*

Marianne This really is something new! Who do they think I am? What wrong have I done? – How do I look today? I hate this gown! – What did he mean, you will reduce me to a violence! What violence? – What violence? – I wish my mother were here. But what good would that do? She agrees with every word he says. I wish I could lash out at someone! (*She overturns the chairs*.) I really am very stupid! This is Octave coming. – I wish he could find him here. – Ah! So this is how it starts! I was told it would happen. – I knew it. – I was expecting it! Patience, have patience! He has a punishment in mind for me! I wonder what it is? I should really like to know what he intends!

Enter **Octave**.

Marianne Sit down, Octave, I have something to say to you.

Octave But where should I sit? All the chairs have their legs in the air. – What has just happened here?

Marianne Why, nothing.

Octave Truly, cousin, your eyes tell me different.

Marianne I have reflected on what you said concerning your friend Cœlio. Tell me, why does he not speak for himself?

Octave The reason is quite simple. – He wrote to you and you tore up his letters. He sent someone to see you, and you refused to listen. He has arranged concerts for you and you left him standing in the street. You see, he has gone to the devil. And it stands to reason.

Marianne So he thought of you?

Octave Yes.

Marianne Well then, tell me about him.

Octave Seriously?

Marianne Yes, seriously, of course. Here I am. I am listening.

Octave Is this a joke?

Marianne What a pitiful advocate you are! Speak, whether it's a joke or not.

Octave Why are you glancing all around you like that? You really are in a temper!

Marianne I wish to take a lover, Octave . . . Or if not a lover, at least a cavalier. Whom do you suggest? I shall abide by your choice: Cœlio or any other, it matters little. – From tomorrow – from this evening. – Whoever has a fancy to sing beneath my windows will find my door ajar. Well? Nothing to say? I tell you I will take a lover. Look, here is my scarf in pledge: whoever you wish shall return it to me.

Octave Marianne! Since you have called me over and agreed to listen for a moment, whatever the reason for this sudden acquiescence, in Heaven's name do not change your mind again. Allow me a moment more to talk to you.

He falls to his knees.

Marianne What do you wish to say?

Octave If ever man in this world were worthy to understand you, worthy to live and die for you, that man is Cœlio. I have never been worth much, and in all fairness I must admit that the passion I am pleading finds in me a disreputable spokesman. Oh, if you only knew at what sacred altar you are worshipped like a god! You, so young, so beautiful and still so pure, handed over to an old man whose senses now are dead and who never had a heart! If only you knew, what a rich fund, what wealth of happiness lies in you and him . . . in the fresh dawn of youth, in life's celestial dew, in the first encounter of twin souls! I would rather not dwell on his sorrows, on the gentle melancholy heart of a man undismayed by your severity and ready to die without complaint. Oh yes, Marianne, die he will. What can I say? What can I invent to lend my words more force? The language of love is unknown to me. Look into your own soul. It can speak to you of his. Is there any power that can move you? You who know how to entreat the Lord, is there a prayer to express the feelings that fill my heart?

Marianne Stand up, Octave. If anyone came by, would they not think, to hear you, that truly you pleaded for yourself?

Octave Marianne, Marianne! For Heaven's sake, do not smile! Do not ignore the first spark of love that could set your heart on fire! This generous whim, this precious moment will slip away. – You have pronounced the name of Cœlio. You have, you say, thought about him. If this is a mood or a fancy, for my sake, don't change it. – The happiness of one man rests upon it.

Marianne Are you so sure I have no cause to smile?

Octave Yes, you are right. I know in how false a light my friendship can appear. I know what I am. I feel sure such language in my mouth must sound like mockery. You doubt that my words are sincere. Perhaps at this moment I have never been so bitterly aware of the small trust I inspire in others.

Marianne Why say that? You see I listen to you. Cœlio does not please me and I want nothing of him. Speak to me of another, of anyone you will. Choose for me among your friends a cavalier worthy of me. Send him to me, Octave. You see how I count on you.

Octave Oh woman, three times woman! Cœlio does not please you . . . when the merest stranger might. The man who has loved you a whole month long, who shadows your every step, who would willingly give his life at a word from your lips, such a man does not please you! He is young and handsome, rich and worthy of you on every score: but he does not please you when the merest stranger might.

Marianne Do as I tell you, or never see me more.

Exit.

Octave (*alone*) Your scarf is very pretty, Marianne, and your little caprice born of anger is a charming treaty of peace. – It would not take much vanity for me to understand it. A touch of perfidy would suffice. But it is Cœlio who will reap the benefit.

Scene Four

At **Cœlio's**

Cœlio, *a* **Servant.**

Cœlio He waits below, you say? Let him come up. Why not tell him to come at once?

Enter **Octave.**

Cœlio Well, friend, what news?

Octave Bind this token round your right arm, Cœlio. Take up your guitar and your sword. Marianne is yours.

Cœlio In Heaven's name, don't mock me.

Octave It will be a beautiful night. The moon will soon rise over the horizon. Marianne is alone and her door is ajar. You are a lucky lad, Cœlio.

Cœlio Is it true? . . . Really true? . . . Either you restore me to life, Octave, or you have no pity.

Octave Not gone yet? I tell you it is all agreed. One song beneath her window. Just pull your cloak round your face, so her husband's spies don't know you. Be fearless, that others may fear you. And prove to her, if she demurs, that it's rather too late in the day.

Cœlio Oh, God! My strength fails me.

Octave Mine too. For I have only half eaten today. – To reward me for my pains, ask them as you go out to bring me up some food. (*He sits down.*) Have you any Turkish tobacco? You will probably find I'm still here tomorrow morning. Come on, my friend, off you go! You can embrace me when you return. Off with you now! Night falls apace.

Exit **Cœlio.**

Octave (*alone*) Write on your tablets, God of justice, that in your Paradise this night shall be counted in my favour. Is it then true you have a Paradise? That woman was beautiful, I swear, and her fit of anger well became her! What can have caused it? Of that I know nothing. – What matters how the ivory ball falls upon the number we have chosen? To filch a mistress from a friend is too common a trick for me. Marianne or some other woman, what do I care? What is important is to have supper! It is clear that Cœlio has been fasting. – How you would have hated me, Marianne, if ever I had loved you! How you would have slammed your door in my face! Compared to me, how like a Sylvanus, an Adonis, your graceless husband would have seemed! – What is the reason for all this? Why does the smoke from this pipe drift more to the right than the left? There lies the reason for everything . . . Mad! Stark raving mad is the man who reckons up his chances and sets reason on *his* side! Heavenly justice holds in her hands a pair of scales. The balance is perfectly just, but all the weights are cheats. On one side a golden coin, on the other a lover's sigh, on this one a cold in the head and on that one a change in the weather. And all our human actions rise and fall as they are governed by these capricious weights.

Servant (*entering*) Here is a letter addressed to you, sir. It's so urgent that your servants brought it here. We were advised to deliver it this evening, wherever you were.

Octave Let us see what this can be. (*He reads.*) 'Do not come this evening. My husband has posted assassins

round the house and if they find you, you are lost.
Marianne.' Unhappy that I am, what have I done? My
cloak! My hat! Please God, it is not too late! You, follow
me, with all the servants not yet in their beds. Your
master's life is at stake.

He runs off.

Scene Five

Claudio's *garden. Night.*

Claudio, *two* **Cut-throats**, **Tibia**.

Claudio Let him enter. Then, when he reaches those
bushes, pounce upon him.

Tibia And what if he comes the other way?

Claudio Then wait for him at the corner by the wall.

Cut-Throat Yes, sir.

Tibia Here he comes. Look, sir, see how long his shadow
is! He is a good tall man.

Claudio Let us withdraw apart and strike when the right
moment comes.

Enter **Cœlio**.

Cœlio (*knocking at the shutter*) Marianne! Marianne! Are
you there?

Marianne (*appearing at the window*) Fly, Octave, fly! Did
you never receive my letter?

Cœlio God in Heaven! What name did I hear?

Marianne The house is surrounded by assassins. My
husband saw you come in this evening and overheard our
conversation. If you stay a minute longer, you are sure to
die.

Cœlio Is this a dream? Am I Cœlio?

Marianne Octave! Octave! Stay not in Heaven's name!
May you still have time to escape! Tomorrow at midday go
to a confessional box in church. I shall be there.

The shutter is closed.

Cœlio Oh, Death, since you are here, come to my aid!
Octave, treacherous Octave, may my blood be on your
head! You knew the fate that awaited me here and sent me
in your place. Your wish will be granted. I open my arms
to you, Death. And so I end my sorrows.

Exit. Muffled cries and distant sounds are heard in the garden.

Octave (*off*) Open up or I'll break the gate down!

Claudio (*opening, nursing his sword*) What do you want?

Octave Where is Cœlio?

Claudio I do not think it is his habit to sleep within this
house.

Octave If you have murdered him, Claudio, take care!
With these very hands I shall break your neck.

Claudio Are you sleepwalking or mad?

Octave Are you not so yourself to be walking about at his
hour, nursing a sword?

Claudio Search this garden, if such be your will. I have
seen no one come in here. And if anyone had wished to do
so, it seems I should have the right to deny him entry.

Octave (*to his servants*) Come and search everywhere!

Claudio (*in a whisper to* **Tibia**) Is all accomplished, as I
directed?

Tibia Yes, sir. Rest assured. They can search to their
hearts' content.

Exeunt.

Scene Six

A cemetery.

Octave *and* **Marianne** *beside a tomb.*

Octave Only I in all the world did know him. Here is his
perfect image, this alabaster urn, draped in its mourning
veil. Thus did tender melancholy veil the perfections of a
delicate and gentle spirit. For me alone this life of his, so
mute, held nothing of a mystery. The long evenings we
spent together seem like fresh oases in an arid desert.
They brought the only drops of morning dew that ever
touched my heart. Cœlio was the better part of me, which
has returned to Heaven with him. He was a man born out
of his time: though acquainted with pleasures, he loved
solitude best. And knowing how deceptive our illusions
are, he preferred his own illusions to reality. Happy would
she have been, the woman who could have loved him.

Marianne Would she not be happy, Octave, the woman
who loved you?

Octave I know not how to love: Cœlio alone knew that.
The ashes that lie within this tomb are all that I have
loved on earth, and all I shall ever love. He alone knew
how to spring in the hearts of others those founts of
happiness that lay within himself. He alone had the gift of
boundless devotion. He alone would have dedicated his
life to the woman he loved, as easily as he would have
braved death for her. I am but a heartless libertine. I have
no respect for women. The love I inspire in others is like
the love I feel for myself: the fleeting frenzy of a dream. I
do not have the secrets he possessed. My gaiety is like an
actor's mask: my old heart is wiser, but my jaded senses
will have none of it. I am just a renegade: even his death is
unavenged.

Marianne How could it have been, but at the risk of your
life? Claudio is too old to accept a challenge, and too
powerful in the city to go in fear of you.

Octave If I had died for him, as he for me, Cœlio would have avenged me. His tomb is rightfully my own: it is I they laid to rest beneath this cold stone, it is I they sharpened their swords for, it is I they killed. Farewell to the gaiety of my youth, my carefree follies, my wild and joy-filled life at the foot of Mount Vesuvius! Farewell to raucous banquets, evening conversations and serenades 'neath gilded balconies! Farewell to Naples and its women, to torchlight masquerades and tardy suppers in the shady woods! Farewell to love and friendship! My place on this earth stands empty.

Marianne But not in my heart, Octave. Why say you: farewell to love?

Octave I love you not, Marianne. It was Cœlio who loved you.

Fantasio

Fantasio (1 January 1834)

translated by BRIAN SINGLETON

Characters

The King of Bavaria
The Prince of Mantua
Marinoni, *his aide-de-camp*
Rutten, *the King's Private Secretary*
Fantasio
Spark
Hartman } *Young townsmen*
Facio
Elsbeth, *the King's daughter*
Elsbeth's governess
Officers, Pages *etc.*

Setting: Munich

Act One

Scene One

At Court.

The **King** *surrounded by courtiers,* **Rutten**.

King My friends, it has been a long time since I announced the betrothal of my dearest Elsbeth to the Prince of Mantua. Today I am pleased to tell you that this evening perhaps, or tomorrow at the very latest, the same prince will be arriving at the palace. I declare today a public holiday; let the prison gates be opened; let the people spend the night rejoicing. Rutten, where is my daughter?

Exeunt courtiers.

Rutten She is in the gardens with her governess, Sire.

King Why have I not seen her today? Is she happy or unhappy with the wedding arrangements?

Rutten The princess's expression seemed to me veiled with a tinge of melancholy. But then doesn't every young girl dream on the eve of her wedding day. And Saint-John's death has affected her.

King Do you think so? The death of my fool? A hunchbacked and nearly blind court jester!

Rutten The princess loved him.

King Tell me, Rutten, you've met the prince. What kind of man is he? I'm afraid I'm giving him what I cherish most in the world, and I don't even know him.

Rutten I spent very little time in Mantua.

King Be honest. Through whose eyes can I see the truth if not through yours?

Rutten Truth, Sire, I can say nothing of the nature or character of the noble prince.

King It's like that, is it? You hesitate, you, a courtier! How this room would be swimming in praise, hyperbole and flattering metaphors if the prince, who tomorrow will become my son-in-law, had seemed to you worthy of the title! Have I made a mistake, my friend? Have I made the wrong choice?

Rutten Sire, the prince could be regarded as the finest king in the world.

King The art of politics is a fine cobweb in which poor helpless flies struggle valiantly. I will not sacrifice my daughter's happiness for anything.

Exeunt.

Scene Two

A street.

Spark, Hartman *and* **Facio** *around a table, drinking.*

Hartman Since today's the day the princess gets married, let's raise our glasses, raise our pipes and raise the roof!

Facio Why don't we go and join the crowd in the streets and knock a few Chinese lanterns off the heads of those loyal subjects?

Spark Why can't we just have a quiet smoke?

Hartman I'm not having a quiet anything. Even if I have to hang in the belfry like a clapper in a church bell, I'm going to ring in the holiday. Where the hell has Fantasio got to?

Spark Yes, let's wait for him. We don't want to do anything without him.

Facio Ah, he always finds us. He's probably blind drunk in some pub in Cheap Street. Come on, one for the road!

He raises his glass. Enter an **Officer**.

Officer Gentlemen, would you mind moving on somewhere else if you don't want your revelry disturbed.

Hartman Why's that, officer?

Officer The princess is at this very moment on the terrace there and I'm sure you'll understand that it wouldn't do if your shouting were to reach her.

Exit **Officer**.

Facio Now hold on . . .

Spark What's the difference if we carouse here or somewhere else?

Hartman Who knows if we'll be allowed to carouse somewhere else? He'll have some little upstart spring up from the gutter to tell us to go carousing with the fairies.

Enter **Marinoni** *in an overcoat.*

Spark The princess has never acted the tyrant in her life. God keep her! If she doesn't want us to carouse it's because she's sad or she's singing. Leave her be.

Facio Huh! See that fellow there in the overcoat – he's fishing for something. The angler wants to join us.

Marinoni (*approaching*) I am new in town, gentlemen. Tell me, why all the celebrations?

Spark Princess Elsbeth is getting married.

Marinoni And she is a beautiful woman, I presume.

Hartman As beautiful as you are handsome.

Marinoni And loved by her people, I would venture, for the whole town seems lit up.

Hartman You are not far wrong, my good man, all these Chinese lanterns are lit as you see and, as you so wisely remarked, are nothing but illumination.

Marinoni Might I ask if the princess is the reason for these celebrations?

Hartman The one and only reason. We could all get married at once and this stupid town wouldn't bat an eyelid.

Marinoni Happy the princess who knows how to make her people love her.

Hartman Chinese lanterns don't make the people happy, my dear simple stranger. That doesn't stop the very same princess from being as flighty as a wagtail.

Marinoni Really, did you say flighty?

Hartman Correct, my dear stranger. The very word.

Marinoni *takes his leave.*

Facio Who the devil was that gibbering Italian? Look – he's going to another group. There's spy written all over him.

Hartman He's nothing of the sort. He's a fool to make fun of.

Spark Here's Fantasio.

Hartman What's the matter with him? He's lolloping about like a lawyer. Either I'm mistaken or he's up to something.

Facio Well friend, what are we going to do this beautiful evening?

Fantasio (*approaching*) Absolutely everything you wouldn't find in a Romantic novel.

Facio I was saying we should join the crowd and have a bit of fun.

Fantasio We should really get ourselves some false noses and fireworks.

Hartman Grab the girls, pull the townspeople by their tails and break their lanterns. Well? Come on, let's go.

Fantasio Once upon a time there was a king of
Persia . . .

Hartman Come on, Fantasio.

Fantasio I'm not going. I'm not going.

Hartman Why not?

Fantasio Give me a glass of that. (*He drinks.*)

Hartman You've got spring in your cheeks.

Fantasio True. And winter in my heart. My head is like
a disused chimney without a fire. Nothing but ashes and a
draught. Phew! (*He sits down.*) I'm fed up seeing everyone
have a good time. I wish this big, heavy sky was a huge
woollen scarf to wrap around the ears of this stupid town
and its stupid people. Come on, let's see. For goodness
sake, tell me some old story or some corny joke.

Hartman Why?

Fantasio To make me laugh. I don't laugh at anything
new these days. Maybe I'll laugh at something I know.

Hartman You're not good company this evening. You
look a bit down.

Fantasio I'm both. It's because I've just left my mistress.

Facio Will you join us, yes or no?

Fantasio I'll join you if you join me. Let's stay a while
and have a chat about this and that, about our new
clothes.

Facio No. If you're tired standing then I'm tired sitting.
I want to lark about outside.

Fantasio I wouldn't know how to lark about. I'm going
to have a smoke under the chestnut trees with my friend
Spark who is going to keep me company. Isn't that right,
Spark?

Spark Whatever you say.

Hartman Well, bye then. We're going to celebrate.

Exeunt **Hartman** *and* **Facio**. **Fantasio** *sits down with* **Spark**.

Fantasio The sunset is ruined this evening. Nature looks pathetic. Look at that valley down there, those four or five dark clouds climbing the mountain. I used to paint landscapes like that, when I was twelve, on the cover of my schoolbooks.

Spark The tobacco's good. So's the beer!

Fantasio Am I boring you, Spark?

Spark No. Why do you ask?

Fantasio You're boring me to death. Isn't that what happens when you see the same faces every day? How are Hartman and Facio going to celebrate?

Spark They're lively lads who can't sit still in the one place.

Fantasio Isn't *The Arabian Nights* a wonderful story. Oh Spark, dear Spark, if only you could take me to China. If only I could shed my skin for an hour or so. If only I could be that man there going by.

Spark That would be a bit difficult.

Fantasio He seems charming. Look at him, his beautiful silk breeches, and beautiful red flowers on his waistcoat, his watch chain beating against his belly while his coat-tails flap around his legs. I'm sure that man has thousands of ideas in his head which are completely alien to me. His inner being is known only to him. I'm afraid everything men say to each other sounds the same, the ideas they exchange are the same in every conversation; but inside all of these individual machines there are so many hidden places, so many secret compartments! He's carrying a whole world inside him, an unknown world which is born and which dies in silence. How lonely all these human bodies are.

Spark Come on now, drink up and stop tormenting your brain.

Fantasio For three days now there's only one thing I've found amusing. My creditors have obtained a warrant for my arrest and if I set foot in my own house four heavies will grab me by the neck.

Spark That sounds a bundle of fun. Where are you going to sleep tonight?

Fantasio With the first girl that comes along. Do you know, my furniture is to be sold off in the morning. Why don't we buy some of it?

Spark Do you need some money, Henry? Do you want me to help you out?

Fantasio Fool! If I had no money I wouldn't be in debt. I'd like to have a ballet dancer for a mistress.

Spark She'd bore you to death.

Fantasio Not in the least. My imagination would be filled with pirouettes and white satin slippers. One of my gloves would be left on a seat in the balcony from New Year's Day to New Year's Eve and I would hum the clarinet solos in my dreams as I await my death from eating too many strawberries in the arms of my beloved. Are you aware, Spark, that we have no station in life, we don't have a profession?

Spark Is that what's getting you down?

Fantasio There's no such thing as a depressed fencing master.

Spark You sound as if you've seen it all before.

Fantasio Ah, to have seen it all before you really have to have put yourself about.

Spark Well then?

Fantasio Well then what? Where do you want me to go? Look at that old smoky town. There isn't a square, or a street or an alley that I haven't hung around thirty times and more; there isn't a paving stone these worn out shoes haven't seen, not a house where I don't know the girl or the old lady whose stupid face is always to be seen at the window. I couldn't take one step without retracing yesterday's steps. Well, my friend, I know every inch of my brain better than I know this town. I know every nook and cranny, I have exhausted every street, every gap in my imagination a hundred times over, I have wandered a hundred times over in every direction in this decrepit brain of mine which I alone inhabit. I've got drunk in every pub, I've lorded it like a king in a golden carriage, I have ridden a quiet mule like any honest citizen, and now I daren't even go into town with a little torch in my hand like some thief.

Spark I don't understand why you torment yourself so much. When I smoke I think only of tobacco; when I drink I think of Spanish wine or Belgian beer; when I kiss my mistress's hand my thoughts enter the tips of her slender fingers and send electric currents right through her. I only need the scent of a flower to excite me, and in the whole of nature the tiniest creature is enough to turn me into a bee and make me flit about here and there with new-found pleasure each time.

Fantasio That's enough. Can you fish?

Spark If I like it I can do it.

Fantasio But can you catch the moon in your teeth?

Spark I don't think I'd like that.

Fantasio Ha ha! What do you know about it? Catching the moon in your teeth isn't something to be sneered at. Let's go to the casino.

Spark No, I don't really want to.

Fantasio Why not?

Spark Because we'll lose our money.

Fantasio God Almighty, what are you thinking of? You conjure up all sorts of horrible things to torture yourself with. Do you always look on the dark side, you miserable sod? Lose our money! Have you no faith, or hope? You really are an appalling atheist. You sicken my happiness, and look at me full of the joys of spring. (*He begins to dance.*)

Spark Do you know there are times when I really wonder if you're mad.

Fantasio (*still dancing*) Someone give me a bell, a glass bell.

Spark Why do you want a bell?

Fantasio Didn't the philosopher say that a man buried in deep thought is like a diver under his bell in the middle of the mighty ocean. I have no bell, Spark, no bell, and I'm dancing like Jesus Christ on the mighty ocean.

Spark Why don't you become a journalist or a novelist, Henry. It's still the only effective way to relieve your misanthropy and dull your imagination.

Fantasio I want to be craving for lobster in mustard sauce, for a girl, for a certain type of crystal. Spark, why don't we build a house for the pair of us.

Spark Why don't you write down all your dreams. It would make a nice little book.

Fantasio A sonnet is worth more than a long poem, and a glass of wine is worth more than a sonnet. (*He takes a drink.*)

Spark Why don't you go away for a while. To Italy.

Fantasio I've already been.

Spark But don't you think it's a very beautiful country?

Fantasio They've got this huge fly there that bites you all night long.

Spark Go to France.

Fantasio You can't get a good Rhine wine in Paris.

Spark Go to England.

Fantasio I'm there already. Do the English actually have a home of their own? I'd rather see them here than over there.

Spark Go to the devil then.

Fantasio Oh, if there was a devil in heaven. If there was a hell, I'd really blow my brains out. What a miserable creature man is. He can't even jump out of the window without breaking his legs. He has to play the violin for ten years to become a halfway decent musician, to learn to be a painter, a publican, to learn to make an omelette. Spark, I've got this urge to sit on top of a parapet and watch the river flowing by underneath and then count one, two, three, four, five, six, seven, and on and on till I die.

Spark The way you're talking would make many people laugh, but it gives me the creeps. It's like the history of our century. Eternity is a big open space where one century after another has flown across the sky like baby eagles and disappeared. Our century is now at the edge of the nest, but its wings have been clipped and it waits for death watching the space into which it is afraid to fly.

Fantasio (*singing*)
 You say I mean life to you
 Please let me be your soul
 For the soul springs eternal
 And life is but a day.

Do you know of a better love song than that, Spark? It's a Portuguese love song. Every time I think of it I want to love someone.

Spark Anyone in particular?

Fantasio I don't know. Some beautiful shapely girl, like the women in the paintings of the Dutch Masters; something as soft as the west wind, pale as the moonlight, dreamy as the wenches you see in Flemish paintings serving one last drink to the big-booted traveller who sits

as straight as a post on his big white horse. What a
beautiful thing the last drink is, a young woman on the
doorstep, a fire to light up the room, dinner in the oven,
the kids asleep, all the tranquillity of a calm, quiet life in
the details of a painting; and the man out of breath but
steady on his saddle having travelled twenty miles and
with another thirty to go, a drop of brandy and a farewell.
The night is dark, the weather threatening, the forest
dangerous. The woman gazes after him a while and as she
returns to her fire mutters the solemn blessing of the poor:
'God keep him!'

Spark If you were in love, Henry, you would be the
happiest man on earth.

Fantasio Love doesn't exist anymore, my friend. Its wet-
nurse, religion, has drooping breasts like an old moneybag
with a shilling at the bottom. Love is the communion
bread you break in two at the foot of the altar. There is no
altar or love anymore. Long live nature! There's still some
wine. (*He drinks.*)

Spark You're going to get drunk.

Fantasio I'm going to get drunk. You said it.

Spark It's a bit late for that.

Fantasio What do you call late? Is midday late? Is
midnight early? When does your day begin? Let's stay,
Spark, please. Let's drink, chat, analyse, reason, talk
politics. Let's devise a government. Let's catch all the
bugs flying round the candle and put them in our pockets.
Do you know that steam-powered canons are beautiful
things in matters of philanthropy?

Spark What do you mean?

Fantasio Once upon a time there was a king who was
wise, very wise. Happy, very happy.

Spark And . . . ?

Fantasio The only cloud on his horizon was not having any children. He ordered prayers to be said in all the mosques.

Spark Get to the point.

Fantasio I'm thinking of my beloved *Arabian Nights*. That's how they all begin. Well, Spark, I'm drunk. I have to do something. Tra la la! Tra la la! Come on, get up.

A funeral passes by.

Fantasio Hey there, lads. Who are you burying? You don't usually have funerals at this time of night.

Bearers We are burying Saint-John.

Fantasio Saint-John is dead? The king's fool is dead? Who has replaced him? The Minister of Justice?

Bearers The position is vacant. You can fill it if you want.

Exeunt.

Spark You really asked for that. What were you thinking of stopping them like that?

Fantasio There was nothing wrong in what he said. It was a piece of friendly advice which I'm going to heed straightaway.

Spark You're going to be the court jester?

Fantasio This very evening, if they want me. Since I can't go home, I'm going to watch the performance of that royal comedy tomorrow, and from the royal box itself.

Spark Very clever, aren't you! You'll be recognized and the footmen will throw you out. Aren't you the godson of the late queen?

Fantasio Very stupid, aren't you! I'll have a hump and a ginger wig like Saint-John and no one will recognize me even if I have three dozen godfathers on my tail. (*He knocks on a shop door.*) Hello there, good sir. Open up, if you haven't already gone out with your wife and your puppies.

Tailor (*opening his shop*) What is it you want, sir?

Fantasio You are the king's tailor, are you not?

Tailor At your service.

Fantasio Did you use to tailor for Saint-John?

Tailor Yes, sir.

Fantasio Did you know him to see? Did you know which side he wore his hump, how he trimmed his moustache and what kind of wig he wore?

Tailor Is this a joke?

Fantasio This is no joke, my man. Let's go to the back room, and if you don't want your coffee poisoned in the morning, mind you stay as silent as the grave about this.

He exits with **Tailor**, *followed by* **Spark**.

Scene Three

An inn on the road to Munich.

Enter **The Prince of Mantua** *and* **Marinoni**.

Prince Well, Colonel?

Marinoni Your Highness?

Prince Well, Marinoni?

Marinoni Despondent, flighty, over the moon, obedient to her father, likes peas.

Prince Write it down. I can only understand fully in long hand.

Marinoni (*writing*) Despon . . .

Prince Write softly. I have been dreaming of an important plan since dinner.

Marinoni There you are, as you requested, Your Highness.

Prince Good. I will call you my close friend. In my whole kingdom I know no other writing more beautiful than your own. Sit over there. Well, my friend, do you think you know the secret of the temperament of the princess, my future wife?

Marinoni Yes, Your Highness. I have been all over the palace and these notes contain the gist of the various conversations in which I interfered.

Prince (*looking at his reflection*) I seem to be powdered like a commoner.

Marinoni You are dressed splendidly.

Prince What would you say, Marinoni, if you saw your master dressed in a simple green tailcoat.

Marinoni Your Highness is mocking my gullibility.

Prince No, Colonel. I would have you know that your master is one of the most romantic men around.

Marinoni Romantic, Your Highness?

Prince Yes, my friend – I have bestowed upon you the title of friend. My family would be apoplectic if they knew of the important plan I am contemplating. I will pretend to arrive at Court as a simple aide-de-camp. It is not sufficient to send a man to sound out public opinion on the future Princess of Mantua (and that man, Marinoni, is you), I want to see with my own eyes.

Marinoni Really, Your Highness?

Prince Don't be horrified. A man like me should only have a broadminded and enterprising close friend.

Marinoni There is only one thing that seems to stand in your way, Your Highness.

Prince And what is that?

Marinoni The idea of disguise could only belong to the glorious prince who rules over us. But if my gracious sovereign is mixed up with the staff, who will the King of Bavaria honour with a magnificent banquet in the gallery?

Prince You are right. If I am in disguise, someone must take my place. It is impossible, Marinoni. I never thought of that.

Marinoni Why is it impossible, Your Highness?

Prince I can, of course, lower my princely dignity to the rank of colonel. But do you really believe that I could consent to elevate someone or other to my rank. And besides, do you think that my future father-in-law would forgive me?

Marinoni The king seems to me a sensible and thoughtful fellow, and a pleasant one at that.

Prince Ah, it is with great regret that I must renounce my plan. To enter this new court without pomp or ceremony, to observe everything, to approach the princess under a false name, and perhaps to woo her. Oh, I'm distraught. It's impossible. Marinoni, my friend, try on my ceremonial dress, I cannot resist it.

Marinoni (*bowing*) Your Highness!

Prince Do you think that in years to come people will forget such an occasion?

Marinoni Never, my gracious Prince.

Prince Come, try it on.

Exeunt.

Act Two

Scene One

King of Bavaria's *garden.*

Enter **Elsbeth** *and her* **Governess**.

Governess I have shed tears, floods of tears.

Elsbeth You are so good-hearted. I, too, loved Saint-John. He was so full of life. No ordinary fool.

Governess To think that the poor man went to heaven on the eve of your wedding, the man who would talk only of you from lunch till supper, all day long. Such a cheerful, funny boy who could make us love ugliness and whom we couldn't help admiring.

Elsbeth Don't speak to me of my wedding. It makes me suffer even more.

Governess You do know that the Prince of Mantua arrives today. I hear he is an Adonis.

Elsbeth What are you saying, my dear! He is hideous and stupid. Everyone here knows that.

Governess Really, I heard he was an Adonis.

Elsbeth I didn't ask for an Adonis, my dear. But it is a cruel thing sometimes to be nothing but the daughter of a king. My father is the most wonderful man. The wedding he is preparing will ensure peace in his kingdom. His reward will be the blessings of the people. What shall I have but his own blessing, and nothing more.

Governess There is sadness in your voice.

Elsbeth If I refused the prince, war would soon break out again. It is a great misfortune that these peace treaties are always signed with tears. I wish I could be strong-willed and put up with the first man who came along, when politics demands. To be mother of a nation consoles the stout-hearted but not the weak-willed. I am only a poor dreamer. Perhaps your novels are to blame, the ones you always keep in your pockets.

Governess Please tell no one, I beg you.

Elsbeth I know little about life, but I have many dreams.

Governess If the Prince of Mantua is like you say, God will not permit this business to go ahead, I'm sure.

Elsbeth Do you think so? God leaves men alone, my poor friend, and treats our bleatings as he would a sheep's.

Governess I'm sure that if you refuse the prince, your father will not force you.

Elsbeth No, he will definitely not force me. And that is why I am sacrificing myself. Do you want me to tell my father to go back on his word and to score out with one stroke of a pen his respectable name on a contract which will ensure the happiness of thousands? What does the unhappiness of one matter. I will allow my good father to be a good king.

Governess *begins to cry.*

Elsbeth Don't cry for me, dear. You might make me cry, too, and a royal fiancée should not have red eyes. Don't worry yourself about it. After all, I will be a queen, how about that? Perhaps I will come to like my finery, my carriages in my new court, who knows? Fortunately for a princess there are other things in a marriage besides a husband. Perhaps I will find happiness amongst my wedding presents.

Governess You are a real paschal lamb.

Elsbeth Come along, my dear. Let's have a laugh about it and only cry when the time comes. I hear the Prince of Mantua is the most ridiculous creature in the world.

Governess If only Saint-John were here.

Elsbeth Ah! Saint-John, Saint-John!

Governess You loved him a lot, my child.

Elsbeth It's strange. My mind and his were sewn together with the finest thread which seemed to come from my heart. His continual mocking of my romantic notions drove me wild, while I can scarcely bear people who always agree with me. I don't know what it was about him, his eyes, his gestures, the way he took his snuff. He was a strange man. When he talked to me he painted beautiful pictures before my eyes. His words brought life to the strangest things as if by magic.

Governess He was a real Yorick.

Elsbeth I don't know about that but he had a real sparkling wit.

Governess There are pages toing and froing. I think the prince will soon be here. You must go back to the palace and change.

Elsbeth Please leave me alone for a little while more. Go and see to what I need. Alas, my dear, there is little time left to dream.

Governess Lord, is it possible that this marriage will take place if it is not to your liking? A father sacrifice his daughter! The king would be like the Old Testament Jephthah if he did it.

Elsbeth Don't speak ill of my father. Go, my dear, and see to what I need.

Exit **Governess**.

Elsbeth (*alone*) There appears to be someone behind those bushes. Is it the ghost of my poor fool I see sitting in the grass among the bluebells? Answer me. Who are you? What are you doing there? Picking flowers? (*She moves to a little rise.*)

Fantasio (*dressed as a fool with hump and wig*) I'm an honest flower picker who bids good day to your beautiful eyes.

Elsbeth Why are you dressed like this? Why have you come with this large wig to mimic a man I loved? Are you practising to be a fool?

Fantasio May it please Your Most Serene Highness, I am the king's new fool. The head butler received me favourably. I was presented to the king's valet. The kitchen boys have been looking after me since yesterday evening, and I am humbly picking flowers waiting for my wit to come.

Elsbeth I doubt if you'll ever pick that particular flower.

Fantasio Why? It can come to an old man just as a young girl can lose it. Sometimes it is difficult to distinguish between a flash of wit and gross stupidity! Talk, talk, talk. That's the most important thing. The worst marksman can hit the bull's-eye if he shoots 780 times a minute, just as well as a clever marksman who takes one or two well-aimed shots. All I ask is to have enough food to fill my belly and I will look at my shadow in the sun to see if my wig is growing.

Elsbeth And so there you are dressed in Saint-John's cast-offs? You are right to speak of your shadow. As long as you wear that costume it will always remind me of him more than you, I think.

Fantasio At the moment I am composing an elegy that will decide my fate.

Elsbeth In what way?

Fantasio It will prove conclusively that I am the best in the world or it will be nothing at all. I am in the process of shattering the universe, of making it an acrostic; the moon, the sun, the stars are fighting to appear in my verse like spectators outside a music-hall.

Elsbeth Poor man. What a job you are undertaking, being witty by the hour. Have you no arms or legs? Would you not be better ploughing the land than your own brain?

Fantasio Poor child. What a job you are undertaking, marrying a fool you have never seen. Have you no heart or head? Would you not be better selling your dresses than your body?

Elsbeth You are a brazen fellow, Mr Newcomer.

Fantasio Can you tell me the name of that flower, please?

Elsbeth A tulip. What are you trying to prove?

Fantasio A red or a blue tulip?

Elsbeth Blue, it looks like.

Fantasio Not at all. It's a red tulip.

Elsbeth Are you trying to dress mutton up as lamb? You don't have to, just to say that one shouldn't argue about taste or colours.

Fantasio I am not arguing. I am telling you that this tulip is red, and yet I admit it's blue.

Elsbeth And how do you work that out?

Fantasio Like your marriage contract. Who can tell whether it was born red or blue? The tulips themselves don't know. Gardeners and solicitors are doing such extraordinary transplants that turn apples into pumpkins, and donkeys' thistles into artichokes which end up with mayonnaise on a bishop's silver platter. The tulip was really expecting to be red, but it has got married and is quite surprised to be blue. That's how the whole world changes when man gets his hands on it. And poor Mother Nature must laugh at herself heartily sometimes when she reflects her continual masquerade in her lakes and seas. Do you think it smelt of roses in Moses' heaven? It only smelt of green hay. The rose is the daughter of civilization. It is a marquess like you and me.

Elsbeth The pale flower of the hawthorn can become a rose and a thistle can become an artichoke. But a flower cannot turn into another one. So what does it matter to nature? You can't change it. You either dress it up or kill it. The tiniest little violet would die rather than let someone artificially alter the shape of its stem.

Fantasio That's why I consider a violet more important than a princess.

Elsbeth There are certain things which even fools have no right to mock. Be careful. If you were listening in to my conversation with my governess, watch yourself.

Fantasio No, not myself. My tongue. You've got the wrong sense. You've lost your senses.

Elsbeth Don't play on words if you want to earn your keep. And don't compare me to a tulip if you want to keep your job.

Fantasio Who knows? A play on words cures many an ill. And to play on words is just another way of playing on thoughts, actions and lives. Everything is a play on words down here, and it's just as difficult to understand the look on the face of a four-year-old child as the gibberish you hear on the stage these days.

Elsbeth You seem to be looking at the world through a rather warped prism.

Fantasio Everyone has his spectacles but no one knows precisely the colour of the lenses. Who can tell exactly whether I'm happy or sad, good or bad, joyful or tearful, witty or stupid?

Elsbeth One thing's for certain. You're ugly.

Fantasio No more certain than your beauty. Here comes your father with your future husband. Who can tell if you will marry him?

Exit.

Elsbeth Since I cannot avoid the Prince of Mantua, I would be as well to go and meet him.

Enter the **King,** **Marinoni** *dressed as the* **Prince,** *and the* **Prince** *dressed as his aide-de-camp.*

King Allow me to introduce my daughter. Forgive the gardener's outfit. I am but a simple man who rules over others and our easygoing etiquette has us dress like our simple people.

Marinoni Permit me to kiss this charming hand, Ma'am, if this favour is not too great for my humble lips.

Elsbeth Your Highness will excuse me if I go back to the palace. I will see him this evening at the reception in a manner more fitting.

Exit.

Prince The princess is quite right. What divine modesty.

King (*to* **Marinoni**) Who is this aide-de-camp who keeps shadowing you? I cannot bear his inept commentary on everthing we say. I beg you, send him away.

Marinoni *whispers to the* **Prince.**

Prince (*to* **Marinoni**) It's very clever of you to persuade him to dismiss me. I will try to meet up with the princess and to have a few words in her ear without revealing anything.

Exit.

King My friend, this aide-de-camp is an imbecile. What are you doing with a man like that?

Marinoni Em, can we proceed a little further, if Your Majesty will allow. I think I see a rather charming pavilion in the trees.

Exeunt.

Scene Two

Another part of the garden.

Enter the **Prince**.

Prince My disguise is a wonderful success. I watch as she falls in love with me. Up to now everything is as I wish. The father seems a fine king, although too simple, and I would be surprised if I didn't please him straightaway. I see the princess returning to the palace. Luck is on my side.

Enter **Elsbeth**, *the* **Prince** *approaches.*

Prince Your Highness, permit me, as faithful servant to your future husband, to offer you sincere congratulations which my humble and devoted heart cannot suppress in your presence. Happy are the noble people in the world. They can marry you, I cannot. That is totally impossible. I am of humble birth. The only thing in my favour is a name which strikes terror in the hearts of the enemy; a pure unsullied heart beats beneath this simple uniform. I am a poor soldier riddled with bullets from head to toe. I haven't a penny to my name. I am lonely, exiled from my native soil like from my heavenly home, I mean from my perfect heaven. I have no woman's heart to press against my own. I am damned and silent.

Elsbeth What do you want of me, my dear man? Are you mad or are you asking for money?

Prince It would be difficult to find the words to express my feelings. I saw you walk alone along this path. I believed it my duty to throw myself at your feet and accompany you as far as the gate.

Elsbeth I am grateful to you. Now please be good enough to leave me in peace.

Exit.

Prince (*alone*) Was I wrong to approach her? But I had to, since my plan is to seduce her beneath this disguise. Yes, I was right to approach her. Yet her response was not very pleasant. Perhaps I shouldn't have spoken to her so keenly. But I had to, since her marriage is almost assured and I am supposed to be unseating Marinoni. But her response was not very pleasant. Is she hard-hearted and false? I must have my wits about me and sound things out.

Exit.

Scene Three

An anteroom.

Fantasio *is lying on the carpet.*

Fantasio How delightful it is to play the fool! I think I was drunk last night when I put on this costume and entered the palace. But really and truly, sound reason never inspired me as much as this act of folly. Here I am accepted, adored, signed up and what's even better, forgotten. I come and go in the palace as if I'd lived here all my life. Just now I met the King. He didn't so much as look at me. His fool was dead and he was told, 'Sire, here's another.' It's wonderful. Thank God, now my mind's at rest. I can talk as much twaddle as I like with no one to stop me. I am one of the King of Bavaria's pets and if I want, as long as I keep my hump and my wig, I can live till I die among the spaniels and guinea-fowl. My creditors will just have to bide their time banging their heads against my door. I am as safe here under this wig as I would be in the West Indies.

I think I see the princess through this mirror in the next room. She's fixing her veil. Two big tears are trickling down her cheeks. There, one drops like a pearl onto her breast. Poor mite! I overheard her conversation this morning with her governess. Really, it was an accident. I was sitting on the lawn with only a mind to sleep. Now there she is crying and hasn't a clue I'm watching her. If only I was versed in rhetoric. I would muse profoundly on the misery of the crown, on this poor lamb with a pink ribbon round her neck to lead her to slaughter. This young girl is a romantic, I don't doubt, and it is a cruel thing for her to marry a man she doesn't know. And yet she sacrifices herself in silence. Chance is a fickle thing. Why did I have to get drunk, stumble across Saint-John's funeral, assume his costume and his place, and commit the craziest act in all creation, and then just happen to see through this mirror the two solitary tear-drops which she will shed on her bridal veil.

Exit.

Scene Four

A garden path.

The **Prince, Marinoni**.

Prince You're nothing but a fool, Colonel.

Marinoni Your Highness is most dreadfully mistaken about me.

Prince You are a complete idiot. Could you not have prevented it? I confide in you the greatest plan ever hatched for many a year and you, my best friend, my most faithful servant, you heap stupidity upon stupidity. No, no, it's no use, it's totally unforgivable.

Marinoni How could I have prevented Your Highness from attracting the trouble which is the natural result of the role you are playing? You ordered me to take your name and to behave like the real Prince of Mantua. Can I stop the King of Bavaria insulting my aide-de-camp. You were wrong to meddle in our affairs.

Prince I really appreciate a rogue like you sticking your nose in and giving me orders.

Marinoni Think carefully, Your Highness, either I am the prince or the aide-de-camp. I am acting on your instructions.

Prince Telling me I am an upstart in front of the whole court for wanting to kiss the princess's hand. I feel like declaring war and going back home to lead my armies.

Marinoni Remember, Your Highness, that this insult was addressed to the aide-de-camp, not the prince. Do you think you can command respect in this disguise?

Prince Enough. Give me back my clothes.

Marinoni (*removing* **Prince**'s *costume*) If my sovereign so requires, I'm ready to die for him.

Prince Really, I hardly know what to do. On the one hand I am furious with what has happened to me, on the other I am loathe to give up my plan. The princess does not appear to respond indifferently to the double meaning in the words with which I constantly pursue her. Already I have managed on two or three occasions to whisper the most unbelievable things in her ear. Come along, let's think about it for a while.

Marinoni (*still holding* **Prince**'s *costume*) What shall I do, Your Highness?

Prince Put it back on and let's go to the Palace.

Exeunt.

Scene Five

Elsbeth, *the* **King**.

King My child, answer frankly: are you happy or unhappy with this marriage?

Elsbeth That, Sire, you must answer yourself. I am happy if you are happy. I am unhappy if you are unhappy.

King The prince seems an ordinary man. You can't say much about him. The only thing, to my mind, not in his favour is his aide-de-camp. He may be a prince but there's nothing noble about him. He is neither attractive nor repulsive. What more can I say? A woman's heart holds secrets which I can never know. Sometimes she creates the strangest heroes, she latches so remarkably onto one or two sides to a man presented to her, that it is impossible to judge for oneself, as long as one has no sensitivity to guide one. Tell me straight what you think of your fiancé.

Elsbeth I think that he is the Prince of Mantua and that war will break out again tomorrow between you and him if I don't marry him.

King There's no doubt about that, my child.

Elsbeth So I think I will marry him and put an end to war.

King May the blessings of my people be your father's thanks. Oh my sweet child! I will be happy with this union. But I would not care to see sadness in those beautiful eyes which belies resignation. Think on it a few days more.

Exit. Enter **Fantasio**.

Elsbeth There you are, poor boy. Are you happy here?

Fantasio Like a bird in the sky.

Elsbeth You would have been better to say like a bird in a cage. This palace is a rather beautiful cage, but it's still a cage.

Fantasio The size of a palace or a room doesn't change the extent of a man's freedom. The body moves where it can. Imagination sometimes spreads its wings as big as the sky in a dungeon as big as your hand.

Elsbeth So you are a happy fool.

Fantasio Very happy. I chat with puppies and the kitchen boys. There is a nasty little lap-dog no taller than that in the kitchen which tells me delightful things.

Elsbeth In what language?

Fantasio In the purest of styles. He would not make a single grammatical mistake in the course of a year.

Elsbeth May I hear a few words in this style?

Fantasio To be honest, I don't want to. It is a strange tongue. Not only lap-dogs speak it. The trees and even the grains of wheat know it, too, but the daughters of kings don't know it. When is your wedding?

Elsbeth In a few days all will be over.

Fantasio You mean it all will have just begun. I intend to give you a present.

Elsbeth What kind of present? I'd like to know.

Fantasio I intend to give you a pretty little stuffed canary which sings like a nightingale.

Elsbeth How can it sing if it's stuffed?

Fantasio It sings to perfection.

Elsbeth I think you're going out of your way to poke fun at me.

Fantasio Not at all. My canary has a little bird-organ in its tummy. If you press gently on a little button under its right foot it will sing all the famous arias like a diva.

Elsbeth This invention is in your head, I think.

Fantasio Not at all. It's a court canary. There are many well-brought-up young girls who behave no differently.

They have a little button under their left arm, a pretty little diamond button like a fop's watch. The tutor or governess presses the button and straightaway you see the lips form a gracious smile, a charming little stream of sugar-sweet words comes out in a soft whisper and all the social niceties begin to dance like nimble nymphs on points around the magic fountain. The fiancé gawks. The assembled company whispers sympathetically and the father who is secretly very happy looks proudly at the golden buckles on her shoes.

Elsbeth You always seem to return to the same themes. Tell me, fool, what have these poor girls done to you that you satirize them so cruelly? Do you have no respect for fulfilling one's duty?

Fantasio I really respect ugliness. That's why I have a great respect for myself.

Elsbeth Sometimes you seem to know more than you can say. Where do you come from? Who are you? I ask because in the one day you've been here you already know how to unlock secrets which princes themselves will never know exist. Is your madness aimed at me or at chance?

Fantasio Chance. I speak a lot to chance. He is my dearest confidant.

Elsbeth He seems to have taught you what you ought not to know. I can only think that you have been listening to my conversations and spying on me.

Fantasio Who knows? What does it matter?

Elsbeth More than you think. While I was in my room putting on my veil I suddenly heard footsteps behind the tapestry. If I am not greatly mistaken those footsteps belonged to you.

Fantasio You can rest assured that it is a secret between your handkerchief and me. My discretion is equal to my curiosity. What pleasure could I take in your troubles? What trouble would your pleasure cause me? You are this and I am that. You are young and I am old. Beautiful, and I am ugly. Rich, and I am poor. You see we have nothing at all in common. What does it matter to you that chance has forced two wheels to cross on the main road which are not on the same track and cannot leave the same mark in the dirt? Can I help it if one of your tears fell on my cheek when I was sleeping?

Elsbeth You speak to me in the shape of a man whom I once loved. That's why I listen to you despite my better judgement. My eyes think they see Saint-John; but perhaps it is a spy they see.

Fantasio And what good would it do me? If it was true that you were shedding tears over your wedding and if I learnt it by chance, what would I gain by telling everyone? I wouldn't get a penny for it and you wouldn't be sent to your room. I can fully understand how dreadful it must be to marry the Prince of Mantua, but really it's none of my business. Tomorrow or the day after you will have left for Mantua with your wedding dress, and I will still be here on this stool in my old breeches. Why do you think I've got something against you? I have no reason to wish you dead. You never lent me any money.

Elsbeth But if chance has made you see what I want kept hidden, should I not throw you out in case another accident occurs?

Fantasio Do you think you can compare me to the confidant of a tragic heroine? Are you afraid I shall shadow you with my wagging tongue? Don't throw me out, I beg you. I am enjoying myself here. Look, here's your governess with her pockets full of secrets. I'll prove to you that I won't listen. I'll go to the kitchen to eat the plover's wing the head butler set aside for his wife.

Exit.

Governess (*entering*) Do you know the most terrible thing, my dear Elsbeth?

Elsbeth What are you trying to say? You're trembling.

Governess The prince is not the prince, and neither is his aide-de-camp. It's a *complete* fairy tale.

Elsbeth What are you trying to tell me?

Governess Shush! One of the prince's own officers has just told me. The Prince of Mantua is a real Almaviva. He is disguised and hidden amongst his aides-de-camp. No doubt he wanted to look at you and get to know you like in a fairy tale. The noble lord is disguised as Lindor. The man presented to you as your future husband is only an aide-de-camp called Marinoni.

Elsbeth It's impossible.

Governess There's absolutely no doubt about it. The noble lord is disguised. It is impossible to recognize him. It is truly amazing.

Elsbeth You say you got it from an officer?

Governess One of the prince's officers. You can ask him yourself.

Elsbeth Did he not point out which of the aides-de-camp was the real Prince of Mantua.

Governess He was shaking all over, the poor man, don't you know, with what he was telling me. He confided his secret to me because he wanted to be nice to you and he knew that I would warn you. It's definitely true about Marinoni but as for the real prince, he wouldn't name him.

Elsbeth It's food for thought, if it's true. Come, take me to the officer.

Enter a **Page**.

Governess What is the matter, Flamel? You seem out of breath.

Page This will really crack you up. I daren't speak in front of Your Highness.

Elsbeth Tell me. What's the matter?

Page Just as the Prince of Mantua was riding into Court ahead of his Chief of Staff his wig flew up in the air and then suddenly disappeared.

Elsbeth Why? What stupidity!

Page I'll die if I'm not telling the truth. The wig flew up into the air on the end of a hook. We found it in the kitchens beside a broken bottle. We don't know who played the trick on him. But the prince was so furious that he swore if the joker was not put to death he would declare war on the king, your father, and burn and butcher the lot of us.

Elsbeth My dear, come and listen to this. I don't think I can keep a straight face.

Enter another **Page**.

Elsbeth Well, what's the news?

Page Ma'am, the king's fool is in prison. It was he who removed the prince's wig.

Elsbeth The fool in prison? At the prince's command?

Page Yes, Your Highness.

Elsbeth Come, dear Mother. I must speak to you.

Exit with **Governess**.

Scene Six

The **Prince, Marinoni**.

Prince No, no, let me reveal my true self. It is time I burst forth. Things cannot go on like this. God damn it, a royal wig on a hook! Are we amongst barbarians in the Siberian desert? Is there not one ounce of decency and civility left on earth? I am so angry I think my head will explode.

Marinoni Such violent behaviour will lose you everything.

Prince And what about the father, the King of Bavaria, the monarch celebrated in all the royal journals last year! This man who outwardly appears so decent, so temperate in his expression, and who starts laughing at his son-in-law's wig flying in the air. Well Marinoni, I know it was your wig that was sent flying, but it was the Prince of Mantua's, was it not, since they believe that you are he. When I think that it could have been me, in flesh and blood, my wig might have . . . It was divine providence which gave me the idea of dressing up. When the idea entered my head, 'I must dress up', destiny had already predicted this fatal event. It was destiny that saved me from an unbearable affront on the ruler of my peoples. But heavens, I can contain myself no more. I have betrayed my dignity too long. Since the divine and human majesties have been mercilessly desecrated and mutilated, since men can no longer tell the difference between good and evil, since the king of thousands bursts out laughing like a publican at the sight of a wig, Marinoni, give me my clothes.

Marinoni (*removing costume*) If my sovereign so commands, I am ready to suffer for him a thousand tortures.

Prince I am aware of your devotion. Come along. I'm going to give the king a piece of my mind.

Marinoni Are you refusing the princess's hand? It was quite obvious she had her eye on you over dinner.

Prince Do you think so? Now I'm more and more confused by the minute. Come along. Let's go see the king.

Marinoni (*holding costume*) What shall I do with it, Your Highness?

Prince Put it back on for the moment. You will give it back to me afterwards. They will be even more petrified when they hear me speak like a prince in this dark tail coat.

Exeunt.

Scene Seven

A prison.

Fantasio, *alone.*

Fantasio I don't know if there's such a thing as divine intervention but it's fun to believe in it. There was a poor little princess who was going to marry this vile dog against her will, a provincial prig whom chance had crowned, like the eagle dropping the tortoise on Aeschylus. Everything was ready. The candles were lit, the intended powdered, the poor little mite had made her confession. She had wiped away the two charming tears I saw this morning. Give or take a sermon or two, the misery of her life was ready to be settled. The fate of two kingdoms, the peace of two peoples depended on it. And then I came along disguised with a hump, drunk once again, in our good king's kitchens, and hooked his dear ally's wig on the end of a string. Really, when I'm drunk I feel I can do anything. Now the marriage has fallen through and everything is up in the air. The Prince of Mantua has demanded my head in exchange for his wig. The King of Bavaria considered the punishment too harsh and only agreed to imprisonment. The Prince of Mantua is so stupid, thank God, that he would rather be drawn and quartered than give in. And so the princess remains single, at least for the time being. Now if that doesn't contain the subject of an epic poem in twelve stanzas, then I don't know what does. Pope and Boileau have written marvellous verse on subjects much less important. Ah, if I were a poet I would paint the scene of the wig flying about in the air. But if you actually do things like that, you don't want to write about them. And so posterity will do without.

He falls asleep.

Enter **Elsbeth** *and her* **Governess**, *carrying a lamp.*

Elsbeth He's asleep. Close the door softly.

Governess You see, there is no doubt. He has taken off his false wig and his deformity has disappeared with it. There he is as he is, as his people see him on his triumphal mount. It's the noble Prince of Mantua.

Elsbeth Yes, it's him. My curiosity is satisfied. I wanted to see his face and nothing else. Let me lean over him. (*She takes the lamp.*) Psyche, don't drop the oil.

Governess He is as beautiful as the baby Jesus.

Elsbeth Why did you give me so many novels and fairy tales to read? Why did you plant so many strange and mysterious flowers in my head?

Governess You really are excited now!

Elsbeth He's waking up. Let's go.

Fantasio (*waking up*) Am I dreaming? I'm holding the hem of a white dress.

Elsbeth Let me go!

Fantasio It's you, Princess. If it's the pardon of the king's fool you bring to me from heaven, allow me to put on my hump and wig. It will only take a moment.

Governess Prince, it really doesn't become you to deceive us like that. Don't put the costume back on. We know everything.

Fantasio Prince! Can you see one?

Governess What's the use pretending?

Fantasio I'm not pretending one little bit. What makes you call me prince?

Governess I'm showing respect to Your Highness.

Fantasio Ma'am, I beg you to explain to me what this good woman is saying. Is this some crazy misunderstanding. Are you making a fool of me?

Elsbeth Why do you ask when you yourself were making fools of us?

Fantasio So, am I a prince by some stroke of luck? Are you casting doubt on my mother's honour?

Elsbeth Who are you, if not the Prince of Mantua?

Fantasio My name is Fantasio. I am an honest citizen of Munich.

He shows her a letter.

Elsbeth An honest citizen of Munich! Then why are you disguised? What are you doing here?

Fantasio Ma'am, I beg you to forgive me.

He falls to his knees.

Elsbeth What does this mean? Get up, man, and go. I am giving you a pardon which you perhaps do not deserve. Who put you up to it?

Fantasio I cannot tell you the reason for my action.

Elsbeth You cannot tell me, and yet I want to know.

Fantasio Forgive me, I daren't tell you.

Governess Let's go, Elsbeth. Don't expose yourself to conversation unworthy of you. This man is a thief, or an upstart who is going to speak to you of love.

Elsbeth I want to know the reason why you put on this costume.

Fantasio Don't do this to me, please.

Elsbeth No, speak, or I'll lock you up in here for ten years.

Fantasio Ma'am, I'm crippled with debts. My creditors have taken out a writ against me. As I speak, my furniture is being sold. If I wasn't in this prison I'd be in another. I was to be arrested last night. Not knowing what to do with myself, how to escape the clutches of the bailiffs, I thought of putting on this costume and taking refuge at the king's feet. If you set me free I'll be collared. My uncle is a miser who lives on potatoes and radishes and lets me die of starvation in all the pubs in the kingdom. Since you want to know, I owe twenty thousand écus.

Elsbeth Are you telling me the truth?

Fantasio If I'm lying, I'll pay it all back.

Sound of horses.

Governess I hear horses. It's the king himself. If I could signal to a page. (*She shouts out of the window.*) Hey, Flamel, where are you going?

Page (*off*) The Prince of Mantua is leaving.

Governess The Prince of Mantua!

Page Yes, war has been declared. There was a dreadful scene between him and the king in front of the whole court, and the wedding with the princess is off.

Elsbeth Do you hear that, Mr Fantasio? You have ruined my wedding.

Governess The Lord God Almighty! The Prince of Mantua is going and I never saw him.

Elsbeth If war has been declared, it is a tragedy.

Fantasio You call that a tragedy, Your Highness? Would you rather have a husband who goes to blows over a wig? Ma'am, if war is declared it will give us something to do. Our men of leisure will don uniforms. I'll take my hunting rifle, if it hasn't been sold. We will go on a tour of Italy, and if you should stop at Mantua it will be as a true queen, with just our swords to lead the way.

Elsbeth Fantasio, do you wish to remain my father's fool? I will pay your twenty thousand écus.

Fantasio I would like that very much. But really, if I'm forced I might jump out of the window one of these days and run away.

Elsbeth Why? You know Saint-John is dead and we really do need a fool.

Fantasio I like this job more than any other, but I cannot hold down any job. If you think it worth twenty thousand écus to be rid of the Prince of Mantua, give me the money but don't pay my debts. A gentleman without debts would be ashamed of himself. I never considered being solvent.

Elsbeth Well, I shall give you the money but take the key to my garden. If ever you get tired running from your creditors, come and hide in the bluebells where I found you this morning. Mind you take your wig with you and your coat of many colours, and don't ever let me see you without this deformity and these silver bells. Because that's how I came to like you. You will be my clown again for as long as you please and then you'll return to your own life. You may go now. The door is open.

Governess How could the Prince of Mantua have gone without me seeing him?

Lorenzaccio

Lorenzaccio (23 August 1834)

translated by DONALD WATSON

Translator's Note

This version was first made in collaboration with students and colleagues of the French and Drama Departments of the University of Bristol, where, in 1974, it was produced in an abridged form lasting three and a half hours, with other students in the cast drawn from the Bristol Old Vic Theatre School. Some of these performers have since had successful careers in the professional world, such as Diana Hardcastle, Veronica Hyks, Paul Evans, Graham Callan, Jack Klaff, to name but a few. It was directed by a French and Drama student, Hassan el Geretly who, after working for several years in the French theatre, now holds an important position in the theatre in Cairo.

Acted versions of this play often require cutting and reshaping. This is a translation of the entire play and has been completely revised.

A compromise has been made in the treatment of proper names between French, Italian and English usage. But it is assumed that 'de' Medici' is pronounced in the Italian, not the French, style with the stress on the first syllable of 'Medici'.

Characters

Alexander de' Medici, *Duke of Florence*
Lorenzo de' Medici (Lorenzaccio) ⎫
Cosimo de' Medici　　　　　　　　⎬ *his cousins*
Cardinal Cibo
Marchese Cibo, *his brother*
Lord Maurizio, *Chancellor of the Council of Eight*
Cardinal Baccio Valori, *Papal Envoy*
Julian Salviati
Philip Strozzi
Peter Strozzi　　　　　⎫
Thomas Strozzi　　　　⎬ *his sons*
Leon Strozzi, *Prior of Capua* ⎭
Robert Corsini, *Governor of the Citadel*
Palla Ruccellai　　　⎫
Alamanno Salviati　⎬ *Republican nobles*
Francesco Pazzi　　⎭
Bindo Altoviti, *Lorenzo's uncle*
Venturi, *a burgher*
Tebaldeo, *a painter*
Scoronconcolo, *a swordsman*
The Council of Eight
Giomo the Hungarian, *the Duke's henchman*
Maffio, *a citizen*
Maria Soderini, *Lorenzo's mother*
Catherine Ginori, *Lorenzo's young aunt*
Marchesa Cibo
Louisa Strozzi, *Philip Strozzi's daughter*
Goldsmith, *Silk Merchant*
Two Court Ladies *and a* German Officer
Two Tutors *and two* Boys
Pages, Soldiers, Monks, Courtiers, Exiles, Apprentices,
Servants, Citizens, *etc.*

Setting: Florence and Venice, 1537

Act One

Scene One

A garden by moonlight. One villa at the front, another at the rear.

Enter the **Duke** *and* **Lorenzo,** *muffled in cloaks with* **Giomo** *holding a lantern.*

The Duke Let her keep me waiting another fifteen minutes and I'm going. It's devilish cold out here.

Lorenzo Don't be so impatient, Your Highness.

The Duke She should have left her mother's house by now. It's midnight and still no sign of her.

Lorenzo If she doesn't come, call me an idiot, and her old mother an honest woman.

The Duke By the Pope's holy guts! They're cheating me out of a thousand ducats!

Lorenzo We only advanced half the sum. I'll vouch for the girl. There's no mistaking that wide-eyed innocent look. What's more tempting to the connoisseur than the chance to corrupt an infant? To divine the making of a whore in a fifteen-year-old girl? To prepare the ground for the seeds of vice and tend them with fatherly care, with a few friendly words in the ear and a gentle caress of the chin? To say all or nothing, according to her parents' disposition. Then gently guide her budding fancies, till the phantoms that haunt her are clothed in flesh and blood, till she can fondle what she fears and despise all that protects her. It doesn't take as long as you think. The secret lies in knowing exactly when and how to strike. And what a prize this girl is! Perfect in all Your Highness

needs to spend a delectable night. So coy and bashful! A
kitten tempted by sweetmeats, but afraid to sully her
paws. Fresh and clean, respectable as a Flemish
housewife. Born of decent folk, what's more, but whose
modest means never allowed her a sound education. No
depth to her principles, only a thin veneer. Yet what a
seething river in spate surges under that thin layer of ice,
ready to crack at every move you make! Never did a
flowering shrub give promise of choicer berries, never
have I scented in the air of a child a more exquisite odour
of lechery.

The Duke Devil take it! I can't see any signal. And I've
got to be at that ball of the Nasi's. He marries off his
daughter today.

Giomo Let's go right up to the house, my Lord. As we're
only abducting a girl half paid for already, why don't we
rap on the window?

The Duke Come on then. Our Hungarian's right.

They move away. Enter **Maffio**.

Maffio In my dream I thought I saw my young sister
cross the garden, covered in jewels and holding a dim
lantern. I woke with a start. God knows it was merely an
illusion, but so strong I couldn't sleep again. The windows
of the villa where she sleeps are shut tight as usual, thank
heaven! And I can just see the faint glow of her lamp
through the leaves of our old fig-tree. Now my crazy fears
have died down, my heart's not beating so fast and I feel
quite calm. I must be out of my mind. My eyes are full of
tears, as if my poor sister had really been in danger. –
What's that I hear? Who's that moving between the
branches?

Maffio's *sister passes in the distance.*

Is that my sister or her phantom? Carrying a dark lantern
and wearing a pendant that flashes in the moonlight.
Gabriella! Gabriella! Where are you going?

Giomo *and the* **Duke** *return.*

Giomo That must be her dear brother, walking in his sleep. Lorenzo will let your fair one into the palace by the postern gate. What have we to fear?

Maffio Hey, who's there? Stay where you are!

He draws his sword.

Giomo Honest varlet, we're your friends!

Maffio Where's my sister? What are you up to here?

Giomo Your sister's been dislodged. Open your garden gates for us, you gallant rogue!

Maffio Draw your sword and defend yourself, assassin!

Giomo (*leaping at him and disarming him*) Stop that now! Not so fast, you fool!

Maffio What shame! Wretch that I am! If there are still laws in Florence, and justice on this earth, by all that's true and holy, I'll throw myself at the feet of the Duke, and he'll have you both strung up.

Giomo The feet of the Duke?

Maffio Yes, yes, I know that ruffians like you murder whole families and get away scot-free. But if I die, do you hear, I won't die like the rest without a word. If the Duke hasn't found out yet that this city is a forest of bandits and poisoners and girls who've been dishonoured, here's one man who'll tell him so. With blood and iron, I'll bring you two to justice!

Giomo (*sword in hand*) Should I run him through, Highness?

The Duke What's this? Run the poor man through! Go back to bed, my friend. Tomorrow we'll send you a few ducats.

Exit.

Maffio Alexander de' Medici!

Giomo The man himself, good varlet. If you value your ears, I shouldn't brag about his visit.

Exit.

Scene Two

A street at dawn.

Masked revellers are leaving a palace blazing with light. A **Silk Merchant** *and a* **Goldsmith** *are opening their shops.*

Merchant Hey there, Mondella old chap! It's a windy day to hang out my cloth.

He spreads out pieces of silk.

Goldsmith (*yawning*) My head's bursting. To hell with their revelling! I never closed my eyes all night.

Merchant Nor did my wife, neighbour. The poor soul twisted and turned like an eel. Devil take it, when you're young, you don't want to sleep when you hear the violins.

Goldsmith Young! Young! You're a fine one to talk with a beard like yours. But, God knows, their damned music doesn't tempt *me* to dance.

Two Apprentices *pass.*

1st Apprentice It's really great fun. You slip between the soldiers by the door and watch the guests come out, all dressed in their multicoloured clothes. Look! That's the Nasi house. (*He blows on his fingers.*) My fingers are frozen, holding this briefcase.

2nd Apprentice And will they let us get close?

1st Apprentice What right have they to stop us? We're citizens of Florence. Look at the crowd round the door! Pages, horses and liveries, all going in and out. You have to be in the know. I can recognize all the important folk. Then you note what they're all wearing and next day in the studio you say: 'I can't keep awake, I spent the night at a ball at Prince Aldobrandi's or at Count Salviati's. The prince was dressed this way, the princess that way.' And you tell no lies! Come on, hold on to my cape!

They take up a place near the door.

Goldsmith Did you hear those gawping little rascals? If any of *my* apprentices got up to such tricks . . . !

Merchant All right, Mondella old man! When pleasure costs nothing, youth has nothing to lose. I love to see these young monkeys looking so wide-eyed . . . I was like that, sniffing the air with my nose out for news. It seems that Nasi girl's a lively wench, so the Martelli boy is a lucky lad. They'll make a fine Florentine family! How grand all these great lords look! I admit I like these festivities. When you're lying quiet in your bed, with the window curtain tucked back, now and then you peep out, as the torches come and go in the palace. And it costs you nothing to catch a few strains of the music being played at the ball. And you say to yourself: Aha! Those are my silks dancing, those fine silks the good Lord gave me, worn on the darling bodies of all those good and lusty lords.

Goldsmith There's many a dancing silk that's not been paid for, my good friend! And they're the ones no one minds sprinkling with wine and scraping against the walls. It's fair enough for great lords to have their fun – that's what they're born for. But there's more than one kind of fun, if you get my meaning.

Merchant Yes, I know. Like dancing and riding and tennis and plenty more besides. But what exactly, Mondella old chap, do you really mean?

Goldsmith Never mind. *I* know. Listen here. All our palaces have never faced a sterner test than today. The ancestors of our present lords just maintained them to keep out the rain. But the old buildings really have to prove their strength, when their grandsons have downed too much wine.

Merchant There's sound sense in a glass of good old wine, Mondella. Why not step into my shop? I've a length of velvet to show you.

Goldsmith Sound sense and good health too. And it's a fine sight, my friend, to see it swallowed by a man who's earned it by the sweat of his brow. Gaily the glass is raised, a flick of the wrist and down it goes to cheer the heart of an honest family man. But all these young rakes at court are shameless drunken sots, steeped in bestiality. What good's it going to do them? You don't please anyone, even yourself. And you certainly don't please God.

Merchant A rowdy carnival, no doubt about that. And their damned balloon ruined my stock. Fifty florins' worth. The Strozzi paid up, thank God!

Goldsmith The Strozzi! Heaven confound the scoundrels who dared attack their nephew! He's the finest man in Florence, Philip Strozzi.

Merchant That didn't stop his son, Peter, dragging that foul balloon round my shop. Three great stains on a velvet brocade. By the way, Mondella, shall I see you at Montoliveto?

Goldsmith It's not my habit to keep up with our fairs. Still I'll go to Montoliveto for piety's sake. It's a holy pilgrimage, my friend. To wash away all our sins.

Merchant We should treat it with reverence, it's true. And we merchants do better business there than on any other day of the year. It's grand to see all those good ladies lingering after Mass to choose among our silks. God bless His Highness! It's a fine institution, the Court.

Goldsmith The Court! The people bear that burden on their backs. Not so long ago Florence was still a fine strong edifice. All those great palaces, the homes of our noble families, were its pillars, not one of which was one inch taller than the rest. Each and all together supported

an old and well-constructed dome. And we could walk
beneath it without fear that any stone might fall upon our
heads. But then – don't breathe a word of this – two
clumsy architects, two outsiders, interfered and ruined it:
the Pope and the Holy Roman Emperor. Charles V made
his entrance by breaching one of the walls. Then they both
agreed to move one of those pillars I mentioned, the
Medici family in fact, and make a bell-tower of it. Like an
evil mushroom the tower sprang up in the space of a single
night. And you know what came next? As the old building
was now rocking in the wind, being top-heavy and minus
one of its legs, they replaced the missing pillar with a
botched-up, formless lump of mud and spittle, which they
called the Citadel. The Germans settled in like rats in a
cheese full of holes. And while they play dice and drink
their acid Rhenish wine, it doesn't do to forget that
they've got their eye on us. The old gentry of Florence can
protest as much as they like, our merchants and all the
citizens can shout themselves hoarse, but the Medici use
their garrison to rule us. Like a cancerous growth that
devours an infected stomach, they're gnawing at our
vitals. It's thanks to those halberds parading round that
platform that a bastard who's only half a Medici, a ruffian
heaven intended for a ploughhand or a butcher's boy, now
sleeps in our daughters' beds, consumes our wine, breaks
our windows and wreaks havoc everywhere. And to think!
For that privilege we pay him our taxes!

Merchant A plague on it! How you go on! You seem to
know it all by heart. But I wouldn't repeat that to
everyone if I were you, Mondella old chap!

Goldsmith And what if they did banish me, like so many
others? Life in Rome is as good as life is here. To hell
with their wedding, the dancers and the revellers!

He goes in. The **Merchant** *joins the crowd. A* **Townsman**
and his **Wife** *pass by.*

Wife Young Martelli is a handsome man, and rich.
Nicolo Nasi is lucky to have a son-in-law like that. There,

you see! The ball is still in full swing. Look at all those lights.

Townsman What about us and *our* daughter – when shall we see her married?

Wife How bright everything is. And still dancing at this hour – that's what I call a celebration! They say the Duke is there.

Townsman To turn day into night and night into day is a convenient way to keep honest folk at arm's length. A fine idea, I must say, to have halberds at the door for one's wedding! May the good Lord save this town! Every day from that damned fortress, those German dogs launch some cursed new invention.

Wife Look at the lovely mask! Oh, what a beautiful dress! But I'm afraid it all costs so much money and we're too poor.

Exeunt.

Soldier (*to the* **Merchant**) Out of the way you pig! Let the horses through!

Merchant Pig yourself, German devil!

Soldier *hits him with his pike.*

Merchant (*moving off*) That's how they keep the terms of our surrender! Beating the townsfolk up, the bastards!

He goes back to his shop.

1st Apprentice (*to his friend*) Do you see that one who's taking off his mask? That's Palla Ruccellai. He's a fine fellow. The small man next to him is Thomas Strozzi, who they call Masaccio.

Page His Highness' horse!

2nd Apprentice Let's go – the Duke's coming out!

1st Apprentice Oh, he won't eat you! (*More people crowd round the door.*) There's Nicolini. And that one's Corsini, the Governor of the Citadel.

The **Duke** *appears, dressed as a nun, with* **Julian Salviati,** *dressed the same way. Both are masked.*

The Duke (*mounting his horse*) Are you coming, Julian?

Salviati No, Your Highness, not yet.

Whispers something to the **Duke.**

The Duke All right, all right! Steady!

Salviati She's lovely, like a demon. Leave it to me. If I can get rid of my wife.

He returns to the ball.

The Duke You're drunk, Salviati. Devil take it, you can't walk straight!

Exit with his suite.

1st Apprentice It won't last much longer now the Duke's gone.

Guests *are leaving on every side.*

2nd Apprentice All these colours, pink, green and blue make me feel quite dizzy.

Townsman It looks as if the supper went on a long time. Those two over there can't take any more.

The **Governor** *mounts his horse, which is struck on the shoulder by a broken bottle.*

Corsini Damnation! Who in hell's name threw that?

Masked Guest Can't you see, Lord Corsini? Look up at that window: it's Lorenzo in his nun's habit.

Corsini Lorenzaccio, the Devil take you! You've injured my horse! (*The window closes.*) A plague on the drunkard and his scurvy tricks! A scoundrel who has not smiled three times in his life, playing silly pranks like a young kid out of school!

Exit. **Louisa Strozzi** *leaves the house with* **Julian Salviati.** *He holds her stirrup. She mounts her horse. A* **Groom** *and a* **Governess** *follow her.*

Salviati You show a fine leg, my girl! The sun shines out of you and burns me to the marrow of my bones.

Louisa My Lord, that's no way for a cavalier to talk.

Salviati What eyes you have, dear heart! And what lovely moist fresh shoulders to caress! What would you accept to let me be your chambermaid tonight? And take your shoe off that pretty little foot?

Louisa Let go of it, Salviati!

Salviati No, per Bacco! Not till you tell me when we bed together.

Louisa *strikes her horse and gallops off.*

Masked Guest (*to* **Salviati**) That young Strozzi girl has gone off with her face bright red. You've made her wild, Salviati.

Salviati Nonsense. A young girl's anger is gentle rain at dawn.

Exit.

Scene Three

The **Marchese Cibo**'s *Palace.*

The **Marchese,** *dressed for a journey, the* **Marchesa,** *their son* **Ascanio,** *and* **Cardinal Cibo** *seated.*

Marchese (*embracing his son*) I should have liked to take you with me, my boy, with your big sword trailing between your legs. But be patient. Massa isn't far away and I'll bring you a nice present back.

Marchesa Farewell, Laurent. Come home soon!

Cibo Why so tearful, Marchesa? Anyone would think my brother was off to Palestine. I doubt he'll be in much danger in his own domain.

Marchese Don't find fault, brother, with these glorious tears.

He kisses his wife.

Cibo I prefer to see honest emotion expressed in other ways.

Marchesa Is honest emotion, Cardinal, not to find expression in tears? Must they be uniquely reserved for fear and repentance?

Marchese Heavens, no! Love springs the finest tears of all. Don't wipe them from my face! Leave it to the wind on the road and they'll dry in their own time. Why, my dear, are you forgetting to send your greetings to the places you love best? Am I not, as usual, to make a great impassioned speech to the rocks and cascades of my ancestral homeland?

Marchesa Poor little waterfalls!

Marchese It's true, dear heart, they weep profusely without you. (*Lowering his voice.*) They were happier once, Ricciarda, weren't they?

Marchesa Take me with you!

Marchese An old soldier like me may look mad enough to do it, but not quite. We'll say no more – I'll only be away a week. I'd rather my dear Ricciarda saw her gardens when they're quiet and peaceful, with no sign of my farmers trampling her favourite pathways in their muddy boots. I have to see about my tenants and their cattle, check those old tree trunks of mine – which always make me think of your father, Alberio – and count every blade of grass that grows in my woods! As soon as I see the first flower show itself, then I'll call a halt and come and fetch you.

Marchesa It's so dear to me, the first flower that appears on our beautiful lawn. I always think the poor little things will never come up again.

Ascanio Father, which horse are you taking with you?

Marchese Come with me into the courtyard and I'll show you.

Exeunt. The **Marchesa** *remains alone with* **Cardinal Cibo**. *A silence.*

Cibo Was it not today you wanted me to hear your confession, Marchesa?

Marchesa May I leave it till this evening? If Your Eminence is free. Or tomorrow, whichever you prefer. My thoughts are not my own, just at the moment.

She goes to the window and waves goodbye to her husband.

Cibo If a faithful servant of God were allowed to feel regret, I'd envy my brother's lot. Such a short uncomplicated journey, quietly doing the rounds on one of his estates. Absent for a week. Yet what grief at his departure – or should I say 'sweet sorrow'? Happy's the man who can still inspire such love after seven years of marriage. It is seven years, isn't it Marchesa?

Marchesa Yes, Cardinal. My son is six now.

Cibo Were you at the Nasi wedding yesterday?

Marchesa Yes, I was.

Cibo And the Duke, dressed as a nun?

Marchesa The Duke in the habit of a nun? Why insist on that?

Cibo I was told that's the costume he wore. Perhaps I was misinformed.

Marchesa It's true. He did. Ah! Malaspina, there's nothing sacred in these sorry times.

Cibo In a moment of folly, a man can still wear the habit of one of our convents, without meaning to be hostile to the Holy Catholic Church.

Marchesa It's not the intention, but the example that is dangerous. I don't look at it as you do. I was revolted. Of course, I can't know for sure what's done or isn't done according to your mysterious rules. God knows where they lead us! Those who hammer and twist their words, to serve their own designs, tend to forget that words stand for thoughts and thoughts give rise to actions.

Cibo That's as may be. The Duke is young, Marchesa, and in the coy robes of a nun I dare say he looked ravishing.

Marchesa Quite perfect. All that was missing were a few drops of the blood of Hippolytus, the cousin he murdered.

Cibo And the cap of Liberty, I suppose? How my dear sister-in-law hates poor Duke Alexander!

Marchesa And you, his right-hand man, don't you care that Florence's Duke is a lieutenant of Charles V? That just as Valori is the Pope's ecclesiastical envoy, Alexander is his political agent? You are my husband's brother, don't you care that here in our own city, *our* sun casts German shadows from the Citadel? Don't you care that debauchery acts as pimp to domination? That its clashing cymbals drown the people's cries? Oh no! If need be, to muffle that sound, your clergy would set all their bells ringing and so alert, if ever it fell asleep, the imperial eagle on our humble rooftops.

Exit.

Cibo (*alone. Lifting the tapestry and calling softly*) Agnolo!

Enter a **Page**.

Anything new today?

Agnolo This letter, Monsignor.

Cibo Give it to me.

Agnolo Your Eminence, I know it's a sin.

Cibo It's no sin to obey a priest of the Roman Catholic Church. (**Agnolo** *hands him the letter*.) It amuses me to listen to the poor Marchesa's outbursts, and then watch her run off to a loving rendezvous with her precious tyrant, bathed in republican tears. (*He opens the letter and reads.*) 'Surrender, or you bring disaster on me, yourself, and both our houses.' The Duke has a laconic style, but it's not without vigour. Has the Marchesa been won over, yes or no? It's not easy to tell. Two months of courtship, almost assiduous. That's a lot for Alexander. It should be enough for Ricciarda Cibo. (*He returns the letter to* **Agnolo**.) Put it back in your mistress's room. Not a word, as usual, eh? Put your faith in me.

He offers his hand for the page to kiss and leaves.

Scene Four

A courtyard in the **Duke's** *Palace.*

Duke Alexander *on the terrace.* **Pages** *exercising horses in the yard. Enter* **Valori** *and* **Lord Maurizio**.

The Duke (*to* **Valori**) Did Your Eminence have news this morning from the Court of Rome?

Valori Paul III extends a thousand blessings on Your Highness and sends his most fervent wishes for your prosperity.

The Duke Nothing but wishes, Valori?

Valori His Holiness fears lest the duke should create new dangers for himself by being too indulgent. The people are not yet used to absolute rule. I believe the Emperor spoke in similar vein to Your Highness on his last visit.

The Duke By God, you've got a fine horse, Lord Maurizio, eh? Excellent rump!

Maurizio Superb, Highness.

The Duke So, my good Apostolic Envoy, there are still a few rotten branches in the city that need pruning. The Pope and Caesar may have made me into a king. But, by Bacchus, the sceptre they gave me looks far more like an axe. All right then! Come on, Valori, what's on your mind?

Valori Highness, I am a priest. If the message my office compels me to convey must lend itself to so harsh an interpretation, my heart forbids me to add one word more.

The Duke Yes, yes. I know your honesty and worth. I swear you are the only honest priest I have ever known in my life.

Valori One's habit does not indicate more or less honesty, my Lord. More men are good than are wicked.

The Duke So you propose no further explanation?

Maurizio May I speak, my Lord? It is quite easy to explain.

The Duke What, then?

Maurizio The disorders of the Court disturb the Pope.

The Duke What's that you said?

Maurizio I said, the disorders of the Court, Your Highness. The Duke alone is judge of his own conduct. It's Lorenzo de' Medici the Pope reclaims as a fugitive from justice.

The Duke From justice? He never offended a Pope, so far as I know. Except my late cousin, Clement VII. And by now he's roasting in hell!

Maurizio When the libertine, in a drunken frenzy, decapitated the statues of the Arch of Constantine, Clement VII let him find refuge outside the Papal States. Paul III could never pardon this living image of Florentine licentiousness.

The Duke By God, that Farnese Pope's a fine one to talk! If debauchery affronts him so, what the hell does he make of his dear bastard, Peter, and *his* revels with the Bishop of Fano? Whenever poor Renzo's name crops up it's always this mutilation business! I think it's funny, chopping off the heads of all those men of stone. In protecting the arts I am second to none and Florence has the leading artists in Italy. But it escapes me why the Pope makes so much fuss over statues of tyrants he'd excommunicate at once, if they were alive today.

Maurizio Lorenzo's an atheist. He mocks at everything. Your Highness's government will never be secure, unless it wins respect. The people call Lorenzo by the infamous name of 'Lorenzaccio'. They know he's master of your pleasures. It is enough.

The Duke Be silent! You forget, Lorenzo de' Medici is Alexander's cousin.

Enter **Cardinal Cibo**.

The Duke Cardinal, come listen to these gentlemen. They say the Pope is scandalized by the disorders of poor Renzo and claim this brings my government into disrepute.

Cibo Messer Francesco Molza has just treated the Academy of Rome to a great harangue in Latin against the mutilator of the Arch of Constantine.

The Duke Would you put me in a rage? Renzo, a man to stand in fear of? He's a notorious coward, effeminate, the palest shadow of an enervated pimp! A dreamer, who goes round night and day without a sword, lest he be frightened by its shadow. A philosopher, what's more, a scribbler, a rotten poet who can't even write a sonnet! No, no, as yet *I'm* not afraid of shadows. By Bacchus, what do I care for Latin speeches and the malicious gossip of the mob! I love Lorenzo, and by the Holy Corpse of God, in my court he will remain.

Cibo Were I, Highness, to fear this man, it would not be for Florence or your court, but for yourself.

The Duke Cardinal, is this a joke? Shall I tell you the truth of it? (*He speaks confidentially to him.*) Whatever I learn of those damned exiles, and all those stubborn republicans hatching plots around me, I owe it to Lorenzo. He wriggles his way in everywhere, and tells me everything. Hasn't he even found some means of contact with the hellish Strozzi clan? Yes, of course he's my go-between. But I tell you, if his activities harm anyone, they don't harm me. Look!

Lorenzo *appears below under an arcade.*

The Duke See that puny little body, this walking aftermath of last night's orgy! See his leaden eyes, his feeble little hands, scarce firm enough to lift a fan. That gloomy face, which sometimes smiles but never finds the strength to laugh. Is that a man to fear? Come now, really! You can't be serious about him. Hey, Renzo! Come up here. Lord Maurizio has a bone to pick with you.

Lorenzo (*climbing the staircase to the terrace*) Friends of my cousin, good day, gentlemen.

The Duke Lorenzo! We've been talking of you for at least an hour. Have you heard the news? They're excommunicating you, my friend, in Latin! Lord Maurizio thinks you dangerous. So does the Cardinal. As for our worthy Valori, he is too shamefaced to pronounce your name.

Lorenzo Dangerous? Who for, Eminence? The ladies of the night or the Saints in Paradise?

Cibo Dogs at court can go mad with rabies, like other dogs.

Lorenzo A priest should put his insults into Latin.

Maurizio Those that are made in the Tuscan tongue can be answered.

Lorenzo Lord Maurizio, I didn't see you there. Forgive me. The sun was in my eyes. You seem to be on form and your tunic looks almost brand new.

Maurizio Like your wit. I had it made out of an old doublet my grandfather wore.

Lorenzo Cousin, when you've finished with one of your suburban conquests, send her along to Lord Maurizio. It's unhealthy to live without a woman. Especially a man with a bull's neck and hairs on the back of his hands.

Maurizio A man who claims the right to jest should know how to defend himself. If I were you, I'd look to my sword.

Lorenzo If they told you I was a soldier, they're mistaken. I'm a poor lover of learning.

Maurizio *Your* sword is your sharp wit. It has a cutting edge, but it's far too common a weapon. We all use what we have.

He draws his sword.

Valori A drawn sword, in front of the Duke!

The Duke (*laughing*) To hell with that! Don't stop them! Come on Renzo, I'll be your second. Someone give him a sword!

Lorenzo My Lord, what are you saying!

The Duke What's this? Has your jesting mood vanished already? Are you trembling, cousin? Shame on you! You disgrace the name of Medici. And *you're* legitimate! I'm only a bastard, but I would honour it better than you. A sword! Bring a sword! No one can provoke a Medici so. You, pages! Come up here! The whole court shall see this and I wish all Florence were here.

Lorenzo Your Highness is laughing at me.

The Duke I may have been laughing a moment ago. But now I'm blushing. A sword!

He takes the sword from a page and presents it to **Lorenzo**.

Valori My Lord, this goes too far. A drawn sword in the presence of Your Highness is a punishable offence within the palace.

The Duke Who speaks here when I have spoken?

Valori Your Highness can only have intended to seek a moment's diversion, and that was Lord Maurizio's sole purpose too.

The Duke And can't you see I'm still joking? Who the devil could take this seriously? Just look at Renzo! He's shaking at the knees. He'd have turned paler if he could! Merciful God, what a face! I believe he's going to faint.

Lorenzo *staggers. He holds on to the balustrade, then suddenly slips to the ground. The* **Duke** *bursts out laughing.*

The Duke What did I tell you? The merest glimpse of a sword make him feel quite ill. There, there, my darling Lorenzetta! Shall we ask someone to take you home to mother?

The **Pages** *help* **Lorenzo** *up.*

Maurizio A twofold coward! Son of a strumpet!

The Duke Hold your tongue, Lord Maurizio! I won't have that language in my presence!

Valori Poor young man!

Lord Maurizio *and* **Valori** *go out.*

Cibo (*who has stayed alone with the* **Duke**) You really believe in all this, my Lord?

The Duke I'd like to know why I shouldn't.

Cibo Hm! It's quite extraordinary.

The Duke That's why I believe it. Do you imagine a Medici just for fun would shame himself in public? Besides, it's not the first time it's happened. He could never stand the sight of a sword.

Cibo Extraordinary! Quite extraordinary!

Exeunt.

Scene Five

In front of the Church of San Miniato at Montoliveto.

A crowd is leaving the Church. Enter **Leon Strozzi,** *the Prior of Capua.*

Townswoman (*to her* **Neighbour**) Are you going back to Florence this evening?

Neighbour I never stay more than an hour and I only come here once, on a Friday. I haven't enough money to stop at the Fair. I come for religious reasons, for the salvation of my soul, that's all I come for.

1st Court Lady (*to a second*) What a good sermon he preached! He's my daughter's confessor. (*She goes up to one of the shops.*) White and gold, very smart for the evening. But in the daytime, how do you keep it clean?

The **Silk Merchant** *and the* **Goldsmith** *with some young gentlemen in front of their shops.*

Goldsmith The Citadel! The people will never stand for it. To see that new Tower of Babel suddenly shoot up over the town, and all that horrible foreign lingo! The Germans will never grow strong in Florence. You'd need a tough piece of twine to graft them onto us.

Merchant Come and look, ladies. May I offer your ladyships this stool under my awning?

1st Gentleman Father Mondella, you're of old Florentine stock. In the back of your workshop, when your fingers are busy chasing your precious metals, I bet they still shake with hatred of tyranny.

Goldsmith That's true, Excellency. If I was a great artist, I'd love our noble princes, because they're the only ones who can be the patrons of great works of art. Great artists have no homeland. But as for me, I just make holy chalices and sword-hilts.

2nd Gentleman Talking of artists, in that little tavern over there, can you see that strapping fellow gesticulating to an admiring audience? Banging his glass on the table. If I'm not mistaken, it's that braggart, Benvenuto Cellini.

1st Gentleman Let's go and join in then. When he's had a glass of wine, he's amusing to listen to, and he's probably spinning a fine old yarn.

Exeunt. Two **Citizens** *sit down.*

1st Citizen There's been a riot in Florence?

2nd Citizen Nothing much. A few poor young lads got killed in the Old Market.

1st Citizen A sad thing for their families.

2nd Citizen Can't be avoided, tragedies like that. What else do you expect young folk to do with a government like ours? It gets trumpeted far and wide that the Emperor's at Bologna, and the gaping mob take up the cry: 'Caesar's at Bologna!' with a wink and a knowing look, without a thought what's happening there. Next day they're even more pleased to hear and repeat: 'The Pope's at Bologna with Caesar.' And then what happens? A general celebration, and that's all they can see in it. So one fine day they wake up, their heads reeling with the fumes from Imperial wine, and they see a sinister face at the great window of the Pazzi Palace. They want to know who this character is, and they're told it's their king. The Pope and the Emperor have given birth – to a bastard with power of life and death over our children, and who couldn't even name his own mother!

Goldsmith (*approaching*) You talk like a patriot, my friend. Be careful! Watch out for the German pike!

A **German Officer** *passes.*

Officer Clear off, gentlemen. These ladies want to sit down.

Two **Court Ladies** *enter and sit down.*

1st Lady Is this from Venice?

Merchant Yes, Worshipful lady. Shall I cut you off a few lengths?

1st Lady If you like. Wasn't that Julian Salviati I just saw?

Officer Yes, walking up and down at the door of the church. He's a one for the ladies.

2nd Lady He's an insolent fellow! Show me some silk stockings.

Officer There won't be any trim enough for your legs.

1st Lady That's enough of your nonsense! As you've just seen Julian, go and tell him I want to speak to him.

Officer I shall. And I'll bring him back with me.

Exit.

1st Lady Your officer's as stupid as they come. What's he good for?

2nd Lady You'll learn. There's not a better *man* to be found!

They move away. Enter **Leon Strozzi**, *the Prior of Capua.*

Leon Give me a glass of lemon, my good man.

He sits down.

1st Citizen There's the Prior of Capua. A real patriot for you!

The two **Citizens** *sit down.*

Leon Have you come from Church, gentlemen? What did you think of the sermon?

1st Citizen Very fine, my Lord Prior.

2nd Citizen (*to the* **Goldsmith**) The people love the Strozzi because though they're noble, they're not proud. It's good to see a great lord, isn't it, talking freely to his neighbours, being so affable? It all means far more than one thinks.

Leon To be perfectly frank, I found the sermon rather too fine. I have preached sometimes myself, and I never saw much glory in rattling the window-panes. But one small tear on the cheek of an honest fellow was always for me a pearl of great price.

Enter **Salviati**.

Salviati I was told some women were asking for me just now. But the only skirts, Prior, I can see here belong to you. Have I made a mistake?

Merchant Excellency, there was no mistake. They just left for a moment. I'm sure they'll be back. I've ten lengths of cloth and four pairs of stockings for them.

Salviati (*sitting down*) There's a pretty wench going by. Where the devil have I seen her before? – Hell, yes, I know! In my bed!

Leon (*to the* **Citizen**) Was it not you who signed a letter addressed to the Duke?

1st Citizen Yes, I've nothing to hide. The petition from the exiles.

Leon Were any of your family banished?

1st Citizen Two, Excellency. My father and my uncle. I'm the only man left in the house.

2nd Citizen (*to the* **Goldsmith**) What a slanderous tongue that Salviati has!

Goldsmith Hardly surprising. A man who's half bankrupt, living off the Medici's charity and married to a woman well known for her easy virtue! He'd like every woman to have as bad a reputation.

Salviati Isn't that Louisa Strozzi walking down that slope?

Merchant It is, your Lordship. There aren't many of our noble ladies I can't recognize. If I'm not mistaken, she's holding the hand of her younger sister.

Salviati I met that Louisa last night at the Nasi ball. S'truth, she shows a pretty leg. At the first chance we get, I'm sharing her bed.

Leon (*turning round*) What do you mean by that?

Salviati It's perfectly true. She's quite willing. I was holding her stirrup without a wicked thought in my head. Then suddenly and by accident I caught hold of her leg. And that's how it all started.

Leon Julian, do you know that's my sister you speak of?

Salviati Quite aware of it! All women are made to sleep with men, so why shouldn't your sister sleep with me?

Leon (*rising*) Do I owe you something, my good man?

He throws a coin on the table and goes out.

Salviati I like that worthy prior, going off without his change! And all for a remark about his sister! Anyone would think there's no virtue left in Florence, except in those Strozzis! There he is, turning round. Stare as hard as you like. You don't scare me!

Scene Six

The banks of the River Arno.

Maria Soderini, Catherine

Catherine The sun's started to go down. Crimson rays slanting through the leaves. And you can hear the frogs singing out their angelus among the reeds. It's strange, all the harmonies of evening against the noisy background of the town.

Maria Pull your shawl closer round your neck. It's time we went home.

Catherine Oh, not yet. Unless you're feeling cold, Maria dear. Just look at that lovely sky! How vast and peaceful it all is! God seems to be everywhere! But why don't you look up? Ever since this morning, you've appeared worried.

Maria Not worried, grieved. You must have heard the latest gossip, that dreadful story about Lorenzo? Now he's the talk of Florence.

Catherine Oh, Mother dear! Cowardice is not a crime, any more than courage is a virtue. Why should anyone be blamed for being weak? It's unfortunate for a man that he's always held responsible for an odd moment of panic. Why shouldn't your son have the privilege all we women share? No one loves a woman who never shows fear.

Maria Would you love a cowardly man? You're blushing, Catherine. Lorenzo is your nephew, but what would you think of him if he belonged to a different family. What woman would lean on his arm as she mounted her horse? What man would shake him by the hand?

Catherine Sad it is. But that's not why I pity him. He may lack the courage of a Medici, but I'm afraid he has no heart. He lacks the decency of an honest man.

Maria Let's not talk of that, Catherine. It's only too cruel when a mother is unable to speak of her own son.

Catherine Oh, it's Florence that's ruined him! Didn't I once see his eyes fired with noble ambition? Weren't the days of his youth like a dawn of great promise? And even now, I often seem to see a sudden flash . . . And I can't help believing something still burns within him.

Maria Oh, all that lies so deep! He was so gifted and so fond of solitude. My Renzo will never make a fighter! That's what I used to say when he came home from college with heavy books under his arm. His lips and dark eyes shone with his worship of the truth. He took everything to heart, forever saying: 'Look at this poor man, and that other who's been ruined. What can be done for them?' And the way he admired the great men in his Plutarch! Oh, Catherine, Catherine! How often have I kissed him on the brow and thought of old Cosimo Medici who earned the name of Father of his Country.

Catherine Don't distress yourself so.

Maria I say I don't want to talk about him, yet I can't stop myself. There are some things, you see, a mother can't keep quiet about, until she's silent in her grave. If my son had been a vulgar rake, if that thin drop of Soderini blood he took from me had ever shown its frailty, then I would not despair. But he gave me good reason to foster hopes in him! Oh, Catherine! Even his handsome looks are gone! Like a malignant gas the corruption in his heart has risen to contort his face. His smile, the radiance that blooms like a flower in youth, has fled from his jaundiced cheeks, leaving behind a sarcastic sneer of discontent and overriding scorn.

Catherine Yet in his strange sadness, at times there is some beauty still.

Maria Was he not born to rule? On the throne would he not have united youth and beauty with a scholar's learning, thus crowning all my cherished dreams with gold? Was I so wrong to expect it? Ah, Cattina! To sleep peacefully there are some dreams one should never have dreamt. It's too cruel to have known that enchanted palace, echoing with the songs of angels, where my own son rocked me to sleep. And then to wake up in a blood-stained hovel, with the remains of what was once human among the debris of an orgy while you're locked in the arms of a loathsome phantom which, as it murders you, still calls you by the name of mother.

Catherine Silent shadows are beginning to move along the road. Let's go home, Maria, all these exiles frighten me.

Maria Poor people! They should rather rouse your pity. Oh, is there nothing I see that doesn't drive a thorn into my heart? Must I keep my eyes closed? Cattina dear, I'm afraid once more that this is Lorenzo's work. All these poor townsfolk trusted him. And of all those fathers banished from their homeland, there's not one my son did not betray. The letters they put their names to are all shown to the Duke. Such is the infamous use he makes of the treasured name of his forebears. The Republicans turn to him as heir to the ancient family they always looked to for protection. He keeps open-house for them, and even the Strozzi go to him. Poor grey-haired Philip will come to a sad end too. There isn't one brazen girl, one poor wretch torn from hearth and home, who doesn't cry out to me: 'You are the mother of our woes!' How soon can I lie beneath this earth? (*She beats the ground.*)

Catherine Poor Mother! I can only weep with you.

They move away. The sun has set. Some **Exiles** *form a group in the middle of a field.*

1st Exile Where are you going?

2nd Exile Pisa. And you?

1st Exile To Rome.

3rd Exile And I to Venice. There are two more off to Ferrara. What will become of us all, so far from each other?

4th Exile Goodbye, neighbour. Till times change for the better. (*He moves away.*) Goodbye. As for us, we can go together as far as the Virgin's Cross.

He turns to go out with one of the others. Enter **Maffio.**

1st Exile Is it you, Maffio? What chance brings you here?

Maffio I've come to join you. I'll tell you how the Duke carried off my sister. I drew my sword, and a man like a tiger with the strength of steel leapt at my throat and disarmed me. Then I was ordered to leave the town and given a purse full of ducats.

2nd Exile And where's your sister now?

Maffio She was pointed out to me this evening, leaving some entertainment, in a gown the Empress would envy. May God forgive her! She had an old crone with her, who lost three teeth on the way out. Never in my life have I landed a punch which gave me so much pleasure.

3rd Exile Let's hope their lewd filth chokes them all. Then we'll die happy.

4th Exile Philip Strozzi will write to us in Venice. One day we'll be surprised to find an army at our command.

3rd Exile Long life to Philip! So long as there's one hair on his head, liberty in Italy's not dead.

Some of the group break away. All the **Exiles** *embrace.*

A Voice To better times!

Another To better times!

Two of the **Exiles** *climb onto the terrace from which Florence can be seen.*

1st Exile Farewell, Florence, plague of Italy! Our Mother Florence is sterile. She has no more milk for her sons!

2nd Exile Farewell, Florence the bastard! Hideous spectre of Florence of old! Farewell, nameless scum!

All Farewell, Florence! A curse on the breasts of your women! A curse on the tears you shed! A curse on the prayers in your churches, the bread from your wheat and the air of your streets! Cursed be the final drop of your corrupted blood!

Act Two

Scene One

At the Strozzi Palace. **Philip** *in his study.*

Philip Ten citizens banished from this district alone! Old Galeazzo! And young Maffio too! *His* poor sister corrupted, made into a whore overnight! Poor child! When will the common folk have learnt enough to stop their daughters laughing while their parents weep? Is corruption one of Nature's laws? Are our so-called virtues the clothes we wear only on Sundays? The rest of the week, the girls are at their windows eyeing the young men as they pass, while they sit and sew. Poor humanity! What name should you bear? The one you were baptized with, or the one your race was heir to? And old dreamers like me, what birthmark have we erased from humanity's face in the four to five thousand years we've lived, yellowing with age like the pages of our books? How easy it is for us, sitting quiet in a study, lightly to trace out our designs in fine hair-lines over this white paper! How easy it is to build up towns and palaces with this little compass and a drop of ink! But when the architect, with a thousand great plans on his shelves, starts getting down to the job, his back is too bent and his ideas too set to be able to raise a single stone from the ground. It is hard to accept that man's happiness is nothing but a dream. But that evil is eternal, irrevocable, impossible to change . . . Never! That is unbearable. Why does the philosopher, who works for the good of all, stop to look about him? That's his mistake. The smallest insect flying past his eyes blots out the sun. We must be bolder than that. We need a word like 'Republic'. And were it nothing but a word, then still it would be something, for the people rise up as it echoes through the air . . . Ah, Leon, good day to you.

Enter **Leon Strozzi**, *the Prior of Capua.*

Leon I have come from the fair at Montoliveto.

Philip Was it a good one? Are you here too, Peter? Come and sit down, I've something to say to you.

Enter **Peter Strozzi**.

Leon It was very good, and I quite enjoyed myself, apart from one rather too provoking incident, which I can barely stomach.

Peter What was that then?

Leon Can you imagine? I had just gone into a shop to take a glass of lemon . . . No, it's stupid of me, I should forget it.

Philip What is it that has upset you? You're like a soul in torment.

Leon It's nothing. Just an unpleasant remark. Of no importance.

Peter What sort of remark? Who about? About you?

Leon Not about me exactly. That wouldn't worry me.

Peter Who, then? Come on then, out with it, if you want to say.

Leon I don't. Such things are best forgotten, when you know the difference between a decent man and a Salviati.

Peter Salviati? What did that swine say?

Leon You're right, he's a worthless creature. Does it matter *what* he says? An immoderate man, a lout straight out of the stables, whose wife, by what they say, is the most shameless libertine! Enough of this now, I'll think no more of it.

Peter You will think of it, Leon. And speak of it too. You see, I'm itching to chop off his ears. Who was he slandering this time? Us? My father? By the blood of Christ, I've no love lost for that Salviati. I must know what he said, do you hear?

Leon If you insist, I'll tell you. He said something in that shop, in front of me, that was truly offensive, concerning our sister.

Peter Oh Christ! What kind of words did he use? Out with it!

Leon The coarsest.

Peter Just like a bloody priest! Here am I, hopping with impatience, and you hesitate for words! A spade's a spade, by Heaven, and a word's a word! God has nothing to do with it!

Philip Peter, Peter! Have some respect for your brother.

Leon He said he would share her bed. Those were his words. And that she had promised him.

Peter That she would bed with . . . Oh! A thousand times Death and Damnation! What's the time now?

Philip Where are you off to? You flare up like a tinder-box! What are you doing with that sword? (**Peter** *has just seized hold of one lying around.*) You're wearing your own, anyway.

Peter I'm not doing anything. Dinner's ready. Let's go and eat.

Exeunt.

Scene Two

The porch of a church.

Lorenzo *and* **Cardinal Valori**. *Then* **Tebaldeo**, *a young painter.*

Valori How is it that the Duke has not yet come? Ah, my
good sir, how satisfying for a Christian is the majestic
splendour of the Church of Rome! Here surely an artist
could find his heart's delight, his Paradise? Warrior, priest
and merchant, do they not all discover here what they love
best? The wondrous harmony of the organ, the brilliance
of the tapestries and velvet hangings, the paintings of the
early masters, and the sweet chanting of silver-toned
voices! All this worldy show may shock an austere monk,
sworn enemy of pleasure. But nothing, to my mind, is
finer than a religion that wins men's hearts in such a way.
Why should priests wish to have a jealous God? Religion is
not a bird of prey, but a dove of compassion gently
hovering over all men's dreams and all their loving.

Lorenzo No doubt. What you say there is perfectly true,
and perfectly false, like all else in this world.

Tebaldeo (*approaching* **Valori**) Ah, Monsignor! How
good to hear a man like your Eminence speak thus of
tolerance and enthusiasm for all that's holy! Please allow a
humble citizen of this town, in whom the sacred flame
burns strongly, to thank you for the few words I've just
heard. To catch from the lips of an honest man the words
you cherish in your own heart, what greater joy can one
wish for?

Valori Are you not Tebaldeo, the young Freccia?

Tebaldeo There is small merit in my works. I know
better how to love the arts than practise them. But all my
young days have been spent in churches. Where else can I
admire Raphael and our divine Buonarotti? For days on
end I stand before their works – in ecstasy. The notes of
the organ reveal their thoughts and lead me into
communion with their spirit. As I gaze and listen to the
hymns of the choir, it is as if they were issuing from the
half-open mouths of those figures kneeling so devoutly in
the paintings. Fragrant wisps of incense waft between
them and me in a hazy cloud and I seem to glimpse the
glory of the artist. But it is only soft and gentle smoke and

would be but a sterile perfume, were it not rising up to
God.

Valori You have the spirit of a true artist. Come to my
palace and wrap something under your cloak to show me.
I should like to be your patron.

Tebaldeo Your Eminence does me too much honour. I
am but a humble novice in the Holy Order of painters.

Lorenzo Why not present your work now? What you are
holding looks like a canvas to me.

Tebaldeo That's true. But I dare not show it to such
great connoisseurs. It's a very poor sketch of a very fine
dream.

Lorenzo Do you make portraits of your dreams? I'll have
some of mine sit for you.

Tebaldeo That's a painter's life, the realization of
dreams. The greatest artists painted theirs with their
genius, without distortion. Their imagination was like a
tree full of sap. Its buds easily blossomed into flowers and
flowers into fruit. The fruit soon ripened in the kindly sun
and when ripe just fell to earth without wasting one grain
of their virginal seed. But the dreams of ordinary artists
are, I fear, hard plants to rear. They need watering with
many a bitter tear, before they begin to flourish.

Tebaldeo *shows his picture.*

Valori Very fine, in all sincerity, though not of the
highest merit. Why should I flatter a man who does not
flatter himself? But you have not yet grown your beard,
young man.

Lorenzo Is it a landscape or a portrait? How should one
look at it? This way or that way up?

Tebaldeo Your Lordship is mocking me. It's a view of
our burial-ground, of the Campo Santo.

Lorenzo How far is this removed from immortality?

Valori You should not tease the boy like this. See how much sadder his wide eyes look with every word you say.

Tebaldeo Immortality is a matter of faith. Those to whom God has given wings arrive smiling.

Valori You speak like a pupil of Raphael.

Tebaldeo He was my master, sir. All I have learnt I owe to him.

Lorenzo Come to my house. I'll have you paint the courtesan, Mazzafirra, in the nude.

Tebaldeo I've scant respect for my brush, but no portrait of a courtesan! I respect my art too much to prostitute it.

Lorenzo Your God took the trouble to create her. Why can't you do the same and paint her? Will you make me a view of Florence?

Tebaldeo Yes, my Lord.

Lorenzo How would you set about it?

Tebaldeo I'd set up my easel on the left bank of the Arno. It's from the east you have the best, the widest panorama.

Lorenzo You'd paint the houses, squares and streets of Florence?

Tebaldeo Yes, my Lord.

Lorenzo So why can't you paint a courtesan, if you can paint an evil city?

Tebaldeo I never yet learnt to talk thus of my mother.

Lorenzo Who do you call your mother?

Tebaldeo Why, Florence, sir!

Lorenzo Then you must be a bastard. Your mother's nothing but a whore.

Tebaldeo An infected sore can start corruption in the healthiest of bodies. But from the precious drops of my mother's blood grows a sweet-smelling herb that cures all ills. The divine flower of art sometimes needs manure to enrich the soil and make it fertile.

Lorenzo What are you trying to say?

Tebaldeo The spark of peaceful and contented nations may be pure, but it glows feebly. An angel's harp has many strings. The west wind may play upon the weakest and draw from them sweet harmonies. But only the north wind stirs the silver cord, the finest and noblest of them all, which even responds to the touch of a coarse hand. Suffering is the ally of inspiration.

Lorenzo You mean that great artists spring from an unhappy land. I'll be your alchemist and distil your meaning: the peoples' tears become pearls as they fall. By Satan, I like you, boy. Families reduced to despair, whole nations to desolation – and all that does is stir up our philosopher's grey matter! What an admirable poet. But how do you reconcile this with your piety?

Tebaldeo I don't mock a family's misfortune. Poetry, I say, is the most loving sister of all suffering. I pity unhappy nations. But I still believe they make great artists. Battlefields produce good harvests, and from foul earth spring heaven's cornfields.

Lorenzo Your doublet is threadbare. Would you wear my livery?

Tebaldeo I belong to no one. If thought is to be free, so must the body too.

Lorenzo I've a good mind to tell my man to give you a good thrashing.

Tebaldeo What for, my Lord?

Lorenzo Because the idea appeals to me. Were you lame from birth, or was it an accident?

Tebaldeo I am not lame. What do you mean?

Lorenzo You're either lame or mad.

Tebaldeo Why, my Lord? You make fun of me.

Lorenzo If you are not lame what keeps you in this city? Here, your ideas of freedom are held in such respect that any servant of the Medici can cut you down without redress. You must be mad.

Tebaldeo I love Florence. She is my mother. That is why I stay. Yes, I know a citizen can be killed in the street in broad daylight, if those that govern us would have it so. That is why I wear this dagger in my belt.

Lorenzo Would you strike the Duke, if the Duke struck you? You know it has often pleased him to commit murder without reason, for his sport.

Tebaldeo If he attacked me, I should kill him.

Lorenzo And you dare say that to me?

Tebaldeo Why single me out? I do no harm. I spend my days painting in my workshop. On Sundays I go to the Church of the Annunziata or to Santa Maria, where the monks think I have a good voice. They dress me up in their white robes, with a red cap on my head, and then I sing in the choir, sometimes a solo part. That's the only public appearance I ever make. In the evenings I visit my mistress. Nobody knows me, and I know nobody. What use am I to anyone, alive or dead?

Lorenzo Are you a republican? Do you love your princes?

Tebaldeo I am an artist. I love my mother and my mistress.

Lorenzo Come to my palace tomorrow. I want you to paint me a picture of importance for my wedding day.

Exeunt.

Scene Three

The rooms of the **Marchesa Cibo**.

Cardinal Cibo, *alone*.

Cibo Yes, Farnese, I'll carry out your orders. Your Papal Nuncio can retire into the confines of honest officialdom

while I with firm hand move the shifting sand on which
he dare not tread. That is what you expected of me. I
understand you and shall act in secrecy as you command.
You assessed me shrewdly when, placing me at
Alexander's side, you granted me no title which would
impose on him . . . subservience. While in all ignorance
he obeys my will his suspicious mind will centre on
another. Let him spend his strength on men of shadow,
plump with the shadow of power. I'll be the invisible
link binding him hand and foot to the iron chain that
ties Rome to the Emperor. If my eyes do not mislead
me, it is in this house I shall find the hammer with
which to forge that link. Alexander desires my sister-in-
law; it could well be his love has turned her head. It is
uncertain what may come of this, but I know how *she*
will wish to use it. Who knows how far it could lead, the
influence of a woman, politically inspired, even upon a
man as gross as that strutting iron-clad? So sweet a sin
for so fine a cause, Ricciarda, is not that truly tempting?
To press this lion's heart against your weak one, pierced
with as many arrows as St Sebastian's? To speak with
tear-filled eyes of the sorrows of your homeland while the
adored tyrant runs his coarse hands through your
tumbling hair. To strike from that rock one sacred
spark, is not that worth the sacrifice of wedded honour
and trifles of that kind? Florence would gain so greatly,
what could a docile husband lose? But you should not
have chosen me as your confessor.

Here she is now with her prayer book in her hand. Today
everything will be made clear. Just whisper your secret in
the ear of the priest, the courtier will turn it to good
advantage, but for conscience' sake, he'll never breathe a
word.

Enter the **Marchesa**.

Cardinal (*sitting down*) I am ready.

The **Marchesa** *kneels down beside him on her prayer-
stool.*

Marchesa Bless me, Father, for I have sinned.

Cardinal Have you said your *Confiteor*? We can begin, Marchesa.

Marchesa I accuse myself of fits of anger, of harmful and irreligious doubts concerning our Holy Father the Pope.

Cardinal Continue.

Marchesa Yesterday, when talking to a group of people of the Bishop of Fano, I called the Holy Catholic Church a den of vice.

Cardinal Continue.

Marchesa I welcomed words that threatened the fidelity I swore my husband.

Cardinal Who spoke to you in this way?

Marchesa I read a letter written in that vein.

Cardinal Who wrote this letter to you?

Marchesa I accuse myself of my own actions, not those of others.

Cardinal Daughter, you must answer me if you wish me to feel confident I can give you absolution. Tell me first whether you answered this letter.

Marchesa I answered by word of mouth, but not in writing.

Cardinal What did you reply?

Marchesa I gave the writer of the letter permission to see me as had been requested.

Cardinal What happened during this meeting?

Marchesa I have already accused myself of listening to words contrary to my honour.

Cardinal How did you reply to them?

Marchesa As befits a woman with any self-respect.

Cardinal Did you not hint that you might eventually be persuaded?

Marchesa No, Father.

Cardinal Did you announce to the person in question your resolve not to listen to such words in future?

Marchesa Yes, Father.

Cardinal Is this person pleasing to you?

Marchesa My heart is not touched, I hope.

Cardinal Have you alerted your husband?

Marchesa No, Father. A sensible woman should not disrupt a peaceful home by recounting stories of this kind.

Cardinal You're hiding nothing from me? Nothing took place between you and the person in question which you hesitate to disclose?

Marchesa Nothing, Father.

Cardinal No tender look? No stolen kiss?

Marchesa No, Father.

Cardinal Are you quite sure, my daughter?

Marchesa Does my brother-in-law think I am in the habit of lying before God?

Cardinal You refused to give me the name I asked for just now. But I cannot grant you absolution unless I know it.

Marchesa And why is that? It may be a sin to read a letter. But not a signature! What has the name to do with it?

Cardinal More than you imagine.

Marchesa Malaspina, you want to know too much. Refuse me absolution if you wish. I shall take as my confessor the first priest I find who will absolve me.

She rises.

Cardinal Why so headstrong, Marchesa? Do you think I do not know it is the Duke you speak of?

Marchesa Well, if you know that, why make me say it?

Cardinal Why do you refuse to say it? You surprise me.

Marchesa And how do you intend to use your knowledge, you, my confessor? Are you so anxious to hear this, in order to repeat it to my husband? Yes, I'm sure that's why. It's a mistake to have a member of the family as one's confessor. Heaven is my witness that when I kneel before you I forget that I'm your sister-in-law. But you take care to remind me. Beware, Cibo! You may be a Cardinal, but you should still be mindful of your eternal salvation.

Cardinal Come back here, Marchesa. There's not so much harm done as you think.

Marchesa What are you trying to say?

Cardinal That a confessor should know everything, because he can give direction, and that a brother-in-law should say nothing under certain conditions.

Marchesa What conditions?

Cardinal No, no, a slip of the tongue – that was not the word I intended. I meant that the Duke is powerful, that a break with him could be harmful even to the richest families in Florence. But in experienced hands a secret of importance could grow into an abundant source of profit.

Marchesa A source of profit! In experienced hands! – I stand here like a statue, turned to stone. What are you brewing behind this priestly ambiguity? At times you churchmen string words together in such a way that we lay folk know not what to think.

Cardinal Come back here and sit down, Ricciarda. I've still not given you absolution.

Marchesa Go on talking. It's by no means certain that I want it.

Cardinal (*rising*) Take care, Marchesa. Anyone who tries to brave me to my face should have no chink in his armour. I have no wish to threaten you. There is only one thing left for me to say: find a new confessor!

Exit **Cibo.**

Marchesa (*alone*) This is beyond belief. To walk off, clenching his fists, his eyes blazing with fury! And that talk of experienced hands directing the course of events! What can this mean? I can conceive he should wish to uncover my secret and warn my husband, but if that is not his aim, what does he want of me? To make me the Duke's mistress? To know all, he said, and govern all? That is not possible. There's some darker more mysterious matter in all this. Cibo would not behave like that. No! I am sure he wouldn't. I know him. Those are the ways of a Lorenzaccio. But he! There must be some hidden meaning, deeper and more far-reaching. To think how men reveal themselves after ten years of silence! It's frightening.

Now what I am to do? Do I love Alexander? No, I do not love him. No, I'm sure I don't. I said as much in confession and I was not lying. Why has my husband gone to Massa? Why is the Duke so pressing? Why did I say I no longer wished to see him? Why? – Oh why is there some charm in all this, some magnetic force that draws me on? (*She opens the window.*)

How lovely you are, Florence, but how sad! The cloaked figure of Alexander has entered more than one house at night. A libertine. I know that's what he is. – And why are you involved in all this, Florence. Who is it then that I love? Is it you or Alexander?

Agnolo (*entering*) Madame, His Highness has just come into the courtyard.

Marchesa How very odd! This Malaspina has left me trembling.

Scene Four

In the Soderini Palace.

Maria Soderini, Catherine *and* **Lorenzo** *seated.*

Catherine (*holding a book*) What story shall I read you, Mother?

Maria My Cattina's making fun of her mother. How can I understand your Latin books?

Catherine This one's not in Latin, it has been translated. It's Roman history.

Lorenzo I know my Roman history by heart. Once upon a time there was a young nobleman called Tarquin the Younger.

Catherine Oh, that's a story of blood and violence.

Lorenzo No, it's not. It's a fairy tale. Brutus was obsessed by one idea, a madman, that's all. Tarquin was a good kind duke, who just put on his slippers to go and see if the little girls were sound asleep.

Catherine Are you going to find something wrong with Lucretia too?

Lorenzo She enjoyed the pleasures of sin and the glory of self-immolation. Like a lark, she let herself get caught alive in a trap, and then gently pushed her little knife in her gut.

Maria Even if you do despise women, must you make a
point of defaming them in front of your mother and her
sister?

Lorenzo I respect both of you. But apart from you, the
world fills me with horror.

Maria Do you know what I dreamt last night, my son?

Lorenzo What dream was that?

Maria It wasn't exactly a dream, as I wasn't alseep. I was
alone in a great hall. My lamp was some distance from me,
on a table by the window. I was thinking of the days when
I was happy, when you, my Lorenzino, were a child. I
was peering through the darkness, thinking: he won't be
back till daybreak, that boy who used to spend all his
nights in study. My eyes filled with tears, and I shook my
head as they ran down my face. Suddenly I heard slow
footsteps in the gallery. As I turned round, a man dressed
in black was coming towards me, with a book under his
arm. It was you, Renzo. 'You are back home early,' I
exclaimed. But the spectre sat down near the lamp,
without a word. He opened his book. And then I
recognized my Lorenzino of old.

Lorenzo You really saw him?

Maria As I see you now.

Lorenzo When did he leave?

Maria When you sounded the bell this morning on your
return.

Lorenzo My own spectre? And he went away as I came
home?

Maria He rose sadly to his feet and faded away like the
morning mist.

Lorenzo Catherine, Catherine, read me the story of
Brutus.

Catherine What's wrong? You're shaking all over.

Lorenzo Mother, sit down this evening where you were last night. And if my spectre returns, tell him he will soon see something to astonish him.

A knock.

Catherine It's my uncle Bindo and Baptista Venturi.

Enter **Bindo** *and* **Venturi.**

Bindo (*aside to* **Maria**) I shall try again, one last time.

Maria We'll leave you. May luck go with you!

Exit with **Catherine.**

Bindo Lorenzo, why don't you deny the scandalous rumour that's going round about you?

Lorenzo What rumour?

Bindo It's being said you fainted at the sight of a sword.

Lorenzo Do you believe it, uncle?

Bindo I've seen you fence in Rome. But here, considering how you occupy your time, it wouldn't surprise me if you'd sunk lower than a dog.

Lorenzo It's true, that rumour. I did faint. Good day, Venturi. What are you charging for your merchandise today? How's business?

Venturi My Lord, the business I control may manufacture silk, but by calling me a merchant you insult me.

Lorenzo You're right. I only meant to remind you that at college you had already formed the innocuous habit of selling silk.

Bindo I have made Signor Venturi cognizant of the projects that now preoccupy so many families in Florence.

He is a firm friend of liberty and I insist, Lorenzo, that
you treat him as such. The hour for jesting has passed. At
times you have informed us that this great trust the Duke
has in you was on your part nothing but a trap. Is this true
or false? Are you one of us, or are you not? This is what
we must know. All our great families have realized that
the Medici despotism is neither just nor tolerable. What
law compels us to allow this arrogant house to rise up
uncontested over the ruins of our privileges? We have
never received our freedom, promised under the terms of
our capitulation. The power of Germany makes itself felt
and grows more absolute from day to day. It is time to call
a halt and gather our patriots together. Will you answer
this appeal?

Lorenzo What have you to say, Signor Venturi? Speak.
Say something, while my uncle gets his breath back. If
you love your country, seize this chance!

Venturi My Lord, I think the same and have no other
word to add.

Lorenzo No other word? Not one fine resounding little
word? You can't be acquainted with true eloquence. You
take one nice little word, not too short, not too long, and
around it like a top you spin a fine-sounding phrase. Then
you throw back your left arm in such a way that your
gesture lends to the folds of your gown a certain dignity
tempered with grace. Your sentence is released and
unwinds like a twanging cord, while the little top spins
free and hums delightfully. You could almost pick it up,
like children in the street, and nurse it in the hollow of
your hand.

Bindo Insolent boy! Answer, or get out of here!

Lorenzo I am with you, uncle. Can't you see from the
cut of my hair that I'm a republican through and through?
See the shape of my beard. Never doubt one single
moment that love of country pervades every stick of
clothing that I wear, even the most intimate.

A bell is rung at the main door of the palace. The courtyard fills with **Pages** *and horses.*

Page (*entering*) The Duke!

Enter the **Duke**.

Lorenzo You do me too much honour, my Prince. Deigning to visit your humble servant in person.

The Duke What men are these? I've something to say to you.

Lorenzo May I have the honour of presenting to Your Highness my uncle, Bindo Altoviti. He regrets that a long stay in Naples has not allowed him to cast himself sooner at your feet. This other gentleman is the illustrious Baptista Venturi who manufactures silk, though he never sells it. Let not the unexpected presence of so great a prince in such a humble house cause you embarrassment, dear uncle. Or you, worthy Venturi. What you beg for will be granted, or you would have every right to say that my gracious sovereign has no ear for my petitioning.

The Duke What are you after, Bindo?

Bindo Highness, I am confused that my nephew . . .

Lorenzo The post of Ambassador in Rome is vacant at the moment. My uncle fondly hoped with your good grace that he might obtain it. In all Florence there's not a single man who can bear comparison with him, when it comes to the devotion and respect he owes the Medici.

The Duke Is that so, Renzino? Well, my dear Bindo, that's settled then. Come to the palace tomorrow morning.

Bindo Highness, I am speechless. How can I express my . . .

Lorenzo And Signor Venturi, though he never sells his silk, begs a warrant for his workshops.

The Duke What sort of warrant?

Lorenzo Your coat of arms over the door and your letters patent. Grant him this, my Lord, if you love those who love you.

The Duke That is in order. Is that all? Go, gentlemen, and peace be with you.

Venturi Highness!. My cup is overflowing. What can I say that . . .

The Duke Let these two people pass.

Bindo (*leaving, aside to* **Venturi**) An infamous trick to play!

Venturi What will you do?

Bindo What the devil can I do? I've been named for the post.

Venturi This is terrible!

Exeunt.

The Duke The Cibo woman's mine.

Lorenzo That's a great pity.

The Duke Why?

Lorenzo Because it'll disappoint the others.

The Duke Oh no, it won't! She's boring me already. But tell me, mignon, who's that beautiful woman arranging flowers at that window? I've been seeing her constantly as I go by, for a long time now.

Lorenzo Where's that?

The Duke In the palace. Over there, opposite.

Lorenzo Oh, she's nothing.

The Duke Nothing! You call an arm like that nothing? By the devil's guts, what a Venus!

Lorenzo She's just a neighbour.

The Duke A neighbour I'd like to accost! Good Lord, if I'm not mistaken, it's Catherine Ginori.

Lorenzo No.

The Duke I know it is! It's your young aunt. Plague on it! I'd forgotten how attractive she is. Why don't you bring her to supper?

Lorenzo Difficult. She's a dragon of virtue.

The Duke Don't you believe it! There's no such thing for men like us.

Lorenzo I'll ask her, if you like. But I warn you she's a blue-stocking. And she talks Latin.

The Duke Good for her! But you don't need Latin to make love! Come over this way, from the gallery we'll see her better.

Lorenzo Another time, mignon. It's late and I've no time to waste. I've got to go to the Strozzi.

The Duke What? That mad old man?

Lorenzo Yes, that silly old infamous fool. There's no curing him of his strange mania for opening his purse to all those vile exiles. Every day these starving beggars gather at his place and get themselves ready for the road. What I plan to do now is go and gobble down his dinner while I give the old gallows' bird repeated assurance of my cordial devotion. I'll have a good yarn to report to you this evening, some charming little prank that'll drag a few of the riff-raff from their beds in the early hours tomorrow morning.

The Duke I'm a lucky man to have you, mignon! I confess I can't see why they let you in.

Lorenzo Of course, you don't know how easy it is to tell a bare-faced lie to an ignorant die-hard! It shows you've never tried. By the way, didn't you tell me you wanted to

give your portrait to someone or other? I've found a
painter for you, a protégé of mine.

The Duke Good, good. But think about your aunt. It's
for her sake I came to see you. Devil take me, I can't get
her out of my mind.

Lorenzo What of the Cibo woman?

The Duke You talk to your aunt about me. I'm telling
you!

Exeunt.

Scene Five

A room in the Strozzi Palace.

Philip Strozzi, Leon Strozzi, Louisa *busy sewing,*
Lorenzo *stretched out on a couch.*

Philip Pray to God that nothing comes of it! How much
implacable undying hatred has begun in just this way
before! Idle chatter from the thick lips of a lecher reeling
from food and wine, enough to start a family vendetta and
draw daggers. You are insulted, so you kill: you have
killed, so you are killed. Soon hate puts down its roots.
Sons are cradled in the coffins of their forebears, and
whole generations spring from the earth, sword in hand.

Leon Perhaps I was wrong not to forget that cruel remark
on my wretched trip to Montoliveto. But how can these
Salviati be endured?

Philip Ah, Leon, Leon! If you had not spread the word,
for Louisa, for all of us, things would be simpler now!
Can't a virtuous Strozzi ignore the jibes of a Salviati?
Must those who live in a marble palace know what
obscenities the populace has written on its walls? Who
cares about the comments of a man like Julian? Will my
daughter find it hard to find an honest husband? Will her
children respect her less? Will I, her father, think of

it, when I'm kissing her good night? What have we come to, if any insolent braggart can make men like us draw our swords? Now all is lost. Peter is furious over what you told us. He has gone off rampaging to the Pazzi. If he meets Salviati, God knows what will happen. Blood will be spilt. Blood, my blood, on the paving-stones of Florence! Oh, why am I a father?

Leon If some remark about my sister, however bad it was, had been *reported* to me, I would have turned my back and that would have been the end of it. But this one was addressed to me. It was so insulting, I did not think the boorish lout knew of whom he spoke. But he knew all right.

Philip Oh yes, they know, the vicious brutes. They know what they're striking at! The old tree-trunk is too resistant. They wouldn't hack at that. But when they attack its youngest shoots, they know what delicate fibres quiver deep within. Oh, my Louisa! What then is reason? My hands tremble at the very thought. Merciful God! Is reason nothing but old age?

Leon Peter's too violent.

Philip Poor Peter! How that red flush rose in his face! How he shook as he heard you quote the insult to his sister. I must have been mad to let you speak. Peter was pacing the room, anxious, furious, out of his mind – up and down, as I am now. As the pure blood rose to his blameless head, I watched him in silent pride. Another true member of his race, I thought. My eldest, another patriot. Oh, Leon, I cannot help being a Strozzi too.

Leon Perhaps there is less danger than you think. There's every chance he won't meet Salviati tonight. Tomorrow we'll see things in a clearer light.

Philip Don't count on that. Peter will kill him, or he'll get killed himself. (*He opens the window.*) Where are they now? Night has fallen and the town is steeped in darkness.

Those gloomy streets fill me with horror. I'm sure that
somewhere blood is being shed.

Leon Calm yourself.

Philip After the way Peter went out, there's no doubt in
my mind that he's either revenged or dead. I watched him
frown as he took down his sword. He was biting his lips
and the muscles of his arms were tense as an archer's. Yes,
yes, now he's dying or revenged. I'm sure of it.

Leon Don't excite yourself. Close the window.

Philip Very well then, Florence. Teach your pavings the
colour of my noble blood! Forty of your sons have it
running through their veins. And I, the chief of this great
family will lean my white head more than once from one
of these high windows, torn by a father's anguish. More
than once this blood of mine, spilt in your town square,
will be drying in the sun. Perhaps even now you drink it
with indifference. But do not laugh tonight at this old
Strozzi, who is frightened for his child. Don't waste his
family away. The day will come when you will count our
clan and stand at the window with beating heart beside
me, listening to the clashing of our swords.

Louisa Oh, Father! Father! You frighten me.

Leon (*aside to* **Louisa**) Isn't that Thomas roaming about
where those lanterns are? I thought I recognized him, he's
so small. There he is, moving off now.

Philip Poor city, where fathers wait like this for their
children to come home! At this hour there are many exiles
who have taken their cloaks and swords to come here
through the darkness. Those that wait for them are not
torn by doubt. They know they will die tomorrow of
privation, if the cold does not kill them tonight. Whereas
we, in our rich palaces, wait to be insulted before we draw
our swords! A drunkard's loose remark taunts us to send
our children and our friends out through that gloomy
maze of streets! But we don't shake the dust from our

weapons for the sake of our public woes. People take
Philip Strozzi for an honest man, because he does good
without opposing evil. And now I, a father, what would I
not give to know that somewhere in this world there was
one man able to return my son to me and punish the insult
to my daughter in the due process of the law? But why
should anyone oppose the evil that threatens me, when I,
who had the power, did not prevent it threatening others?
I was hunched over my books, turning my country into a
dreamland of all I admired in the Ancient World. The
walls screamed out to me for vengeance, and I stopped my
ears to steep myself in meditation. It has needed tyranny
to slap me in the face to make me ripe for action. And
now my vengeance has grey hair.

Enter **Peter** *and* **Thomas** *with* **Francesco Pazzi**.

Peter It's over. Salviati is dead.

He kisses his sister.

Louisa How horrible! You're covered in blood.

Peter We laid in wait for him at the corner of the
Bowmen's Street. Francesco stopped his horse. Thomas
hit him in the leg, and I . . .

Louisa Stop it! Be quiet! It makes me shiver. Your eyes
are starting from your head. Your hands look hideous.
Your whole body's shaking, and you're as pale as death.

Lorenzo (*rising*) You're beautiful, Peter. You're as tall as
vengeance.

Peter Who said that? Why are you here, Lorenzaccio?
(*He goes to his father.*) When will you shut your doors to
this miserable wretch? Don't you realize what he is?

Philip It's all right. I know all about it. And I don't just
mean that Maurizio affair. If Lorenzo's here, it's because I
have good reason to receive him. We'll discuss it at the
proper time and place.

Peter (*between his teeth*) Ha! Reason to receive that scum!
One of these days I could find reason, and a good one too,
to toss him out the window. Say what you will, it chokes
me to see that leper lounging round our house.

Philip Peace! Enough now! Peter, you're too headstrong!
God grant your escapade tonight may not bring us to
disaster! But first you must be hidden.

Peter Hidden! By all the saints, why should I be hidden?

Lorenzo (*to* **Thomas**) And then you hit him on the
shoulder? Tell me a little more about . . .

*He takes him off to a window embrasure where they talk
quietly together.*

Peter No, Father, I won't hide myself away. This insult
was made in public, in an open square. I struck him down
in an open street. And tomorrow morning it will be a
pleasure to tell the whole town about it. Since when
should one hide oneself away for having avenged one's
honour? It would suit me perfectly to walk abroad with
my sword drawn, and still dripping with blood.

Philip Come this way, I must talk to you. You weren't
wounded, my boy? No hurt received in all this?

Exeunt.

Scene Six

*The **Duke**'s palace.*

*The **Duke**, partially clad, **Tebaldeo** painting his portrait.*
Giomo *playing his guitar.*

Giomo (*singing*)
   Cupbearer, when I have drawn my last breath,
   Carry my heart to my well-belov'd lass.
   To the devil with pious prayers and a Mass.
   Don't let her summon the black priest of death.

It's naught but water when tear follows tear.
Tell her to unstop a wine-barrel's womb.
Let them sing drinking-songs over my bier
And I'll answer them back from deep in the tomb.

The Duke I know I had something to ask you. Tell me,
Hungarian, what had that fellow done to you? The one I
saw you beating up with so much gusto.

Giomo Hell, I don't know. And he couldn't tell you now
either.

The Duke Why, is he dead?

Giomo As I went by just now, I got the idea they were
burying him.

The Duke When my Giomo hits, he hits hard.

Giomo You can talk. I've seen you kill a man more than
once with just one blow.

The Duke You don't say! I must have been drunk. When
I'm half-seas over, even my mildest blows are lethal. (*To*
Tebaldeo.) What's the matter with you, boy? Is your
hand shaking? You're pulling a terrible face.

Tebaldeo Nothing, my Lord, may it please Your
Highness.

Enter **Lorenzo**.

Lorenzo How's it going? Are you content with my
protégé? (*He picks up the* **Duke**'s *coat of mail from the sofa.*)
That's a nice coat of mail, mignon! It must be pretty hot
to wear.

The Duke If it vexed me, I wouldn't wear it. It's steel
mesh. Even the keenest file couldn't cut through a single
link. Yet it's as light as a piece of silk. I don't suppose
there's another like it in the whole of Europe. So I never
take it off. Hardly ever.

Lorenzo Do you think it would stop a dagger?

The Duke Sure it would.

Lorenzo Now I come to think of it, you always do wear it under your tunic. Out hunting the other day, when we were on the same horse, and I was behind, holding on to you, I could feel it quite distinctly. It's a sensible habit.

The Duke It's not that there's anyone I don't trust. As you say, it's become a habit. A soldierly habit.

Lorenzo That costume's magnificent. And the perfume on those gloves! But why are you posing half dressed? Your coat of mail would have looked most effective. You were wrong to take it off.

The Duke It was what the painter wanted. Besides, it's always better to reveal the throat when one's posing. Think of all those Romans.

Lorenzo Where the devil's my guitar? I must play a treble accompaniment to Giomo.

Exit.

Tebaldeo Highness, I shall do no more today.

Giomo (*at the window*) What on earth is Lorenzo up to? Standing there gazing at the well in the garden. That's hardly the place to look for his guitar.

The Duke Give me my clothes. Where's my coat of mail got to?

Giomo I can't find it. I've looked, but it's disappeared.

The Duke Renzino had it a minute ago. He must have thrown it down in some corner as he went out. Superbly careless as usual.

Giomo It's incredible. No sign of it. Completely vanished.

The Duke Come on now, you're dreaming. That's impossible.

Giomo   Look for yourself, my Lord. The room's not that big.

The Duke   Renzo was holding it over there by the sofa.

Enter **Lorenzo**.

The Duke   What have you done with my coat of mail, then?

Lorenzo   I put it back where it was. Wait – no, I put it down on that armchair. No, on the bed, oh, I don't know. But I found my guitar. (*He sings to his own accompaniment:*) 'Good day, Lady Abbess . . .'

Giomo   In the garden well, I suppose? You looked quite absorbed leaning over it just now.

Lorenzo   I'm never happier than spitting down a well to make rings in the water. It's my only pastime. (*He goes on playing.*) 'Good morning, Abbess of my heart . . .'

The Duke   My coat of mail lost! I can't get over it! I've only taken it off twice in my life, except to go to bed.

Lorenzo   Oh, forget it, forget it! We can't have the son of a Pope turn into a valet. Your servants will find it.

The Duke   The devil take you! It was you who lost it!

Lorenzo   If I were the Duke of Florence, I'd find something better than coats of mail to occupy my mind. By the way, I've talked to my dear aunt about you. It's all going fine. Come over here and I'll whisper in your ear.

Giomo   (*quietly to the* **Duke**) It's odd to say the least. Someone's taken your coat of mail.

The Duke   Oh! It'll turn up.

He goes and sits next to **Lorenzo**.

Giomo   It's not natural disappearing like that to spit in the well. I'd like to find that coat of mail again. There's a rusty old doubt at the back of my mind I'd like to be rid

of. Pooh! But it's only Lorenzaccio! It must have fallen
under a chair.

Scene Seven

In front of the **Duke**'*s Palace.*

Enter **Salviati** *limping and covered in blood with two men
holding him up.*

Salviati (*shouting*) Duke Alexander! Alexander de'
Medici! Alexander! Open your window! See how your
supporters are treated!

The Duke (*at his window*) What's this dreadful row?
Who's that, in the mud and filth, stumbling up to the
walls of my palace?

Salviati The Strozzi have murdered me. I've come to die
at your gates.

The Duke Which of the Strozzi? And why?

Salviati Because I said their sister was in love with you,
noble Duke. The Strozzi thought she'd been insulted
when I said she fancied you. Three of them set upon me.
One of them I didn't know, but I recognized Peter and
Thomas.

The Duke Get my men to help you up here. By
Hercules! Those cut-throats will spend the night in prison,
and tomorrow morning I'll have them hanged.

Salviati *is let into the palace.*

Act Three

Scene One

Lorenzo's *bedroom*.

Lorenzo *and* **Scoronconcolo** *fencing*.

Scoronconcolo Master, have you had enough of this play-acting yet?

Lorenzo No! Cry out! Come on, louder! See what you can make of this one! Die, you rascal!

Scoronconcolo Murder! He's going to kill me! Cut my throat!

Lorenzo Die, die, die! Kick, then!

Scoronconcolo Help, guards! Help me! That hellish Lorenzo is killing me!

Lorenzo Die, you scum! I'll stick you like a pig, I'll bleed you! Run him through the heart! He's ripped open! – Go on, Scoronconcolo, shout! Hit him, then, kill him! Tear his guts out! Let's cut him in pieces and eat him. Eat him! I'm in up to the elbow! Now dive into his throat! Roll him over! Let's bite him, get our teeth in! Devour him!

He falls exhausted.

Scoronconcolo (*wiping his brow*) That's a rough game you've invented, Master. You're a real tiger. Like a billion thunderclaps, your roaring echoes like a cave full of lions and panthers!

Lorenzo The day of blood shall be my wedding day! Oh! Glorious Sun! The sun has been parched and leaden long enough. But soon you will be drunk with his blood. Oh!

Vengeance! The nails of my vengeance have grown long
enough by now. Now the teeth of a Ugolino can't wait to
sink in that skull!

Scoronconcolo Are you delirious? In a fever?

Lorenzo Coward, coward – pander – that little weakling
and fathers and daughters – goodbyes, endless farewells –
along the banks of the Arno – urchins spell it out on the
walls. Laugh, old man, in your white nightcap! Laugh out
loud! Can't you see how my nails have been growing? Ah!
His skull! That skull!

He faints.

Scoronconcolo Master, you must really have an enemy!
(*He throws water into his face.*) Come on, master, there's no
need to go mad like this! Some people are decent and
loyal. I'll never forget the good you've done me. If you
have an enemy, Master, you just tell me, I'll take care of
him and no one will suspect a thing.

Lorenzo It's nothing. I told you, I just wanted to frighten
my neighbours.

Scoronconcolo With all this rampaging about in here,
knocking everything over, they must have got used to our
infernal din by now. I bet you could slaughter thirty men
in that passage, then trundle them over your floor, and not
a soul would turn a hair. If you want to frighten the
neighbours, you're going the wrong way about it. The first
time, perhaps. But now they just simmer with fury and
don't even bother to rise from their chairs or go and look
out of their windows.

Lorenzo Are you sure?

Scoronconcolo You've an enemy, Master. Haven't I seen
you stamping your foot and cursing the day you were
born? Don't I have ears? When you're in a rage, haven't I
distinctly heard one sharp little word, Vengeance? I tell
you, Master, you're losing weight – you don't even joke as
you used to. There's nothing worse for the digestion than

a hearty meal of hate. Take any two men under the sun, isn't there always one who resents the other's shadow? Your doctor's here in my scabbard. Let me cure you.

He draws his sword.

Lorenzo Has that doctor ever cured you?

Scoronconcolo Quite a few times. In Padua once, a young girl told me . . .

Lorenzo Show me your sword. Yes, my lad, it's a fine blade.

Scoronconcolo Try it out and you'll see.

Lorenzo You've diagnosed my disease, all right. But, for this enemy, I don't want a sword that's been used on others. The weapon that kills him will be baptized in his blood alone and will bear his name for ever.

Scoronconcolo What is his name?

Lorenzo Who cares? Are you faithful to me?

Scoronconcolo For you, I would nail Christ back on his cross.

Lorenzo I'll trust you then. I'm going to do it in this room. That's why we've been kicking up all this row every day, so our dear neighbours won't be surprised. Now listen carefully and make no mistake. If my first blow strikes home you leave him to me. But I'm a mere flea to that wild boar, so if he fights back, I'll rely on you to hold him down. No more than that, do you hear? He's mine. I'll give you the details later.

Scoronconcolo Amen!

Scene Two

In the Strozzi Palace.

Enter **Philip** *and* **Peter**.

Peter It makes me want to cut off my right hand, to

think I missed that swine, Salviati, when I was striking such a strong blow for justice. There's no one who'd not have rejoiced that at least one Salviati would never roam the streets again. But when the cunning devil fell, he lay there like a spider, with his crafty legs curled under him, playing dead to stop me finishing him off.

Philip What do you care that he's still alive? Your revenge is all the greater. They say his wounds are so bad that till the day he dies he won't forget them.

Peter I know that's the way you take it. You see, you may be a good patriot, Father, but being a patriarch suits you even better. I should keep out of this, if I were you.

Philip What's going on in that head of yours now? Can't you be still for half an hour without plotting some new mischief?

Peter No, in hell's name, I can't. Half an hour's too long in this poisonous atmosphere. The sky weighs down on me like the vaulted roof of a prison cell. In our streets I seem to breathe nothing but the jibes and belches of drunken sots. Goodbye, I have business to attend to.

Philip Where are you going?

Peter Why do you want to know? I'm off to the Pazzi.

Philip Wait for me then. I'm coming too.

Peter Not now, Father. It's not the right moment for you.

Philip Tell me the truth.

Peter Just between ourselves, there'll be about fifty of us there, the Ruccellai and others, who don't exactly cherish the Bastard.

Philip And so?

Peter Avalanches are sometimes started by a stone no bigger than the top joint of one's finger.

Philip But you've reached no firm decision? Made no plan? Taken no precautions? You're like children playing with life and death. Matters like this have shaken the world. Thousands have grown old thinking such thoughts which have caused numberless heads to roll at the feet of the executioners! Providence itself is dumb with terror and, fearful to intervene, leaves it up to men to bring such projects to fruition. Yet you mull it over, while you try out your swords and drink your Spanish wine, as though you were assessing a horse or a masquerade! Do you know what makes a republic? The craftsman in his workshop, the labourer in his field, the citizen in the market-place, the life of a whole community and in God's justice the simple happiness of men. But you are children, who can barely count up to five upon your fingers!

Peter Any festering sore can be cured if you lance it.

Philip Cured! Cured! Don't you know that even the slightest operation needs a doctor? That to draw one drop of blood from a patient's arm requires a whole world of science and a lifetime's experience. Last night when you concealed your naked blade beneath your cloak, do you think I felt no rage myself? As you are her brother, am I not the father of my Louisa? Don't you realize what it cost me to hold back? Only fathers know that: children will never know. We'll talk about this again, if you become one some day.

Peter You've learnt the art of loving, why can't you learn to hate?

Philip And how do these Pazzi serve God? They invite their friends to conspire together as if for a game of dice. Friends who might slip, as they cross their courtyard, on the Pazzi blood shed long ago when their grandfathers challenged these Medici. What? Are their swords still thirsty? What plot are you hatching this time? What are you after now?

Peter Why go back on your own words? Haven't I heard you a hundred times say the same things as we do? Do you think we don't know what preys on you, when your servants wake in the morning to see the lights in your windows still burning? Men like you who go without sleep don't die without speaking their mind.

Philip What are you trying to say? Answer me!

Peter We're plagued by the Medici. A man with snake-bite can't wait for a doctor. He must cauterize the wound himself.

Philip And when you've overthrown the system we have, what will you put in its place?

Peter One thing's for sure: it could never be worse.

Philip Learn to count on your fingers, I say.

Peter It's easy to count the heads of a Hydra.

Philip So you're determined to take action?

Peter To hamstring the assassins of Florence.

Philip And you will act, irrevocably?

Peter Goodbye, Father. Let me go – alone.

Philip Since when have old eagles stayed in the nest, when their young go in search of prey? Oh, my children, who have the strength I once had in my glorious youth, who are now what young Philip was before, show me I have not grown old in vain. Take me with you, my son. I see you will take action. I will make you no long speeches, just a few words. This grey head of mine may still contain something worth hearing. Two words and I'll be done. I won't embarrass you. I'm not in my dotage yet. Don't leave without me, my boy. Just wait for me to fetch my cloak.

Peter Come then, my noble Father. We shall kiss the hem of your robe. You are the father of us all. Come, old gardener of Florence, and see your life's dreams stretching out towards the sun. Come and watch the plant you love spring out of the soil you sowed. Freedom is ripe for plucking.

Exeunt.

Scene Three

A street.

A **German Officer,** *with* **Soldiers** *surrounding* **Thomas Strozzi.**

Officer If we don't find him at home, we'll find him with the Pazzi.

Thomas Have a good look, don't spare yourself! You'll pay for it in the end!

Officer No threats now. I'm carrying out the orders of the Duke. I've nothing to fear from anyone.

Thomas Imbecile! Who dares arrest a Strozzi on the word of a Medici!

A group of people is forming around them.

1st Townsman Why arrest this gentleman? We know him well, it's Philip's son.

2nd Townsman Let him go! We'll answer for him!

1st Townsman Yes, yes, we'll answer for the Strozzi. Let him go free or watch out! We'll have your ears off.

Officer Out of the way, you rabble, let the Duke's justice pass, or we'll cut you to pieces with our halberds.

Enter **Peter** *and* **Philip.**

Peter What's up? What's this infernal din? What are you doing there, Thomas?

1st Townsman Stop him, Philip! Stop him taking your son off to prison!

Philip To prison! On whose orders?

Peter To prison? Do you know who we are?

Officer Seize that man!

The **Soldiers** *arrest* **Peter**.

Peter Let me go, bastards, or I'll stick you like pigs!

Philip On whose orders are you acting, sir?

Officer (*showing the* **Duke**'s *warrant*) Here's my warrant. I have orders to arrest Peter and Thomas Strozzi.

The **Soldiers** *push back the people, who start throwing stones at them.*

Peter What are we accused of? What have we done? Help me, friends. Let's give these swine a beating.

He draws his sword. Enter another detachment of **Soldiers**.

Officer Come help me! Lend me your aid! (**Peter** *is disarmed*.) March off! The first one who comes too near gets a pike through his guts! That'll teach them to mind their own business!

Peter You have no right to arrest me without an order from the Council of Eight. I don't give a damn for Alexander's orders! Where's the order from the Council of Eight!

Officer Your case comes up before them. That's where we're taking you.

Peter If that's so, I've nothing more to say. What am I accused of?

2nd Townsman What's this, Philip? You let them lead your children off before the Council of Eight?

Peter Answer me! What am I accused of?

Officer That's no concern of mine.

The **Soldiers** *go off with* **Peter** *and* **Thomas**.

Peter (*as he leaves*) Have no fear, Father. The Eight will send me home to supper, and all the bastard will get for his justice is what it costs him.

Philip (*alone, sitting down on a bench*) I have many children, but not for long, if it goes on like this. What have we come to then, if an act of revenge as just as Heaven itself is punished as though it were a crime? The two eldest sons of a family as old as this city imprisoned like common bandits of the open road! The grossest of insults avenged, a Salviati chastised, and they bring out their pikes and their halberds! Why should my sword not spring from its sheath? If the sacred process of judgement and the law has become a shield for pimps and drunkards, then the assassin's weapons, axe and dagger, must needs protect all decent men. Oh Christ! Justice transformed into a bawd. The honour of the Strozzi attacked in a public place, and a sovereign court pronounces on a ruffian's boorish jibes! A Salviati hurls his wine- and blood-stained glove at the noblest family in Florence, and when chastised he draws for his defence the executioner's official sword! And by the sun's light, only fifteen minutes ago I spoke out against any idea of revolt! With these words of peace fresh on my lips, this is the bread they offer me! I must now flex the muscles of my weary arms, and this old body, bent with old age and learning, must straighten up for action!

Enter **Lorenzo**.

Lorenzo Are you begging for alms, Philip, sitting there at the corner of the street?

Philip I'm begging alms from all just men. I am a beggar starved of justice and my honour is in tatters.

Lorenzo What change will come over the world and what new gown will Nature wear, if the mask of anger falls over the serene and noble face of Philip? What can my good old father be lamenting? For whom are you shedding the most precious of gems, the tears of a man without fear, without reproach?

Philip You must rid us of the Medici, Lorenzo. I know you're a Medici yourself, but only in name. If I have ever really known you, faithful and impassive I have watched you playing out your hideous little game. But now is the time when the actor must disgorge the man. If there has ever been a decent instinct in you, let it be shown today. Peter and Thomas are in prison.

Lorenzo Yes. Yes. That I know.

Philip And is this your answer? Is this your true face, man without a sword?

Lorenzo What do you want of me? Tell me, and then you'll have my answer.

Philip Action! But of what kind I cannot say. What means can one employ? What leverage exert to prise up that citadel of death and topple it into the river? What's to be done, what resolution taken, what men can be called upon? I cannot know that yet. But we need action, action, action! Oh Lorenzo! This is the time! Have you not been labelled a heartless cur, slandered and defamed? But if, in spite of all, I have kept my door, my hand, my heart open for you, speak now and say if you have deceived me. Did you never tell me of another Lorenzo who hides behind the Lorenzo I see before me? A man who loves his country and is devoted to his friends? You used to say that and I believed you. Speak, speak now. The time has come.

Lorenzo May the sun descend upon my head, if I am not what you take me for!

Philip To laugh at a desperate old man, my friend, is to invite misfortune. If you're in earnest, take action! The promises I've had from you would commit God himself. On account of those promises I welcomed you. Even the prodigal son in a fit of mad folly would not have acted out such a filthy, leprous role as the part you're playing: and still I welcomed you. When the stones of Florence screamed out as you passed, when every step you took left pools of human blood behind, I called you by the sacred name of friend, made myself deaf to trust you, blind to love you. I let the shadow of your evil reputation fall across my honour, and even my children doubted me when they traced in my hand the hideous contact with yours. Be honest with me, as I have been with you. Take action, for you are young and I am old.

Lorenzo Peter and Thomas are in prison. Is that all?

Philip Oh, heaven and earth! Yes, that is all. Nothing to speak of. Two of my own children will sit on the bench reserved for thieves. As many times as the number of my grey hairs I have kissed their dear heads, which I shall find tomorrow morning nailed to the fortress gates. Yes, that is all, it's true. No worse than that.

Lorenzo Do not speak to me this way. The sorrow that devours my heart would make the blackest night appear like brilliant sunshine.

He sits down next to **Philip**.

Philip It is impossible I let my children die. You must see that. If my arms and legs were torn from my body, Philip's mutilated members would, like the dragon's join up and grow again to rise in vengeance. I know it all too well! The Council of Eight! A tribunal composed of men of marble! A forest of phantoms, through which the dismal wind of doubt blows from time to time, stirring them for a moment into life, but only to be resolved into one word of judgement. And against that one word, in all conscience, there's no appeal! And these are men who eat and sleep, have wives and daughters! Oh, let them kill and slaughter as they like, but not my children! Not my children!

Lorenzo Peter is a man: he'll speak out and gain his freedom.

Philip Oh, Peter, my first-born!

Lorenzo Go home and stay quiet in the house. Or better still, leave Florence. You can rely on me for everything, if you leave Florence.

Philip I, an exile? You think *I* could spend my last hour in the bed of a wayside inn? Oh God! And all this for one remark from a Salviati!

Lorenzo I would have you know that if Salviati tried to seduce your daughter, it was not for himself alone. Alexander has one foot in that man's bed, where he exerts his seigniorial rights over prostitution.

Philip And we do nothing! Oh Lorenzo, Lorenzo! You have some firmness in you, tell me what can be done. I am weak. My heart is too concerned in all this. My spirit fails me, can't you see? I've wasted my strength in meditation, turned like a horse in a wine-press in endless circles too often to be fit for battle. Give me your advice and I shall take it.

Lorenzo Go home, my friend.

Philip Now I know for sure what I must do: go straight to the Pazzi. There I shall find fifty young men all resolute and sworn to action. I shall speak to them with dignity, as befits a Strozzi and a father, and they will listen. This evening I'll invite forty members of my family to supper and tell them what has passed. Then we shall see, we'll see! All is not lost yet. Let the Medici be on their guard! Farewell, I'm going to the Pazzi. I was about to go there with Peter anyway, when they arrested him.

Lorenzo There are many forms of demon, Philip. The one that tempts you now is not the demon you should fear the least.

Philip What do you mean?

Lorenzo Take care, this demon is more beautiful than Gabriel himself. Like the strings of the lyre, words like freedom, homeland, mankind's happiness resound as he approaches, shaking the silver scales on his flaming wings. He makes the earth fertile with his tears and in his hand he holds the martyr's palm. His words purify the air about his lips. His flight is so swift that none can say where he is bound. Take care! Once in my life I saw him cross the sky. I was absorbed in my books, but the touch of his fingers set the hairs on my head quivering like feathers. We had better not tell whether I heeded him or not.

Philip I find it hard to understand you, and I fear to, though I don't know why.

Lorenzo Have you no other thought in mind but the rescue of your sons? Examine your conscience. Is there no other idea, more terrible and more far-reaching, that whirls you on in its chariot to join this youthful gathering?

Philip Why, yes! I want this injustice to my family to be a beacon in the fight for freedom. I shall go for myself, and for everyone's sake!

Lorenzo Take care, Philip. The thought of mankind's happiness has crept into your mind.

Philip What do you mean? Has the venom that infects your conduct poisoned your innermost thoughts? You who called yourself a flagon that contained a precious draught, is this what you hold inside you?

Lorenzo I am indeed precious to you, for I shall kill Alexander.

Philip You?

Lorenzo I myself. Tomorrow, or the day after. Go home. Try and get your sons released. If you fail, let them suffer a light sentence. I know for sure no other danger threatens them. And I repeat: in a few days from now Alexander de' Medici will no more exist in Florence than the sun shines at midnight.

Philip If that were true, why should I be wrong to think of freedom? Will that not come, when you have done this deed? If you really do it?

Lorenzo Philip, Philip, take care. You carry sixty virtuous years in your grey head. Too high a stake to risk losing in a gamble.

Philip If behind these dark words you're hiding
something I may hear, say on. You intrigue me strangely.

Lorenzo Philip, as I stand before you now, I once was
honest. I believed in virtue and the greatness of mankind,
as a martyr trusts in God. I have shed more tears over
poor Italy's woes than Niobe for her daughters.

Philip Well, Lorenzo?

Lorenzo The days of my youth were pure as gold. For
twenty silent years the lightning gathered in my breast.
And I must have sparked off a thunderbolt, for suddenly,
one night when I was sitting in the ruins of the ancient
Colosseum, I stood up, I don't know why, raised dew-
drenched arms to heaven and swore that one of the tyrants
of my fatherland would meet death at my hands. I was a
peaceful student at the time, only concerned with the arts
and sciences. It's impossible for me to say how such a
strange vow came about. Perhaps that's how it happens
when one falls in love.

Philip I've always had faith in you, yet I seem to be
dreaming.

Lorenzo And so do I. At that time I was happy, my
hands clean, my heart untroubled. My name put me in
line for the throne. To see the fulfilment of all a man
could wish for, I had nothing to do but sit back and watch
the rising and setting of the sun. I had no cause to bless or
curse mankind. But I was good, and to my eternal sorrow
I wanted to be great. I must confess that, much as
Providence urged me to kill a tyrant, no matter who, pride
had a hand in it too. What more should I say? Of all the
Caesars in the world I thought only of Brutus.

Philip Pride in virtue is a noble pride. Why defend
yourself against it?

Lorenzo You would have to be mad to grasp the nature
of the thoughts tormenting me. To comprehend the
feverish exaltation that gave birth to the Lorenzo talking

now, a scalpel would have to lay bare my entrails and my brain. A statue stepping down from its pedestal to mingle with men in a public square would perhaps best describe how I felt the day I first began to live with the idea that I must be a Brutus.

Philip You never cease to amaze me.

Lorenzo First I wanted to kill Pope Clement VII. I was banished from Rome too soon. I started all over again with Alexander. I wanted to act alone, with no help from anyone. I was working for mankind, but among all my philanthropic dreams I stood in proud isolation. So I had to use guile to engage my enemy in single combat. I had no wish to stir up the masses or achieve the garrulous glory of a Cicero, paralysed by words. I wished to tackle the man himself, grapple with a live tyrant at close quarters and kill him. Then bear my bloody sword to the tribune and let the fumes from Alexander's blood rise up those praters' nostrils to stew their turgid brains.

Philip A will of iron, my friend! What a will of iron!

Lorenzo It was an arduous task I set myself with Alexander. Florence was, then as now, soaked in blood and wine. The Emperor and the Pope had made a duke out of a butcher's boy. To approach and please my cousin, I had to wade through the tears shed by countless families. To become his friend and win his confidence, I had to kiss on his thick lips the last dregs of all his orgies. I was pure as a lily, yet I never recoiled from this obligation. What all this did to me, I dare not say. You must know what I suffered. From some wounds it is unwise to remove the dressing. I became cowardly and depraved, an object of shame and disgrace. No matter. That's not the question now.

Philip You lower your head. Your eyes are moist with tears.

Lorenzo No, I am not ashamed. Even in the service of infamy, a plaster mask cannot blush. What I have done is

done. All you shall learn is that my plan has been
successful. Alexander will soon be heading for a certain
place he'll never leave alive. I have reached the end of my
labours. And rest assured, Philip, that when a herdsman
brings the wild bull down upon the grass, it is not
entangled in more nets and nooses than I have cast to
snare my Bastard. To get within striking distance of him,
it would take an army more than a year's campaigning.
But now his heart lies exposed beneath my hand. I have
only to let fall my dagger to pierce it through. Soon it will
all be over. Now do you realize my position and why I
want to warn you?

Philip If what you say is true, then you are our Brutus.

Lorenzo My poor Philip. Once I thought I was a Brutus,
recalling the hollow stick he took to Delphi, which
enclosed a rod of gold. But now I know what men are like
and I advise you not to get embroiled.

Philip Why, why?

Lorenzo Ah! You have lived your life alone, Philip. Like
a shining lighthouse, you have stood motionless on the
shore of the human ocean, gazing into the water at the
reflection of your own brilliance. In your deep solitude,
you found the sea magnificent beneath the splendid
canopy of heaven. You did not count up the waves or
sound the depths. Your trust in God's creation was
complete. Meanwhile I dived straight in. I plunged into
the surging swell of life and, enclosed in my glass diving-
bell, I explored the hidden deep. While you were dazzled
by the surface, I discovered the remains of shipwrecks, the
bones of men and monstrous Leviathans.

Philip Your despair breaks my heart.

Lorenzo I speak like this because I see in you what I was
once, about to do what I myself have done. I don't despise
mankind, but historians in their books are wrong to make
men out to be different from what they are. Life is like a
city. You can live there for fifty or sixty years and see

nothing but its promenades and palaces, so long as you steer clear of its brothels and avoid stopping on the way home by windows in evil back streets. So this is my advice, Philip. If you wish to save your children, then stay quietly at home. It's the best way to see them sent back to you with little more than a reprimand. If you wish by some 'gesture' to serve mankind, then I advise you to chop off your arms, or you'll discover all too soon that no one else has arms to gesture with but you.

Philip I can see how the part you're playing can make you feel like this. The loathsome road you've followed in pursuit of a great ideal has made you believe, as I understand it, that what you've seen is everywhere the same.

Lorenzo I woke from my dreams, that's all. It's a dangerous thing to do, I warn you. I know what life is and, make no mistake, it's a sordid business. If you have any values left, don't get mixed up in it.

Philip That's enough! An old man needs a stick to lean on. Don't tell me mine's a broken reed. I believe in everything that you call dreams. In virtue, morality and freedom.

Lorenzo And there I go, Lorenzaccio, strolling through the street! And the children don't throw mud at me! Their sisters' beds are still warm with my hot sweat. Yet as I pass by, their fathers don't beat me with brooms or attack me with their knives. In ten thousand of these homes, behind locked doors, they'll still be talking till the seventh generation of the night I called on them. Yet not a house will spew out one single ploughman to split me in two like the rotting timber I am! The air that you breathe, Philip, I breathe too. My cloak of rainbow silk lazily trails over the fine sand on our pathways, yet not one drop of poison falls into the chocolate I drink. And oh, Philip! Worse than that: when I stop outside their doors, mothers in their poverty shamefully lift the veils that hide their daughters' faces displaying their beauty to me with a smile more foul than the kiss of Judas. And while I pinch the young girl's chin, in my pocket I'm clenching my fist with fury round four or five filthy pieces of gold.

Philip A tempter should never despise the weak. Why, if you have doubts, do you tempt others?

Lorenzo Am I a Satan? By heaven, when I first assumed my role as a modern Brutus, newly dressed in the uniform of the great brotherhood of vice, I was like a swaggering ten-year-old in the armour of some legendary giant. Corruption to me was a stigma, and only monsters had it branded on their brow. So I announced to all and sundry that my twenty years of virtue had been a stifling mask. And it was then, Philip, that I came close to life. When we came face to face, I saw that everyone was the same. They all dropped their masks. Finding me a worthy partner, Humanity lifted her skirts and exposed to me her monstrous nudity. I've known men as they really are, and it's made me wonder who I'm striving for. When I walked the streets of Florence, with my phantom at my side, I'd look round in search of faces that gave me cause to hope. And I'd ask myself: when I've carried out my plan, will *he* take advantage of it? I've watched the Republicans in their studies and visited our shops. I've kept my ears and eyes open. I've noted how the common people talk, I've seen how tyranny has moved them, and at patriotic banquets I've drunk the wine that breeds high-sounding speeches of sedition. I've tasted the most virtuous of tears – between two kisses. Always I've hoped humanity would show me something honest in her features . . . like a lover before his wedding day, observing his bride-to-be . . .

Philip If all you've seen is evil, then I pity you. But I can't believe you. Evil exists, but not without good, just as there are no shadows without light.

Lorenzo You want to see me as someone who despises men. You wrong me. I know perfectly well there are some good men. But what use are they? What do they *do*? What action do they take? What matter that their conscience is alive, if their arms and hands are dead? Something good can be found in everything. A dog is a faithful friend. You can look on him as the most loyal of all your servants. But when he licks his master with a tongue that stinks of rotten flesh a mile off, you can also tell he's been sniffing round the bodies of the dead. The lesson I have to learn from all this is that I myself am lost, and that men will no more reap benefit from me than they will understand me.

Philip Poor boy, my heart aches for you! But if you're an honourable man, when you've saved your country, you'll find yourself again. It rejoices my old heart, Lorenzo, to think that you are honest. Then you'll be able to throw aside the hideous disguise that so disfigures you, and your metal will shine out as pure as the bronze statues of tyrant-slayers like Harmodius and Aristogiton.

Lorenzo Philip, I was honest once, Philip. A hand that has once raised the veil that hides the truth can never let it fall again. It remains uplifted there till death, forever holding that frightening veil and raising it higher and higher above a man's head, till his eyes are closed by the angel of eternal sleep.

Philip Every sickness can be cured, and vice is a sickness too.

Lorenzo It's too late. I've grown used to my trade. Once I wore vice like a garment; now it's stuck fast to my skin. I'm a pander now all right, and when I mock my fellow humans my cynical jokes are as grim as death itself. To kill Tarquin, Brutus played the madman, and I'm amazed that, doing so, he never lost his reason. Listen, Philip, to what I say: learn from my example and stop working for your country.

Philip If I were to believe you, my sky would grow dark forever, and I'd be condemned to grope my way through the last years of my life. The path you have chosen's a dangerous one. Why shouldn't I choose another which leads to the same goal? I mean to rouse the people and act openly.

Lorenzo Take care, Philip. The man who's warning you knows only too well why. Whichever road you choose, you'll still have mankind to contend with.

Philip I have faith in the Republicans. They are honourable men.

Lorenzo I'll make you a wager. Once I've killed Alexander, it will be easy for the Republicans, so long as they act as they should, to set up the finest republic that's ever flourished on earth. It's theirs for the asking, if the people are behind them. But I bet you neither they nor the people will do anything at all. All I ask of you is, keep out of it. Speak, if you like, but be careful what you say, and still more what you do. Let *me* take action: your hands are clean and I have nothing to lose.

Philip Do it, and then you'll see.

Lorenzo I shall – but remember this: can you see that family sitting round a table in that little house? You'd think they were human beings, wouldn't you? Each one has a body and a soul. But if it entered my mind, all by myself and just as I am now, to go inside and stab their eldest son right there among them not one single knife would be raised against me.

Philip You appal me. With hands like yours, how can your heart stay pure?

Lorenzo Come, let's go home to your palace and try and free your sons.

Philip But feeling the way you do, why go on and kill the Duke?

Lorenzo Why? You ask me that?

Philip If you believe your country will gain nothing from this murder, then why do it?

Lorenzo You stand there and ask me that? Just look at me. Once I was handsome, virtuous and at peace.

Philip You open up a gaping pit of horror!

Lorenzo You ask me why I'm killing Alexander? Would
you rather I took poison or jumped into the Arno? Would
you rather I turned phantom and obtained no answering
sound when I beat upon this hollow frame of bones? (*He is
beating his own chest.*) If I am but the shadow of myself,
would you rather I broke the last thread that links my
heart today with the few remaining fibres of my former
self? Don't you see that this murder is all that's left me of
my virtue? Don't you see that for two years, while I've
been clambering down a rocky precipice, this murder's the
only tuft of grass I've been able to dig my nails in? Or as
I've no more shame, do you think I've no more pride left?
Do you want me to let the riddle of my life fade into
enigmatic silence? Oh yes, it's true that I might spare this
cattle-drover, if I could be restored to virtue, if my
apprenticeship to vice could be effaced. But I love
gambling, wine and women. You understand? If there's
one thing you respect in me, it is perhaps this murder, if
only because you would not do it yourself. You see, for
some time now the Republicans have been hurling mud
and infamy at me. My ears have been burning far too long
and men's curses have turned the bread sour in my
mouth. I've heard enough of their braying voices and
endless chatter. It's high time the world found out about
me, and about itself. Tomorrow, perhaps, I'll have killed
the Duke, thank God! In two days it will all be over. The
mob that circles round me with suspicious eyes, as if
gazing at some curious monstrosity shipped from the
Americas, will soon happily spill out their stock of words.
Whether I am understood or not, whether men take action
or abstain, I will have said my piece. If I don't start them
cleaning their rusty pikes, at least I'll get them sharpening
their pens. And Humanity's cheek will bear the mark of
my sword traced out in blood. They can call me what they
like, a Brutus or an Erostratus, but I don't wish them to
forget me. My whole life hangs on the point of my dagger,
and whether Providence turns her head or not when she
hears me strike my blow, I'm challenging human nature to
turn up heads or tails on Alexander's grave. In two days'

time mankind will be summoned before the Tribunal of
my will.

Philip All this bewilders me, and what you say gives me
both pain and pleasure. But Peter and Thomas are in
prison, and where that's concerned I trust no one but
myself. In vain I try to check my rage, I am too deeply
moved. Although you may be right, I must take action. I
shall call my family together.

Lorenzo Do as you will, but take care. All I ask is that
you keep my secret and do not tell it even to your friends.

Exeunt.

Scene Four

The Soderini Palace.

Enter **Catherine** *reading a letter.*

Catherine 'Lorenzo has surely talked to you about me.
But who else could do justice to a love like mine? Let my
pen now inform you what my tongue never dared to say,
in this note which I'd gladly sign in my heart's blood.
Alexander de' Medici.' Had this not been addressed to
me, I would have thought the messenger mistaken and,
reading it, I can hardly believe my eyes.

Enter **Maria**.

Catherine Oh Mother dear, look at this letter and explain
the mystery to me if you can.

Maria Unhappy girl! He loves you! Where did he see
you? Where did you speak to him?

Catherine Nowhere at all. As I was coming out of
church, a messenger gave it to me.

Maria He says Lorenzo must have told you about him?
Oh Catherine! To have a son like that! One who tries to
make his own mother's sister the mistress of the Duke.

And not even his mistress! Oh, my dear, I cannot even bring myself to say the names such creatures bear. Yes, this is all you needed, Lorenzo, the finishing touch. Come! I intend to take this opened letter to him, and find out before God what answer he will make.

Catherine I thought the Duke was in love with . . . Forgive me, mother, but I thought the Duke loved the Marchesa Cibo. That's what I was told . . .

Maria That is true. He has been in love with her, if he can love at all.

Catherine And he no longer loves her? Oh, how shameless he must be, to reveal such a heart to me! Come, Mother, let's go to Lorenzo's.

Maria Give me your arm. I don't know what's wrong with me the last few days, I've been in a fever every night. In fact, I've hardly been without it for three months now. I've had too much sorrow to bear. Poor Catherine! Why did you make me read that letter? Everything is too much for me now. I'm not young any more. Though it seems, if things were better, I wouldn't feel so old. But all I see, when I look round me, draws me to my grave. Let us go. Support me, my poor child, I won't burden you much longer.

Exeunt.

Scene Five

At the **Marchesa***'s.*

The **Marchesa***, grandly dressed, is before her mirror.*

Marchesa When I think this is really happening, it strikes me as something so new and strange. Life is full of unexpected pitfalls! Can it really be nine o'clock already, and here I am in my finest dress, waiting for the Duke!

Whatever comes of it, I want to test the power I have over him.

Enter the **Cardinal Cibo**.

Cibo You look magnificent, Marchesa. What beautifully scented flowers!

Marchesa Cardinal, I cannot receive you now. I'm expecting a friend, a lady. Please forgive me.

Cibo I'll leave you then, I'll leave you. By what I can see of your boudoir, through that half-open door, it looks a perfect paradise. May I go and wait for you in there?

Marchesa I'm sorry, I'm rather late. No, not my boudoir. Anywhere else you like.

Cibo I'll come back at a more favourable time.

Exit.

Marchesa Always the face of that priest! And why? Why is he always circling about me, like a bald-headed vulture? I find him constantly behind me, whenever I turn round. Can it be an omen that my last hour is near?

Enter a **Page**, *who whispers to her.*

Marchesa Very well, I'm coming. Oh! My poor heart's too proud to play the servant. I'm made of sterner stuff!

Exit.

Scene Six

The **Marchesa***'s boudoir.*

The **Marchesa**, *the* **Duke**.

Marchesa That's how I see the situation. And that way I could love you.

The Duke Words, words! Nothing but words!

Marchesa It all means so little to you men! To sacrifice
one's peace of mind, the sanctity of one's chastity and
honour, sometimes even one's own children. To live for
one person only in this world. Self-sacrifice, in fact, as
that's what they call it. But it's hardly worth the effort.
Why listen to a woman? Frills and furbelows and amorous
intrigues! Can a woman talk of anything but that?

The Duke You talk of your daydreams.

Marchesa Dreams, yes, by Heaven, I've had my dreams.
It's only kings, alas, who don't need dreams. All their
wildest whims come true and even their nightmare fears
get fixed in marble metaphors. Alexander! Alexander!
What power lies in that name: to wish is but to do! Ah,
God himself can say no more than that. When they hear
that name, people join their hands in dread to pray and
pale herds of men listen with bated breath.

The Duke No more of this, my dear. It makes me tired.

Marchesa To be king. Do you realize what that means?
To be armed with a hundred thousand hands! To be one
ray of the sun that dries the tears of mankind! To be the
source of their joy and grief? What a chilling thought that
is! How that old man in the Vatican would tremble if you
spread your wings, like the young eagle you are! Caesar is
so remote and your garrison so loyal to you. Besides, one
can slaughter an army, but not a people. The day you
have the whole nation behind you, when you're the head
of a state that has freely chosen you, when you can say:
'Just as the Doge of Venice weds the Adriatic, so I slip my
golden ring on the finger of my beautiful Florence, and
her children are my children . . .' Do you know how it
feels, when a race of men embraces its benefactor? When a
father proudly points you out to his child?

The Duke It's taxation that matters to me. So long as
they pay their taxes, what do I care?

Marchesa But that's the road to assassination. You'll be
crushed by the paving-stones they rip from the ground.

Have you never seen at the foot of your bed the spectre of posterity? Have you never wondered what those now living in their mothers' wombs will think of you? Yet all the time you're alive, you've only to say the word. Have you forgotten Old Cosimo, the Father of his Country? When one's a king, it's easy to be a great one. Declare Florence independent. Insist that the Emperor observes the treaty to remove his troops. Draw your sword and brandish it! They'll say it dazzles them and beg you to put it by. Just think how young you are! You can still change your destiny. The people's hearts are always full of grateful indulgence for their princes, and the memory of their past mistakes sinks into a deep well of forgetfulness. Your counsellors have misled you and deceived you. But there's still time to speak out. So long as you live, your page in God's book has not yet been turned.

The Duke Enough of this, my dear.

Marchesa But when it *has* been! Oh, then, when some poor reluctant gardener is given a day's wages to water the few wilting daisies around Alexander's tomb, when paupers can breathe freely and look up at a sky from which the dark meteor of your power no longer threatens them, when all who speak of you shake their heads and count around your tomb the graves of those of their families, are you sure that your last sleep will be a peaceful one? Are you sure, you who never go to Mass and care only about taxation, that Eternity is soundless and that the home of the departed holds no echo of our life on earth? When the winds blow away the people's tears, where do you think they go?

The Duke You have very shapely legs.

Marchesa Listen to me! I know you're thoughtless, but you're not an evil man. No, I swear to God you're not. You couldn't be. So look! Take a firm hold on yourself. Just think for one moment. Is there no sense at all in my advice? Am I completely deranged?

The Duke I take in what you say. But what's wrong with what I'm doing? I'm no worse than my fellow princes. Better, I dare swear, than the Pope! With all your speeches you remind me of the Strozzi – and you know how I hate *them*. You want me in rebellion against Caesar! The Emperor, dearest, is my father-in-law. You imagine the Florentines don't like me, I'm sure they love me. But if you *are* right, who should I be afraid of?

Marchesa You fear the Emperor and not your people. Yet hundreds of your own citizens have been killed or dishonoured by you. And you think a vest of chain-mail is all you need for protection?

The Duke Enough of this!

Marchesa Yes, I know I let my tongue run away with me and don't mean what I say. Who doubts, my dear, that you are a brave man? As brave as you are handsome. You've done wrong, but that's because you're young and headstrong. And – I don't know – in a land where the blazing sun beats down on us, too hot-blooded. But I implore you, don't leave me lost and helpless, don't let my poor love for you, my name be added to some infamous roll-call of shame. I'm a woman, it's true, but if I were nothing but my beauty, other women could easily eclipse me. But tell me, just tell me! Do you feel nothing for me, there? (*She taps his heart.*)

The Duke Little devil! Sit down beside me, sweetheart.

Marchesa I suppose I must admit I have ambitions, not for myself but for you! You and my dear Florence! God knows what pain I suffer.

The Duke What pain? What's wrong with you now?

Marchesa No, it's nothing. But listen! Listen to me! I can see I bore you. You count the minutes and turn away your head. Don't go just yet! This may be the last time I shall see you. Now, listen! I have to tell you that everyone names you the new plague of Florence. There's not one hovel without your image pinned to its walls, a dagger through the heart. I may be out of my mind and you may hate me tomorrow. But I don't care. This much you must know.

The Duke Don't make me angry or you'll suffer for it.

Marchesa Yes, I'll suffer for it.

The Duke We'll speak of this again – tomorrow morning if you wish. If I leave now, don't be upset. The hunt is waiting.

Marchesa Yes, I'll suffer for it!

The Duke Why say that? You look miserable as hell. Why the devil do you get involved in politics? Come, come along now! Your little woman's role suits you so well. A real woman. You are too . . . zealous, but that can change with time. Help me on with my coat then, I look almost indecent.

Marchesa Goodbye, Alexander.

The **Duke** *kisses her. Enter* **Cardinal Cibo**.

Cardinal Oh, Highness! I beg your pardon. I thought my sister-in-law was alone. So clumsy of me. The penance shall be mine. Please forgive my indiscretion.

The Duke And what do you mean by that? Now now, Malaspina, that sounds like a priest talking! Such things are not for your eyes, are they? Come along with me. What the hell do you care?

They go out together.

Marchesa (*alone, holding her husband's portrait*) What are you doing now, Laurent? It has just gone noon. You must be walking on the terrace in front of the horse chestnuts. Your plump cattle grazing all round you and the farmhands eating their midday meal in the shade. The sun draws a white mantle of mist from off the lawn. Over the white head of their old master the trees you so carefully tended rustle religiously while our long cloistered walk respectfully echoes to the restful sound of your steps. Oh, my dearest Laurent! I have betrayed your treasured honour and cast doubt and ridicule over the closing years of a noble life. Never again will you clasp to your breast a heart worthy of your own. And when you are back from the hunt, I shall bring you your supper with trembling hands.

Scene Seven

At the Strozzi Palace.

Philip *with the forty members of his family who are having supper.* **Louisa** *is next to him.* **Peter** *and* **Thomas** *are absent.*

Philip Let all the family sit at table.

Guests Why are there two empty chairs?

Philip Peter and Thomas are in prison.

Guests Why? Why?

Philip Because Salviati publicly insulted my daughter here at the Fair at Montoliveto and in front of her brother Leon. Peter and Thomas killed Salviati and Alexander de' Medici arrested them to avenge the death of his pimp.

Guests Death to the Medici.

Philip I have gathered my family together to recount my woes and beg for their help. Let us sup now. Then if you have the stomach for it, let us go out, sword in hand, to demand the return of my sons.

Guests We agree. We'll do it.

Philip It is time for this to end! You know that. Or we'll see our children murdered and our daughters dishonoured. It is time Florence taught these bastards what human rights are. The Council of Eight have no

right to condemn my children. And I could not survive
such shame.

Guests Have no fear, Philip, we are here.

Philip I am the head of this family. How can I permit
these insults? There are as many of us, as there are
Medici. And twenty more families like ours, not counting
the Rucellai and the Aldobrandini. Why should the
Medici murder our children, and we not murder theirs?
One barrel of gunpowder in the cellars of the Citadel, and
that German garrison will be no more. What is left to the
Medici then? There lies their strength. Without it they are
nothing! Are we men? Are they to cut down all our noble
families, as old as Florence itself, and uproot them from
their native land? They have made a start with us. It is for
us to stand firm. Like a bird-catcher's whistle, at one cry
of alarm from us a host of eagles, driven from their nests,
will swoop down over Florence. They are close by,
turning round this city, their eyes fixed on its belfries.
There we'll display the black flag of the plague. At that
signal of death, rallying to the colours of the wrath of
heaven, they'll come swarming in. Tonight, let us first
release my sons. Tomorrow we'll all go together and, with
naked swords, we'll raise an army like ours from every
palace in Florence. Eighty patrician homes will respond to
the call of freedom.

Guests Long live freedom!

Philip As God is my witness, it is violence alone that
forces me to draw my sword. For sixty years I've been a
good and docile citizen, doing harm to none and spending
half my fortune in the service of those in need.

Guests That's true!

Philip The vengeance that drives me to revolt is just. I
am a rebel, because God made me a father. I am not
moved by pride, ambition or self-interest. My cause is a
loyal one, honourable, sacred. Fill your cups and rise. Our

vengeance is a host we can break without fear and share out before God. I drink to the death of the Medici.

Guests (*rising and drinking*) Death to the Medici!

Louisa (*setting down her glass*) Ah! I'm dying!

Philip What's wrong, child? What's the matter? Oh God! My darling daughter! How pale you are! Speak to me! What's wrong? Speak to your father! Help! Quick, a doctor! Quick! Oh! Too late!

Louisa I'm going to die! I'm dying!

She dies.

Philip She's going, friends! She's dying! A doctor! My daughter's poisoned!

He falls on his knees beside **Louisa**.

A Guest Undo her corsage! Give her warm water! If it's poison, she must have warm water.

Servants *rush up*.

Another Guest Slap her hands! Open the windows and slap her hands!

Another Perhaps she's just fainted. She may have drunk something down too quickly.

Another Poor child! How serene she looks! She can't have died like this, so quickly.

Philip Are you dead, my child? My Louisa, my darling daughter, can you really be dead?

1st Guest Here's the doctor.

Enter a **Doctor**.

2nd Guest Make haste, sir. Tell us, is it poison?

Philip She's fainted, hasn't she?

Doctor The poor young girl! She's dead.

Profound silence reigns in the hall. **Philip** *is still on his knees beside* **Louisa,** *holding her hands.*

A Guest It's poison from the Medici. Philip's so still, we mustn't leave him in this state.

Another Guest I'm sure I saw a servant near the table who used to work for Salviati's wife.

Another He must have done it. No doubt about it. Let's go and arrest him.

Exeunt.

1st Guest Philip won't speak to anyone. He is thunderstruck.

Another It's horrible! An appalling crime!

Another It cries to heaven for vengeance! Let's go and cut Alexander's throat.

Another Yes, let's go! Death to Alexander! He's behind it all. We must be mad! He has always hated us. We always act too late.

Another It's not just for himself that Salviati poisoned poor Louisa. He did it for the Duke. They're out to kill us to the last man. Come on, let's go!

Philip (*rising*) You'll bury my daughter for me, won't you, my friends? (*He puts on his cloak.*) In my garden, behind the fig-trees. I say goodbye, my good friends, goodbye. Fare-you-well.

A Guest Where are you going, Philip?

Philip I have had enough. I've had as much as I can take, you see. Two sons in prison and my daughter dead. I can't stay here, I'm going away.

A Guest Going away? With no thought of revenge?

Philip Yes, yes. Just lay my poor daughter in the earth. But do not bury her. I shall see to that in my own way. Some poor monks I know will come tomorrow and take her to her last resting-place. It does no good to gaze at her. She is dead. So it serves no purpose. Goodbye, my friends, go to your home and farewell.

A Guest He has lost his reason. Don't let him leave like this.

Another Terrible! (*Leaving.*) I shall pass out if I stay in here.

Philip Don't manhandle me! Don't make me stay in the same room as the body of my daughter! Let me leave this place.

A Guest Take vengeance, Philip, let us avenge you. Your Louisa will be our Lucretia. We'll force Alexander to drink the last drop of poison in her cup.

Another The new Lucretia! We'll swear over her body that we'll die for freedom! Go home, Philip, and think of your country. Don't retract your words now.

Philip Liberty, vengeance. Fine words all. But I have two sons in prison and now my daughter's dead. If I stay here, I'll be surrounded by death. The main thing is for me to leave and for you to stay quiet. When my door and windows are closed, they'll forget about the Strozzi. If they stay open, I'll have to watch you all fall, one after the other. I am old, you know, it's time I shut my shop. Farewell, my friends, and hold still. Once I've gone, no harm will come to you. I shall go to Venice.

A Guest Stay here tonight. There's a terrible storm.

Philip Don't bury my poor child. My monks will come tomorrow and bear her away. Oh God of Justice! What was my offence?

He runs off stage.

Act Four

Scene One

The **Duke**'s *palace.*

Enter the **Duke** *and* **Lorenzo**.

The Duke I'd like to have been there – there must have been more than one face red with fury. But I can't imagine who could have poisoned this Louisa.

Lorenzo Neither can I. Unless it was you.

The Duke Or one of the Salviati. Philip must be enraged. They say he's left for Venice. Thank God – now I'm free from that old horror. And his blessed family may do me a favour and keep quiet. Do you know they almost started a minor revolution in their district? Two of my Germans were killed.

Lorenzo What upsets me most is that honest Salviati got wounded in the leg. Have you found your coat of mail yet?

The Duke No, I haven't. And it annoys me more than I can say.

Lorenzo Watch out for Giomo, he's the one who stole it. What do you wear instead?

The Duke Nothing. I couldn't stand any other. There are none as light as that one.

Lorenzo That's awkward for you.

The Duke You haven't said anything yet about your aunt.

Lorenzo It must have slipped my mind. She adores you. Tell me when you wish to receive her. She's had stars in her eyes, no rest, since your love first stirred her poor heart. Take pity on her, my Lord, I beg you. Tell me when you wish to receive her, at what time she can come and surrender to you her little gift of virtue.

The Duke Are you serious?

Lorenzo Serious? As grim as death itself. I'd like to see an aunt of mine not want to sleep with you.

The Duke Where could I see her?

Lorenzo In my bedchamber, my Lord. I'll have white curtains round my bed and a bowl of mignonette on my table. At midnight precisely my aunt will be there in her night-gown. I'll write it down for you in your notebook, so you won't forget after supper.

The Duke No fear of that. Catherine's a dish fit for a king. You're a bright lad, all right. But tell me, are you quite sure she'll come? How did you approach her?

Lorenzo I'll tell you, later.

The Duke I'm going to see a horse I've just bought. Till tonight! Come and fetch me after supper and we'll go to your house together. As for that Cibo woman, I've had more than I can take. Yesterday, all through the hunt, I had to hear her droning on again. Goodnight to you, mignon.

Exit.

Lorenzo (*alone*) So it's settled. Tonight he comes home with me, and tomorrow the Republicans will see what they have to do. The Duke of Florence will be dead. I must warn Scoronconcolo. Hurry up, sun, if you're anxious for the news that the night will bring.

Exit.

Scene Two

A street.

Peter *and* **Thomas Strozzi** *coming out of prison.*

Peter I was quite sure the Eight would acquit us both. Come, let's knock on our door and go and embrace our father. That's strange, the shutters are closed.

Porter (*opening the door*) Alas, my Lord: you've heard the news?

Peter What news? Standing there at the door of our deserted palace, you look like a ghost emerging from a tomb.

Porter Is it possible that you've heard nothing?

Enter two **Monks**.

Thomas What could we have heard? We're just out of prison. Tell us what's happened.

Porter Alas, my poor good Lords! It's horrible what I have to say.

Monks (*approaching*) Is this the Strozzi palace?

Porter Yes, who are you looking for?

Monks We've come for the corpse of Louisa Strozzi. See, Philip has given us this authority to take it away.

Peter What's that you say? Whose body are you seeking?

Monks Leave this place, my son. You bear the stamp of Philip on your face. No good news awaits you here.

Thomas What? Is she dead? Dead? O God in heaven!

Goes to one side and sits.

Peter I am more stout-hearted than you think. Who killed my sister? People of her age don't die overnight without an unnatural cause. Tell me who killed her, then I can kill him. Answer me, or you're a dead man too.

Porter   Alas! Who can tell? No one can even guess.

Peter   Where is my father? Come, Thomas, no tears. By Heaven, my heart grows hard, as if turning to stone, a rock of everlasting granite.

Monks   If you are Philip's son, come with us. We will take you to him. He has been at our monastery since yesterday.

Peter   And I am not to know who killed my sister! Listen to me, priests: if you are made in God's image, you can accept my vow. By all the world's instruments of torment, by all the tortures in hell . . . No, I'll say no more. Let's hurry to see my father. O God! God! Let the truth be what I suspect, so I can grind them all like grains of sand beneath my feet. Come, before I lose my strength. Not another word. For now it's a question of revenge, more dreadful than any dreamed up by the wrath of heaven.

Exeunt.

Scene Three

A street.

Lorenzo *and* **Scoronconcolo**.

Lorenzo   Go home now, and don't fail to come at midnight. You will shut yourself in my study till I come and fetch you.

Scoronconcolo   Yes, my Lord.

Exit.

Lorenzo (*alone*)   When I was in my mother's womb, what tiger haunted her dreams? The spectre of myself when young, doting on flowers and fields and Petrarch's sonnets, rises before me, shuddering in horror. Oh God!

At the mere thought of tonight, why does joy burn me like a red-hot brand, so I feel it even in my bones? From what savage entrails am I sprung? What monstrous coupling presided at my birth? What has he done to me, this man? If, hand on heart, I'm honest with myself – who can hear me say tomorrow: 'I have killed him', without asking why I did it? It's strange. Though he's done wrong to others, at least after his fashion he has been good to me. If I had quietly stayed in the deep solitude of Cafaggiuolo, he would never have sought me out. Yet I came to Florence in search of him. But why? Was it my father's ghost urging me on, like Orestes, to track down a new Aegisthus? What offence had he done me, then? It's strange, yet for this I gave up everything. The sole thought of this murder has crumbled my whole life's dreams to dust. Once this assassination stood like a sinister raven in my path, luring me on, and as a man I was ruined. What can it all mean? Just now, as I walked through the square, I heard two men talking of a comet. What I feel here, beneath my ribs, is this the beating of a human heart? Oh, why lately has this question come to me so often? Am I the arm of God? Is there some cloud of glory above my head? When I enter that room, about to draw my sword from its sheath, I fear it may be the flaming sword of Archangel Michael and I turn to ashes as I fall upon my prey.

Exit.

Scene Four

The **Marchese Cibo's** *Palace.*

The **Cardinal** *and the* **Marchesa.**

Marchesa As you wish, Malaspina.

Cibo Yes, as I wish. Consider carefully, Marchesa, before you cross swords with me. Are you like most women, who need to see a gold chain and seal of office before they recognize a man's authority? Are you waiting for some lackey to burst through the door and bellow out my name, before you are ready to admit my power? You must learn that rank and title do not make the man. I am no mere envoy of the Pope, nor an agent of Charles V. I am more than that.

Marchesa Yes, I know. Caesar has sold his shadow to the devil. And the imperial shadow struts about, draped in a scarlet robe. His name is Cibo.

Cibo You are Alexander's mistress. Remember that. And your secret lies in my hands.

Marchesa Do what you will with it. And then we shall discover how a confessor comes to terms with his own conscience.

Cibo You are mistaken. It was not your confession that betrayed you. With my own eyes I saw you embrace the Duke. Even if you had revealed your secret under the seal, it would be no sin for me to speak of what I saw elsewhere.

Marchesa Very well. What then?

Cibo Why did the Duke take such careless leave of you? With a sigh of relief, like a young boy when the school bell sounds. You sated him with your patriotism. Like some insipid sauce it accompanied every dish you served. How prudish your duenna must have been, and what tedious books she made you read. Did you never learn that as a general rule a king's mistress never mentions politics?

Marchesa I admit I was never taught precisely what conversation was required from a king's mistress. And I omitted to seek enlightenment. Nor did I follow the Turkish fashion and eat rice to plump out my figure.

Cibo To hold on to one's lover for rather more than three days hardly demands great learning.

Marchesa If a woman could have learnt from a priest, it would all have been quite simple. Why did you not advise me?

Cibo Shall I advise you now? Take your cloak, go to the Duke's palace and slip into his bedroom. If, when he sees you, he is still expecting a speech, prove to him that on occasion you know better. And if he drowses off with his head on your republican breasts, make sure it is not from boredom. Are you a virgin? Is there no wine from Cyprus left? Can you recall no ribald songs? Did you never read the sonnets of Aretino?

Marchesa Oh God! I have heard such words before, whispered to hideous old hags shivering in the New Market. If you are no priest, are you not a man? Are you so sure there is no one in heaven that you dare make even your crimson robes blush?

Cibo There is nothing more virtuous than the ears of a debauched woman. Pretend not to understand me if you like. But remember that your husband is my brother.

Marchesa What is your purpose in tormenting me like this? I can only vaguely guess. You are contemptible. What do you want of me?

Cibo There are some secrets no woman should know, and yet given some cognizance of them, she may further the interests they hide.

Marchesa Which mysterious thread of your dark thoughts do you wish me to hold on to now? If your designs are as ominous as your threats, speak on. Tell me at least what strand of hair suspends the sword over my head?

Cibo I cannot speak openly, as I don't trust you yet. Suffice it to say that any other woman would have made herself a queen by now. Since you call me Caesar's shadow, you must have noticed it is great enough to eclipse the sun of Florence. Do you know how far a woman's smile may lead her? Do you know what fortunes are founded on roots that lie in a bedchamber? Alexander is the son of a Pope. Take note. And when that Pope was at Bologna . . . But my tongue runs away with me.

Marchesa Be careful that you don't make confession. If you are my husband's brother, I am Alexander's mistress.

Cibo You were, Marchesa. And so were many others.

Marchesa I was. Yes, thanks be to God, that's in the past.

Cibo I knew very well you would try to pursue your own dreams at first. One day, however, you will have to account for mine. Now listen. There is little point in our quarrelling, though you take everything so seriously. Make your peace with Alexander. And as you didn't like it just now when I told you how, there's no need to repeat myself. Be advised by me. In one or two years' time you will be grateful. I have worked long and hard to become what I am now, and I know to what heights one can rise. If I were sure of you, I could tell you things that God himself shall never know.

Marchesa Don't hope for any help from me. Remember that I despise you.

She makes to leave.

Cibo One moment! Wait an instant! Can you not hear the sound of horses' hooves? Is my brother not expected back tomorrow or today? Do you know me as a man to change his mind? Go to the palace tonight, or you will regret it.

Marchesa Well, I can accept that you're ambitious and that your ends justify your means. But won't you speak more clearly? You see, Malaspina, I don't want my 'corruption' to make me despair of everything. If you can persuade me, do so. Talk frankly to me. What is your main intention?

Cibo So you don't despair of letting me persuade you, is that it? Do you think I'm a child, that you only need to rub my lips with honey to unseal them? You must act first. Then it's my turn to speak. When you have played your woman's part and can claim to rule not just the mind of Alexander, Duke of Florence, but your lover Alexander's heart, then I shall inform you of the rest and you'll learn what I'm waiting for.

Marchesa So after reading Aretino for the first stage of my education, I must move on to the book of your secret thoughts? Shall I tell you what you dare not tell me? You only serve the Pope till the Emperor learns that you can serve his interests better than the Pope himself. You hope the time will come when Caesar will have none to thank but you – for enslaving Italy. And when that day comes – the day you long for – the man who rules half the world will doubtless reward you with heaven's paltry legacy – the Papacy. In order to govern Florence, by governing the Duke, you would this very instant turn yourself into a woman, if you could. When poor Ricciarda Cibo has inveigled Alexander into making two or three political manoeuvres, people will soon be saying that, though she controls the Duke, behind her stands her brother-in-law, His Grey Eminence the Cardinal. And who knows, as you say, how far your ship of state may lead you, once it is launched upon an ocean of the people's tears? Isn't that roughly your position? No doubt my imagination cannot reach the same heights as yours, but I believe I am not far wrong.

Cibo Go to the Duke tonight, or you are lost forever.

Marchesa Lost? How's that, then?

Cibo Your husband shall learn the truth.

Marchesa So be it. Do that and I shall kill myself.

Cibo The threats of a woman! Listen to me. Whether you know my mind rightly or not, go to the Duke tonight.

Marchesa No.

Cibo Here is your husband now, just entering the courtyard. By all that's sacred, I'll reveal everything, if you say no again.

Marchesa No, no, no!

Enter the **Marchese**.

Marchesa While you were at Massa, Laurent, I gave myself to Alexander. I did so, knowing full well what sort of man he is and what wretched part I'd cast myself to play. But this priest wants me to assume one that's even more vile. The horrors he proposes are to make me the regular mistress of the Duke. Which Cibo can turn to his own advantage.

She falls on her knees.

Marchese Are you out of your mind? What does she mean, Malaspina? Well? You stand there like a statue. Is this some game you're playing, Cardinal? Well, then? What am I to make of all this?

Cibo Ah! By the body of Christ!

Exit.

Marchese She's fainted. Ho there! Bring some vinegar.

Scene Five

Lorenzo's *bedroom*.

Lorenzo *and two* **Servants**.

Lorenzo When you've put flowers on the table and at the foot of the bed, you can make up a good fire. But see there is not too much flame tonight. Let the coals give off heat, without burning too bright.

Enter **Catherine**.

Catherine Mother is ill. Won't you come and see her, Renzo?

Lorenzo My mother is ill?

Catherine I'm sorry, but I cannot hide the truth from you. Yesterday I received a note from the Duke, saying that you had told me of his love. Reading that letter deeply upset Maria.

Lorenzo Yet I never did speak to you of this. Weren't you able to tell her I had nothing to do with it?

Catherine I did . . . But why does your room look so neat today, so clean and tidy? I thought tidiness wasn't your strong point.

Lorenzo So the Duke has written to you? It's odd I never knew of it. But tell me, what do you make of his letter?

Catherine What do I make of it?

Lorenzo Yes, of Alexander's declaration. What do you make of it, in your innocent little heart?

Catherine What do you expect?

Lorenzo Weren't you flattered? To have so many women envy you? It's such a conquest, a love that elevates you to the rank of mistress of . . . Go, Catherine, go tell my mother I will come to her. Get out of here! Leave me!

Catherine *leaves.*

By Heaven! What a man of wax I am! Has vice, like Dejaneira's tunic, infected the very fibres of my being? I was on the point of corrupting Catherine. I believe I'd defile my own mother if my brain once set itself the task. God knows what bow the gods have strung inside my head or with what force its arrows strike the target. If all men are splinters from some blazing furnace, then the unknown being who created me ignited this frail and puny body not with a spark but a firebrand. I can deliberate and choose, but not retrace my steps once I have chosen! Oh

God! Why do young folk today glory in fashionable vices and children straight from school scurry off to perversion? What filth mankind must be to crowd into cheap dives, panting for lechery, whereas I, who wished to assume a mask only to make me look more like them, and visited these sinks of iniquity with the firm resolve to stay undefiled beneath my sullied garb, I cannot find myself again nor wash my hands clean, even with blood! Yet, poor Catherine, you would die like Louisa Strozzi or fall into the eternal pit like so many others, if it were not for me. Oh Alexander, I have no piety but I devoutly hope you say your prayers before you come to this room tonight. Is Catherine not virtuous? Irreproachable? Yet how many words would it take to turn this artless dove into the willing prey of that tawny gladiator! To think I nearly said too much! How many young girls, cursed by their fathers, now loiter at some street corner or gaze at the reflection of their shaven heads in the cracked mirror of a cell – girls as fine as Catherine till they listened to pimps not half so clever as me! I have committed many crimes and if my life is ever thrown into the scales of judgement there will be on one side a mountain of tears, but on the other perhaps one pure drop of milk from Catherine's breast which will have nourished an honest child.

Exit.

Scene Six

A valley. A convent at the rear.

Enter **Philip** *and* **Peter Strozzi**, *and two monks. Novices are bearing* **Louisa***'s coffin. They place it in a tomb.*

Philip Before she is laid in her last resting-place, let me embrace her. So I used to lean over her bed to give her her good night kiss. Her sad eyes would be half-closed as they are now. But at the first rays of the sun they would open like pale blue flowers. Gently she would rise with a smile on her lips and come to her old father to return that kiss. That heavenly vision brought solace to the painful awakening of a man who is tired of life. Another day, I would think, and still another furrow to be ploughed! But my daughter helped me see the beauty of life, so I could welcome the dawn of a bright new day.

The tomb is closed.

Peter (*off stage*) This way! Come this way!

Philip You will never rise from your bed again, never with bare feet tread this grass to come in search of your father. Oh, my Louisa! God alone knew who and what you were. Apart from me, apart from me!

Peter (*entering*) A hundred men have come from Piedmont to Sestino. Come, Philip, now is not the time for tears.

Philip What do you know, my boy, about the time for tears?

Peter The exiles are all gathered at Sestino. It's time to think of vengeance. Though our army is small, we'll boldly march on Florence. If we can reach the citadel and surprise the guards by night, it will soon be over. By Heaven, the mausoleum I'll raise for my sister will be a better one than this.

Philip I won't go. My friends must go without me.

Peter But we cannot do without you. You know our confederates are counting on your name. Francis I himself expects you to strike a blow for freedom. Here is his letter. He writes to you as head of the Republican movement in Florence.

Philip (*opening the letter*) Tell the bearer to return these words to the King of France: 'The day Philip takes up arms against his homeland Philip will have lost his reason.'

Peter What's this? Another fine-sounding phrase?

Philip A phrase that means what it says.

Peter So you're prepared to jeopardize the exiles' cause for the sake of another fine phrase? Take care, Father, you can't treat this like a passage from Pliny. Think again, before you refuse.

Philip For sixty years I've known how I should answer that letter from the King of France.

Peter This is beyond belief! Would you force me to be blunt with you . . . ? Come with us, Father, I beg you. When I was going to see the Pazzi, did you not ask me to take you there? Was that so very different?

Philip Quite different. An outraged father, sword in hand, rushing from the house with his friends in search of justice is quite different from a rebel who takes up arms against his homeland and goes roaming the country in defiance of our laws!

Peter It wasn't justice we were after! It was to strike down Alexander. What's the difference this time? You cannot love your homeland, or you would take advantage of such a chance as this.

Philip Such a chance! Oh God! You call this a chance! (*He beats on the tomb.*)

Peter Let me convince you.

Philip There is no ambition in my grief. Leave me alone. I've said my piece.

Peter You're a stubborn old man, an inveterate word-spinner, and you'll bring ruin on us all.

Philip Hold your tongue, insolent boy! Get out of my sight!

Peter I dare not say what's in my mind. Go where you will. This time we'll act without you. Never let it be said that our cause was lost for want of a scholar of Latin!

Exit.

Philip Your time is up, Philip! This all means your day is over.

Scene Seven

The bank of the Arno. A long row of palaces is visible.

Enter **Lorenzo**.

Lorenzo The sun is setting now, so I've no time to lose. Even if everything I do here seems like a waste of time. (*He knocks at a door.*) Hallo there! Signor Alamanno! Hallo!

Alamanno (*on his terrace*) Who's there? What do you want?

Lorenzo I have come to warn you that the Duke will be murdered tonight. If you love freedom, make plans with your friends for tomorrow.

Alamanno And who's going to kill Alexander?

Lorenzo Lorenzo de' Medici.

Alamanno Is that you, Renzinaccio? Why don't you come in and sup in my parlour with merry-making friends?

Lorenzo I've no time for that. Get ready to act tomorrow!

Alamanno Don't tell me *you* want to kill the Duke? Get along with you, too much wine has gone to your head.

He goes back into his house.

Lorenzo (*alone*) I think it's a mistake to tell them *I'm* going to kill the Duke. No one believes me. (*He knocks at another door.*) Hey there! Signor Pazzi! Hello there!

Pazzi (*on his terrace*) Who's calling?

Lorenzo I've come to tell you Alexander will be murdered tonight. Tomorrow try and work for the liberty of Florence.

Pazzi And who's to kill the Duke?

Lorenzo That's no matter. Take action anyway, you and your friends. I can't tell the name of the man who'll do it.

Pazzi You're a crazy idiot. Go to the Devil!

He goes indoors.

Lorenzo (*alone*) Even if I don't say it's me, it's clear they still won't believe me. (*He knocks at another door.*) Hey there! Signor Corsini!

Corsini (*on his terrace*) Who's there?

Lorenzo Duke Alexander will be murdered tonight.

Corsini Really, Lorenzo! If you're drunk, go and jest elsewhere. You had no right to injure my horse at the Nasi ball, Devil take you!

He goes indoors.

Lorenzo Poor Florence! Poor Florence!

Exit.

Scene Eight

Open country.

Enter **Peter Strozzi** *and two* **Exiles**.

Peter My father won't come. I couldn't make him see reason.

1st Exile I won't tell my comrades. It's enough to put them to flight.

Peter But why? Take a horse tonight and ride flat out to Sestino. I'll be there tomorrow morning. Tell them Philip refused. But not Peter.

1st Exile Our confederates need Philip's name. Without it we'll do nothing.

Peter My family name is the same as Philip's. Tell them Strozzi will come. That'll do the trick.

1st Exile They'll ask me which Strozzi, and if I don't say 'Philip' nothing will happen.

Peter Idiot! Do as I tell you and don't speak for any but yourself. How do you know in advance that nothing will happen?

1st Exile This is no way to treat people, my Lord!

Peter Go on! To horse and ride to Sestino!

1st Exile But in faith, sir, my horse is tired. I rode twelve leagues during the night. I'm in no mind to saddle up again at this hour.

Peter You're a stupid fool. (*To the* **2nd Exile**.) *You* go. You'll make a better job of it.

2nd Exile My friend's quite right about Philip – his name would be a great help to our cause.

Peter Cowards! Callous boors! Don't you realize? The best help for our cause is the thought of your starving wives and children. Their mouths may be full of Philip's name, but it won't fill their stomachs. What swine you are!

2nd Exile There's no way of coming to terms with so coarse a man. Let's go, comrade.

Peter Go to the Devil, you rabble! And tell your confederates that if *they* don't want me, the King of France does! So they'd better watch out in case I get power over all of you!

2nd Exile (*to the* **1st Exile**) Come on, comrade, let's go for supper. I'm quite worn out, like you.

They go off.

Scene Nine

A square at night.

Enter **Lorenzo**.

Lorenzo I'll tell him it's a matter of modesty and take the torch away. It happens all the time. A young bride, for example, often insists that her husband removes the light, before she enters the bedroom on her wedding night. And Catherine's thought to be most virtuous. – Poor girl! If she is not, in all the world who else is? But what if the shock of all this brought about my mother's death? It might. So be it. What will be will be. Have patience! Still a whole hour to wait, the clock has only just struck. But if you really want it – no, why should you? – Take the torch away if you wish. It's quite simple the first time a woman gives herself. – Why don't you come in and get warm? – Oh Lord, yes! Just a young girl's fancy. How could anyone suspect it's for a murder? They'll be really astonished, even Philip.

So there you are, pale moonface! (*The moon appears.*) If the Republicans were proper men, what a revolution there'd be tomorrow in this city! But Peter's too ambitious. Only the Ruccellai are worth anything at all. – Oh, words, words! These everlasting words! If there is anyone up there, how He must laugh at us all! It really is very funny, quite a joke. – The chatter of inactive men is great for killing corpses and battering at ever-open doors! Men with no arms and no hands! No, no! I won't take the light away. I'll aim straight for the heart. He can watch himself being murdered . . . By the blood of Christ, they'll be at their windows tomorrow. So long as he hasn't thought up some new breastplate, another coat of mail! Accursed invention! It's one thing, taking God on, or the devil, but to fight against bits of interlocking metal is a different story! Damn the armourer's filthy workmanship! – I'll go in after him, and he'll put his sword down here – or there, yes, on the couch. – It's easy enough to roll his

sword-belt round the hilt. It would be best if he felt like
lying down. Lying, sitting or standing? Better, sitting.
First, I'll go out again. Scoronconcolo's hiding in the
study. Then we'll burst in! But I wouldn't want him to
have his back to me. I'll make straight for him. Enough
now! Peace! It will soon be time. – I'd better go to some
tavern. I hardly noticed, but I'm getting cold and I could
drink a flagon. – No, I won't drink. Anyway, they're
closed. Where the hell can I go? Is she a good woman? –
Yes, truly she is. – Even in her shift? – Oh, no, no! Surely
not! – Poor Catherine! – How sad if over all this my
mother died. Even if I'd told her my plan, what good
would it have done? Instead of consoling her, this 'crime'
would have obsessed her till she drew her very last breath.
I don't know why I'm still on my feet, when I'm dropping
with fatigue. (*He sits down on a bench.*)

Poor Philip! His daughter was lovely as the day! Once I
sat beside her under the horse-chestnut, with her small
white hands so busy with a needle! How many quiet days
I've spent beneath the trees! Oh, what serenity, what
peace stretched out before me at Cafaggiuolo! The
caretaker's little girl, Gianetta, was so pretty spreading her
washing out on the grass to dry. How she used to chase
the goats away – and the white one always came trotting
back on its long slender legs. (*A clock strikes.*)

Ah! Now it's time I went. – Evening, mignon. Why don't
you drink a glass with Giomo? – Good wine! Strange, if he
took it into his head to ask: Is your room quiet and
secluded? Can anything be heard in the neighbouring
rooms? That would be amusing. But we've seen to all this.
Yes, really funny if it occurred to him to ask that. I was
wrong about the time. It was only the half that struck.
What's that light shining from the portico of that church?
Men working with blocks of stone. It must take nerve to
chip and chisel like that. They're making a crucifix.
Bravely fitting the parts together! I'd like to see that
marble corpse suddenly spring up and take them by the
throat. And now what's happening to me? It's amazing,

I've a terrible urge to dance! If I let myself go, I could hop about like a sparrow over all that timber and rubble. Hey, mignon, mignon! Put your best clothes on, and wear your new gloves! Tra la la! Look your finest for your beautiful bride! But let me whisper in your ear: watch out for her little knife!

He runs off.

Scene Ten

At the **Duke***'s.*

The **Duke** *at supper,* **Giomo**. *Enter* **Cardinal Cibo.**

Cibo Highness, beware of Lorenzo.

The Duke There you are, Cardinal. Sit down and take a drink.

Cibo Beware of Lorenzo, Duke. This evening he's been to the Bishop of Marzi to ask for post-horses tonight.

The Duke That can't be true.

Cibo I've had it from the Bishop himself.

The Duke Oh, come now! I tell you I've good reason to know that it can't be true.

Cibo I am not easily deceived. It's my duty to warn you.

The Duke Even if it were true, what's so alarming about that? Perhaps he's going to Cafaggioulo.

Cibo What alarms me is this: as I was coming here across the square, I saw him with my own eyes leaping over bits of wood and stone like a madman. I called to him and I must confess he gave me a look that frightened me. You can be sure he's hatching some little plot tonight.

The Duke Well, why should any plot of his be dangerous to me?

Cibo Should one speak one's mind, even when a favourite is concerned? I must inform you that this evening, he quite openly told two of my acquaintances, who were talking on their terrace, that he would murder you tonight.

The Duke Have a glass of wine, Cardinal. Surely you know it's usual for Renzo to be drunk at sunset?

Enter **Lord Maurizio**.

Maurizio Highness, be on your guard against Lorenzo. He told three of my friends this evening that he means to kill you tonight.

The Duke You too, my gallant Maurizio? You believe in fairy tales as well? I thought you too much of a man for that.

Maurizio Your Highness knows I'm not one to take fright without reason. I can prove what I say.

The Duke Sit down then and clink glasses with the Cardinal. – You won't find me ill-mannered, if I go about my business . . .

Enter **Lorenzo**.

The Duke Well, mignon, is it time already?

Lorenzo It will soon be midnight.

The Duke Get them to fetch my sable doublet.

Lorenzo Let's make haste, perhaps your proud beauty's at the rendezvous already.

The Duke Which gloves should I take? For love or for war?

Lorenzo For love, Your Highness.

The Duke So it shall be. I want to be a lusty lover tonight.

Exeunt.

Maurizio What do you say to all this, Cardinal?

Cibo That in spite of men, God's will is done.

Exeunt.

Scene Eleven

Lorenzo's *bedroom.*

Enter the **Duke** *and* **Lorenzo**.

The Duke I'm chilled to the bone. It's cold as hell. (*He takes off his sword.*) Hey, what are you up to there, mignon?

Lorenzo I'm winding the belt round your sword and putting it under your pillow. It's always wise to have a weapon to hand.

He winds the belt round in such a way that it prevents the sword being drawn from its scabbard.

The Duke You know I don't like women who chatter. I've just remembered that Catherine girl is a rare one for talking. To avoid all conversation I'll go and lie on the bed. – By the way, why did you order post-horses from the Bishop of Marzi?

Lorenzo To go and see my brother. He wrote to say he was very ill.

The Duke Well! Go and fetch your aunt then.

Lorenzo In no time at all.

Exit.

The Duke (*alone*) Paying court to women who can only say yes seems remarkably stupid to me. Only fit for a Frenchman. Today above all, when I've eaten as much as three fat monks, I couldn't even manage 'heart of my heart' for the Infanta of Spain herself. I think I'll pretend to be asleep. A bit boorish, but it's the easiest way out.

He lies down. **Lorenzo** *returns, sword in hand.*

Lorenzo Are you asleep, my Lord?

He strikes him.

The Duke You, Renzo?

Lorenzo Rest assured, my Lord.

He strikes again. Enter **Scoronconcolo**.

Scoronconcolo Is it over?

Lorenzo See where he bit my finger. I shall carry till death this ring of blood, this diamond without price.

Scoronconcolo Oh God! It's the Duke.

Lorenzo (*sitting on the window ledge*) What a beautiful night! How clear and pure the air. Now my heart bursts with joy. I can breathe again.

Scoronconcolo Come, master, we've gone too far. Let's get away.

Lorenzo The evening breeze is soft and scented. How the wild flowers are unfolding! Resplendent Nature and eternal peace!

Scoronconcolo The wind will freeze the sweat that soaks your face. Come, my Lord.

Lorenzo Oh, bounteous God, to grant this precious moment!

Scoronconcolo (*aside*) His soul is strangely stirred. It's up to me to make the first move.

He makes as if to go.

Lorenzo Wait, draw these curtains. Now give me the key to this room.

Scoronconcolo Let's hope the neighbours heard nothing!

Lorenzo Have you forgotten they're familiar with our brawling? Come, let's go.

Exeunt.

Act Five

Scene One

At the **Duke**'*s Palace.*

Enter **Valori, Maurizio** *and* **Guicciardini.** *A crowd of* **Courtiers** *are moving around the hall and its antechambers.*

Maurizio Giomo is not back yet since he took that message. It all looks more and more alarming.

Guicciardini He's just coming into the hall now.

Enter **Giomo.**

Maurizio Well? What did you find out?

Giomo Nothing at all.

Exit.

Guicciardini He doesn't want to answer. Cardinal Cibo is shut away in the Duke's study. The news comes to no one but him.

Enter another **Messenger.**

Guicciardini Well, has the Duke been found? Does anyone know what's become of him?

Messenger I don't know.

He goes into the study.

Valori A dreadful business, gentlemen, this disappearance! No news of the Duke at all. Lord Maurizio, didn't you say you saw him yesterday evening? He didn't seem unwell?

Giomo *returns.*

Giomo (*to* **Lord Maurizio**) I can tell you in confidence. The Duke's been assassinated.

Maurizio Assassinated? Who by? Where did you find him?

Giomo Where you told us – in Lorenzo's bedchamber.

Maurizio By the devil's blood! Does the Cardinal know?

Giomo Yes, Excellency.

Maurizio What's he decided? What's to be done? People are crowding round the Palace already. The whole ghastly business has leaked out – we'll be dead men when it's confirmed – they'll slaughter the lot of us.

Servants *carrying food and casks of wine cross the rear of the stage.*

Guicciardini What's all this going on? Are they sharing this out to the people?

Enter a **Courtier**.

Courtier Is it possible to see the Duke, gentlemen? A cousin of mine has recently arrived from Germany and I wish to present him to His Highness. Be good enough to look favourably on him.

Guicciardini Answer him, Signor Valori. I don't know what to say.

Valori This hall gets more crowded every minute with these morning callers hoping to pay their respects, waiting patiently to be admitted.

Maurizio (*to* **Giomo**) Was he laid out there on the spot?

Giomo Faith, yes, in the sacristy. What else could we do? If the people knew of his death they could bring about a lot more. When the time comes he'll receive a public burial. Meanwhile we took him away wrapped up in a carpet.

Valori What's to become of us?

Gentlemen (*approaching*) Will we soon be allowed to offer our services to His Highness? What say you, Gentlemen?

Enter **Cardinal Cibo**.

Cibo Yes, Gentlemen, you may go in an hour or so. The Duke spent the night at a masquerade and at the moment he's resting.

Valets *are hanging up masqueraders' robes at the windows.*

Courtiers Let us withdraw. The Duke is still resting. He spent the night at a ball.

The **Courtiers** *withdraw. Enter the* **Eight**.

Niccolini Well, Cardinal? What's been decided?

Cibo
Primo avulso non deficit alter Aureus,
*et simili frondescit virga metallo.**

Exit.

Niccolini Admirable, I must say, but what does that achieve? The Duke is dead. We have to elect another, and as soon as we can. If we don't have a duke by tonight or tomorrow, we're done for. Just now the people are on the boil.

Vettori I propose Octavian de' Medici.

Cappomi Why him? He's not first in the blood line?

Acciavoli Why not the Cardinal?

Maurizio Are you joking?

Ruccellai Why in fact don't you take the Cardinal? In defiance of all our laws you leave it up to him after all to be sole judge in this matter.

Vettori He's capable of giving good direction.

Ruccellai Let him await an order from the Pope.

---

* 'If the first golden branch is lopped, another will grow with leaves of the same metal.'

Vettori That he has done. The Pope sent his authorization by a courier the Cardinal despatched during the night.

Ruccellai By homing pigeon, I suppose? It takes a courier time to arrive before he has time to come back. Who do they take us for? Children?

Canigiani (*approaching*) Gentlemen, if you take my advice, this is what we should do: elect his natural son, Giuliano, Duke of Florence.

Ruccellai Bravo! A five-year-old child! He is five, isn't he, Canigiani?

Guicciardini (*quietly*) Now we know what sort of man *he* is! It's the Cardinal who put that silly idea in his head. Cibo would act as regent, while the child stuffed himself with cake.

Ruccellai That's a shameful proposal. If you talk nonsense like that, I shall leave this room at once.

Enter **Corsi**.

Corsi Gentlemen, the Cardinal has just written to Cosimo de' Medici.

The Eight Without consulting us?

Corsi The Cardinal has also written to the military commanders at Pisa, Arezzo and Pistoia. Giacomo de' Medici will be here tomorrow with as many men as possible. Alexander Vitelli is already in the fortress with the whole garrison. As for Lorenzo, three couriers have been sent after him.

Ruccellai Why doesn't your Cardinal make himself Duke at once? It's quicker that way.

Corsi I have been charged to beg you to vote on the election of Cosimo de' Medici, under the provisional title of Governor of the Florentine Republic.

Giomo (*to* **Valets** *crossing the hall*) Spread sand round the doorway and be as generous with the wine as with the rest.

Ruccellai Our poor people! What scroungers we make of you.

Maurizio Come gentlemen, your votes. Here are your cards.

Vettori Cosimo is indeed the first in line after Alexander. His nearest relative.

Acciavoli What sort of man is he? I know little about him.

Corsi The best prince in the world.

Guicciardini I'd hardly say that. The most verbose and polite of princes would be nearer the mark!

Maurizio Your votes, my lords.

Ruccellai In the name of all our citizens, I make formal objection to this vote.

Vettori Why?

Ruccellai The Republic has had enough of princes, dukes and lords – here is my vote.

He shows a blank card.

Vettori Your vote is only one vote. We'll do without you.

Ruccellai Farewell, then. I wash my hands of it.

Guicciardini (*running after him*) Good God! Hey, Palla, you're too hasty.

Ruccellai Leave me alone. I'm sixty-two and more, so you can't harm me much longer.

Exit **Ruccellai.**

Niccolini Your votes, gentlemen. (*He unfolds the cards, which have been placed in a hat.*) It's unanimous. Has the courier left for Trebbio?

Corsi Yes, Excellency. Cosimo will be here tomorrow morning, unless he turns us down.

Vettori Why should he?

Niccolini God! If he did, we'd be in a fine state! To reach Cosimo, it's fifteen leagues from here to Trebbio. And with as much again to get back, it could mean a whole day wasted. We ought to have chosen someone who lived nearer.

Vettori It's too late now. Our vote is cast and he'll probably accept. It's all quite bewildering.

Exeunt.

Scene Two

Philip Strozzi *in his study.*

Philip I might have known it. – Peter is collaborating with the King of France. Now he's at the head of some sort of army, ready to gut our city with fire and sword. And our poor name of Strozzi will have lent itself to that! Respected for so long, now it throws up a rebel and a massacre or two. Oh my Louisa! Sleeping peacefully beneath the grass, you're surrounded by the world's forgetfulness, lost in the dark valley where I left you, and you too are forgetful of the world. (*A knock at the door.*) Come in!

Enter **Lorenzo**.

Lorenzo I'm bringing you the finest gem of all to set in your crown.

Philip What's that you've just thrown down? A key?

Lorenzo The key to my room, and in my room lies Alexander de' Medici, murdered by this hand.

Philip Is this really true? I can't believe it.

Lorenzo Try, if you can. I'm not the only one will tell you so.

Philip (*picking up the key*) Alexander is dead? Is that possible?

Lorenzo What would you say if the Republicans offered to let you take his place as Duke?

Philip My dear friend, I'd refuse.

Lorenzo Is this really true? I can't believe it.

Philip Why not? It seems quite simple to me.

Lorenzo As it was for me to murder Alexander. Why won't you believe me?

Philip Our new Brutus! I believe you and embrace you. So our liberties are safe! Yes, I believe you. You are what you said you were. Give me your hand. The Duke is dead! – But there's no hatred in my joy, just the purest and holiest of love, love for my country. And I take God for my witness.

Lorenzo Don't get too carried away! Nothing is safe. Except for me. And the Bishop of Marzi's horses have nearly broken my back!

Philip You must have warned our friends? I expect by now they are sword in hand.

Lorenzo I warned them, yes. With the diligence of a mendicant friar, I knocked at every Republican door. I told them to sharpen their swords, as by the time they woke Alexander would be dead . . . I expect by now they've woken up several times. And duly gone to sleep again. In truth I expect no more of them.

Philip Did you warn the Pazzi? Did you tell Corsini?

Lorenzo Everyone. I think I could have told the moon herself, I was so sure that nobody would listen.

Philip What do you mean?

Lorenzo I mean that they shrugged their shoulders, and back they went to their dinners, their games of dice and their wives.

Philip But didn't you explain the matter to them?

Lorenzo What the hell was there to explain? Do you think I had an hour to spend with each of them? Be prepared, I said. And then I did the deed.

Philip And you think the Pazzi will do nothing? How do you know? You've had no news since you left, and you've been on the road for several days.

Lorenzo I think the Pazzi will be doing something. Fencing practice in their anteroom, with a pause whenever their throats are dry to swallow a glass of sweet wine.

Philip You stick to your wager! Wasn't that what you bet me? I'm more hopeful than you. Don't you worry.

Lorenzo Oh I won't. I know.

Philip Why didn't you show yourself to the people and hold up the Duke's head? They'd have followed you as their saviour and leader.

Lorenzo I left the stag to the hounds. Let them tear him apart.

Philip If you hadn't despised men so, you could have turned them into Gods.

Lorenzo I don't despise them, I know them. I'm perfectly sure there are very few very wicked men, a great many cowards and large numbers who are apathetic. Some are ferocious too. Like the citizens of Pistoia, who seized on the occasion to cut the throats of their chancellors in the open streets in broad daylight. I learnt that less than an hour ago.

Philip In spite of everything I can't stop my heart beating fast. I feel full of joy and hope.

Lorenzo I'm very glad to hear it!

Philip Why take this attitude, when you don't know what's happening? Most men, of course, are not capable of greatness. But all mankind can respond to it. Why deny the history of the world? It's true it takes a spark to start a forest fire, but you only need one flint to make that spark. The glint of one single sword can light up a whole epoch.

Lorenzo I don't deny history, but I wasn't part of it.

Philip If I'm a dreamer, let me call you our Brutus. My friends and fellow-patriots can still, if they will, write a fine deathbed scene for the oldest of the Strozzi.

Lorenzo Why are you opening the window?

Philip Can't you see that courier galloping up the road at full stretch? Lorenzo the Great! My Brutus! I breathe freedom in the air, I can feel it.

Lorenzo Philip, Philip, enough of that! Close that window. It hurts me to listen to you.

Philip People are gathering in the street to hear some proclamation. Hey, there! Giovanni! Go and buy a copy from the town crier.

Lorenzo Oh God! God!

Philip You've gone as white as death, what's wrong?

Lorenzo Didn't you hear?

Enter a **Servant** *with a copy of the proclamation.*

Philip No. Read me what the crier's just proclaimed!

Lorenzo (*reading*) 'To any man, noble or commoner, who shall take the life of Lorenzo de' Medici, a traitor to his country and murderer of his master, in whatever manner and wherever he may be throughout the length and breadth of Italy, the Council of Eight in Florence hereby promises: Primo, four thousand golden florins of immediate receipt; Secundo, an annuity of one hundred florins to him throughout his life, and after his death to his inheritors in line direct; Terzio, the right to practise any office of the law or justice, and entitlement to all charters and privileges of State, notwithstanding his birth, be he a commoner; Quarto, a free pardon in perpetuity for any misdemeanour committed by him, past or future, be it a petty or a criminal offence. – Promulgated and signed by the Council of Eight.' Well, Philip! You didn't want to believe just now that I'd killed Alexander? Now you know I have.

Philip Be quiet! Someone's coming up the stairs. Go and hide in the next room.

Exeunt.

Scene Three

Florence. A street.

Enter two **Gentlemen**.

1st Gentleman Isn't that the Marchese Cibo over there? And isn't that his wife on his arm?

The **Marchese** *and* **Marchesa** *pass.*

2nd Gentleman It hardly looks as though our good Marchese has a vindictive nature! Is there anyone in Florence who doesn't know his wife was mistress to the late Duke?

1st Gentleman They seem quite reconciled now. I think I just caught them holding hands.

2nd Gentleman A pearl of a husband, he must be! And with a good stomach to have swallowed that affront. Like drinking the Arno!

1st Gentleman I know it sets people talking – but I wouldn't advise you to speak to him about it. He's good at wielding any weapon you care to name, and the wits and rhymesters steer well clear of his palace garden. They don't like the smell of it.

2nd Gentleman If he's such a queer fish, mum's the word!

Exeunt.

Scene Four

An inn.

Enter **Peter Strozzi** *and a* **Messenger**.

Peter Those were his very words?

Messenger Yes, Excellency. From the king himself.

Peter Very well.

Exit the **Messenger**.

The King of France, as protector of Italy's freedom, behaves just like a bandit protecting a pretty woman on the road against another bandit. He defends her up to the moment when he rapes her. I've a new road ahead of me, anyway, where good grain is more plentiful than dust. Curse that Lorenzaccio, trying to make a name for himself! Like a frightened bird, my vengeance has slipped through my fingers. There's nothing left for me to do that's worthy of me. We'll make one strong attack on the town, and then I'll leave these weaklings behind me. They think of nothing but my father's reputation and always look me up and down to see what I have that's like him. I was born for something better than to be chief of a band of brigands.

Exit.

Scene Five

Florence. A square.

The **Goldsmith** *and the* **Silk Merchant** *seated.*

Merchant Listen carefully to what I say. Pay attention now. The late Duke, Alexander, was killed this very year, 1536. Now follow me. It's a fact, over and done with, and he was killed in 1536. Aged twenty-six, you notice. That's nothing yet. So he was twenty-six. Right. He died on the sixth day of the month. Aha! Did you know that? Wasn't it on the sixth precisely that he died? Now listen. He died at six o'clock at night. What do you think of that, Mondella, old chap? If that's not a bit odd, I'm no judge at all! So he died at six o'clock at night. Ssh! Not yet! Don't say a word! He was wounded in six places. Well! Now do you get it? Wounded in six places, at six o'clock at night, on the sixth day of the month, when he was twenty-six in the year 1536. And now, just one word more: he'd reigned over us six years.

Goldsmith What is this rubbish you're talking?

Merchant What, what? Have you no head at all for figures? Can't you see what I'm getting at? The supernatural way the coincidence works out?

Goldsmith No. I really can't see what it all adds up to.

Merchant You can't? You really mean you can't see it?

Goldsmith I can't see it amounts to anything at all. How could this possibly help us?

Merchant What it amounts to is that six sixes contributed to Alexander's death. Ssh! Now don't tell anyone this came from me. You know my reputation as a sensible and prudent man. By all the saints, don't injure that! It's more serious than you might think. And I tell you as a friend.

Goldsmith Oh, get away with you! I may be an old man, but I'm not an old woman yet . . . ! That Cosimo arrives today, there's the most obvious result of all this business. Your night of the six sixes has thrown up a fine word-spinner for us! By my life's end, it puts us all to shame! Even the meanest of my workmen, neighbour, were banging their tools on the table when they saw the Eight pass by. And you know what they shouted? 'If you can't or won't take action, you call on us, we'll do it!'

Merchant Your workmen aren't the only ones to shout. There's such a storm of words flying round the town, I've never heard of anything like it.

Goldsmith Some chase after the soldiers, others after the wine they dish out. Their mouths and their brains are soaked in it, so what few fine words and common sense they might have left are all befuddled.

Merchant There are some who would like a new Council and free elections for a Gonfaloniere. A Chief Magistrate at the head of the Republic, as in the old days.

Goldsmith Some of them did, as you say, but none of them took action. When I went to the New Market, old as I am, I got a blow from a halberd in the leg. Not a single soul came to help me. The only ones to show themselves were the students.

Merchant I can well believe it. Have you heard, neighbour? They say Robert Corsini, the Governor of the Citadel, went last night to the Republican gathering at the Salviati palace.

Goldsmith True enough. He offered to hand the fortress over, with its keys, provisions and all, to the friends of freedom.

Merchant And did he, neighbour? Was he able to? It was a noble act of treason.

Goldsmith Indeed it was! They all shouted as they drank their sweet wine and smashed window-panes. But did they even listen to the good man's proposition? As they didn't dare accept his offer, they said they doubted his good

faith. By a thousand million devils, it makes me mad!
Look, there are messengers from Trebbio arriving.
Cosimo can't be far off. Good night, neighbour. My
blood's boiling! I must go straight to the palace.

Exit.

Merchant Then wait for me, neighbour. I'll come with
you.

Exit. Enter a **Tutor** *with the little* **Salviati Boy**, *and another*
Tutor *with the little* **Strozzi Boy**.

1st Tutor *Sapientissime doctor*, how fare you, sir? Is your
treasure in safekeeping? Your precious health, I mean.
And are you still on an even keel in these storm-tossed
times of ours?

2nd Tutor *Signor dottore*, this is a meeting pregnant with
significance: to be greeted with such elaborate erudition
when the ground we walk on cracks with trepidation.
Permit me to clasp a hand whose gargantuan grasp has
conceived masterpieces in our native tongue. Confess. You
recently composed a sonnet.

Salviati Boy Pig of a Strozzi!

Strozzi Boy Your papa got beaten up, Salviati!

1st Tutor Can it be that our Muse's feeble effort has
come to your attention? You, a man so conscientious in his
art, so versatile, so austere? Eyes such as yours roam over
glittering peaks on the horizon. Have they really cast a
glance at the somewhat extravagant emanations of my
fervid imagination?

2nd Tutor Oh, for mercy's sake, if you love art, if you
love us, tell us your sonnet. The town has but one
concern: your sonnet.

1st Tutor Perhaps you will stand amazed that I who at
the start sang the praises, as you might say, of the

monarchy, appear to celebrate, on this occasion, the Republic.

Salviati Boy   Stop kicking me, Strozzi!

Strozzi Boy   Here, Salviati, here come two more, you dog!

1st Tutor   These are my verses, then:
Let us sing of freedom, which blooms more fiercely now . . .

Salviati Boy   Make this ruffian stop it, sir! He's a cut-throat. All the Strozzis are cut-throats!

2nd Tutor   Come on, child, behave yourself!

Strozzi Boy   Creep back on the sly, would you? Take that, you swine! And tell your papa to add it to the gash he got from Peter Strozzi! Poisoner! You're all poisoners!

1st Tutor   Will you be quiet, you little wretch! (*He punches him.*)

Strozzi Boy   Ouch! Oh, he hit me!

1st Tutor
Let us sing of freedom, which blooms more fiercely now
Under a riper sun and skies of pinker hue.

Strozzi Boy   Oh, he clipped me over the ear!

2nd Tutor   You hit him too hard, my friend.

The **Strozzi Boy** *beats the* **Salviati Boy**.

1st Tutor   Oh well, it's no matter!

2nd Tutor   Go on, please go on.

1st Tutor   With pleasure. But those boys will never stop fighting!

The **Boys** *go out fighting and the* **Tutors** *follow them out.*

Scene Six

Venice. **Philip Strozzi***'s study.*

Philip, *with* **Lorenzo** *holding a letter.*

Lorenzo This letter is to tell me that my mother is dead. Come with me, Philip, and we'll take a walk together.

Philip Don't tempt fate, my friend, I beg you. You always go out and about as if that proclamation was no threat to your life at all.

Lorenzo When I was about to kill Clement VII there was a price on my head in Rome. Now I've killed Alexander, it's only natural it should apply all over Italy. If I left Italy, a trumpet would soon sound my doom in the whole of Europe. And when I die, the Good Lord won't fail to paste up my eternal condemnation at every crossroads in His vast domain.

Philip Your sad humour is black as night. You haven't changed, Lorenzo.

Lorenzo No, truly, I haven't. I wear the same clothes, I still walk with the same legs and yawn with the same mouth. Only one wretched thing in me has changed. I feel more hollow and more empty than a tinpot statue.

Philip Let us leave Venice together. Become a man again. You have done many things, but you're still young.

Lorenzo I am older than the great-grandfather of Saturn. Come take a walk with me, I beg you.

Philip Your mind is tortured by inaction. That's what you suffer from. You have much on your conscience, my friend.

Lorenzo Oh, I agree. That the Republicans made no move in Florence was a great failing on my part. That a hundred young students, brave and resolute, got themselves massacred for nothing. That Cosimo, a cabbage-farmboy, has been elected unanimously, oh yes, I admit, I admit these were all unpardonable faults, for which I must be held responsible.

Philip Let us not draw conclusions from an event that is far from over. What counts for you now is to leave Italy. Your work's not finished yet on earth.

Lorenzo I was a murder machine, but for one murder only.

Philip Has nothing ever made you happy apart from this murder? If you were to become an honest man again, would you still wish to die?

Lorenzo Philip, as I told you before: I was honest, once. Perhaps I could be so again, were it not for the boredom that overcomes me. I still love women and wine. That's enough to make me a libertine, it's true, but not enough to make me want to be one. Let us go out, I beg you.

Philip You will get yourself killed on one of your many walks.

Lorenzo It amuses me to watch them. The reward is so enormous it almost gives them courage. Yesterday a strapping fellow, with no hose to cover his legs, followed me along the canal for a quarter of an hour at least. But he couldn't make up his mind to strike me down. The poor man was carrying some kind of knife, long, like a meat skewer. The way he gazed at it, so shamefaced, made me quite sorry for him. He could have been the father of some starving family.

Philip Oh Lorenzo, Lorenzo! You really are sick at heart. I'm sure he was an honest man. Why attribute to cowardice the respect people feel for the misfortunes of others?

Lorenzo Interpret that as you will. I'll take a stroll to the Rialto.

Exit.

Philip (*alone*) I must get one of the servants to follow him. Hey there! Gianni! Pippo!

Enter a **Servant**.

Philip Fetch swords, you and one of your comrades, and keep Lord Lorenzo in sight. Stay a fair distance behind him, but go to his aid if he's attacked.

Servant Yes, my Lord.

Enter **Pippo**.

Pippo My Lord, Lorenzo is dead. A man was hidden by the door, and he struck him from behind as he went out.

Philip Go quickly, he may only have been wounded.

Pippo Can't you see all those people? They've dragged him off and – merciful God! They're throwing him into the lagoon!

Philip Oh horror! How horrible! And no tomb even will ever bear his name!

Exit.

Scene Seven

Florence. The main square.

The public stands are crowded.

Townspeople (*assembling from all sides*) Long live the Medici! The new Duke! The new Duke! Cosimo is Duke!

Soldiers Back, scum!

Cibo (*on a dais, to* **Cosimo de' Medici**) My Lord, you are Duke of Florence. Before accepting from my hands the crown which the Pope and Caesar have charged me to entrust to you, I have been commanded to administer your oaths.

Cosimo And those are, Cardinal?

Cibo To dispense justice without fear or favour. Never to dispute the authority of Charles V. To avenge the death of Alexander. And to deal kindly with the Lord Julius and Lady Julia, his natural children.

Cosima How must these be sworn?

Cibo On the Gospel. (*He offers him the Gospel.*)

Cosimo I swear unto God, and unto you, Cardinal. Now give me your hand.

They advance towards the people. **Cosimo** *is heard speaking from a distance.*

Most mighty and noble Lords, the thanks I render to Your most Gracious and Illustrious Lordships for the Supreme favour they have shown me can but express the promise, most welcome to one so young as I, to keep constantly in mind, not only the fear of God, but justice and fair dealing, and the desire to harm no one, neither in property nor honour, and as for my good government, never to ignore the advice and judgement of their most Wise and Prudent Lordships, to whom I now most devoutly offer and commend myself.

Don't Play With Love

On ne badine pas avec l'amour (1 July 1834)

translated by MICHAEL SADLER

Translator's Note

> Alfred de Musset
> Called his cat pusset
> Not unexpected
> In one so affected.

The temptation with Musset has always been, and not only in clerihews, to concentrate on personality and reputation. He was so young, so clever, so passionate, so public, so debauched. The tabloid press would have loved him, because he did what the readers didn't dare to do. This is the way he lives on in French histories of French literature, in those fascinating, mind-numbing cribs (*Castex et Surer*, *Lagarde et Michard*) which unleash onto the unsuspecting young the reflections of civil servants armed with bottles of formalin. Musset almost impales himself on their pens. In the brilliant and black *Confessions d'un enfant du siècle*, he encourages the pat paradox: he is ardent and disenchanted, enthusiastic and depressed, insouciant and grave, ironic and self-indulgent. Born too late for the Empire and too early for Decadence.

But in 1830, when *La Nuit vénitienne* flopped, Musset turned his back on his public. This 'armchair reflex' means that his famous plays were conceived heedless of his public self. They are private property. As you read, you can imagine him writing fast, angry, drunk, bored. Taking it out on the paper. Things change fast, people go on, go over the top, are vicious, tender. But he hasn't got an audience in mind. These plays, in his mind, are unperformable. In a sense they are even unreadable. Quite often, right in the middle of a moving and dangerous situation, you're not sure you understand what they're saying. In *Don't Play With Love*, the chorus changes character with the rapidity of a litmus paper in a glass of Aloxe-Corton. The two main characters, Camille and Perdican, are deeply unmade. Why is youth so stupid? So he's right about nuns. So she's wrong. Why can't he see that she may be right to be wrong, and that it's easy for him, because it's not him who runs the risk of being discarded, disgraced, pregnant. Propriety was an insurance against life. Can't he see? And then. Can't she see that maybe he's not the world's greatest lover, that he's over-eager, over-demanding and that he's in need of a touch of make-believe surrender. Then Rosette dies and they are stopped too fast in their tracks, congealed in their unmaking, adolescents trapped in larva.

In his presentation of the 1991–2 season at the Théâtre des Amandiers at Nanterre, in the Parisian suburbs, the director Jean-Pierre Vincent, who was staging a Musset revival, said these plays give voice to youth in a way that few others do. He said that there is a lineage which goes from Nerval, who committed suicide, to Büchner, who died at twenty-four, to Rimbaud, who vanished, to Jim Morrison, who died in his bath. Musset, who petered out, belongs to this family.

This play has been performed in this translation twice. Once on Radio Three directed by Peter Kavanagh, once in a production by Jean-Marc Lantéri at the Institut Français in London. The BBC production used the Rossini 'Petite messe solennelle' in the version for two pianos and harmonium. Like *On ne badine pas avec l'amour*, this music is moving and facile, popular and deep, hummable and mysterious.

Young actors (and if you've bought this collection you must, somewhere, be a young actor – your present translator is a largish 'jeune premier' of fifty), read this play . . .

Characters

The Baron
Perdican, *his son*
Blazius, *Perdican's tutor*
Bridaine, *a priest*
Camille, *the Baron's niece*
Sister Pluche, *her governess*
Rosette, *Camille's foster-sister*
Chorus
Peasants, Servants, *etc.*

Act One

Scene One

In front of the castle.

Blazius, Sister Pluche, Chorus.

Chorus Wearing his best clothes, his pens and pencils in a bag at his side, the learned Dr Blazius gently bobs through the cornflowers in bloom on his frisky mule. Like a baby sleeping on a pillow, he lolls on the soft cushion of his belly and, with eyes half closed, mutters Pater Nosters down his triple chins. Good day, Dr Blazius, you've arrived, like some antique barrel, just in time for the grape harvest.

Blazius I bring important news. But anyone wishing to apprehend it must first fetch me a glass of cool wine.

Chorus This is the biggest bowl we've got. The wine is delicious, Dr Blazius. Drink first. Talk afterwards.

Blazius Here is the news. The Baron's young son, Perdican, has just come of age and has been awarded the degree of doctor in Paris. He is returning home to the castle this very day, his mouth so full of the most beautiful and ornate expressions that half the time you haven't the faintest idea what he's talking about. His most gracious person has been transformed into a golden Book of Knowledge. He knows the lot. The merest blade of grass in the mud at your feet, he can tell you its name in Latin. And when it rains or when it's windy, no problem, he knows why. Your eyes will gape as wide as this door here, for instance, when you see him unroll before you scrolls that he has coloured himself with different coloured inks – off his own bat and without breathing so much as a word

to anyone! He is, from top to toe, a priceless diamond.
This is the gist of what I am to announce to his father,
Monsieur le Baron. And I am sure that you will appreciate
that some of this glory rubs off on yours truly, his tutor
since the age of four. Hence, my dear friends, would you
be so kind as to fetch me a stool so that I can alight from
this mule without breaking my neck. The beast is a little
on the restive side and I would not be unpartial to a little
tot before going inside.

Chorus Have another one, Dr Blazius. Get your breath
and your wits back. We've known Perdican ever since he
was born. And as he's coming himself, there was no need
to be so longwinded. Here's hoping that growing up has
not driven the boy out of him!

Blazius Good gracious! The bowl's already empty. What
a surprise! I had no idea I was evacuating the liquid at
such a lick! Farewell! As I trotted along the road I
composed one or two little unpretentious sentences which
are doubtless going to warm the cockles of the Baron's
heart. I am now going to proceed to ring the bell.

Exit.

Chorus And here comes another mule, this one wheezing
for breath as it humps and bumps Sister Pluche up the
steep path. She is frightened out of her wits and so she
hits the poor animal with a stick. But the mule, by way of
reply, just nods its head and chews on a thistle. Her long,
thin legs flay the mule in fury while her hands scratch
away at her rosary. Good day, Sister Pluche. You arrive
like the hot wind which turns the woodland yellow.

Pluche A glass of water, pleb. Serf. Bring me a glass of
water to which has been added a drop of vinegar.

Chorus And where have you come from, Pluche, dear
friend? Your wig is covered in dust. Your quiff is a mess
and your chaste skirt at present affords an unexpected
glimpse of your very respectable garters.

Pluche Hear this, servants. Camille, the beautiful niece of the Baron your master, is today arriving at the castle. She has left the convent, where she has been living, on the express order of your master in order that she might rightfully receive that which is due to her from her mother's inheritance. Her education, thanks be to God, is well and duly completed and those who perceive her will have the distinct joy of admiring a flower whose perfume is composed of wisdom and devotion. There has never, never ever, been one so much a lamb, a dove or an angel as this darling little nun. May the Lord in Heaven guide her every step. So be it. Move aside, pleb. I get the feeling my legs are swollen.

Chorus Pray get yourself sorted out, honest Pluche. And when you next can get on your knees to pray to God, ask for rain. Our wheat is as thin and dry as your shins.

Pluche You brought me water in a bowl which stank of kitchen fat. Ignorant yob. Lout.

Exit.

Chorus We're now going to dress in our Sunday best. And wait for the Baron to call us. Unless I'm much mistaken, there's revels in the air.

Exit.

Scene Two

*The **Baron**'s living room.*

*Enter the **Baron**, **Bridaine** and **Blazius**.*

Baron My dear friend and Very Reverend Bridaine. Allow me to introduce my son's tutor, the Doctor Blazius. Yesterday morning, at precisely eight minutes past twelve, my son came of age and, at the same time, was awarded a unanimous, congratulatory first-class doctor's degree. Dr

Blazius, allow me to introduce the parish priest, the Very Reverend Bridaine, who is also my very dear friend.

Blazius (*bowing*) Doctor, might I add, in literature, botany, and both Roman and canon law.

Baron Go up to your room, dear Blazius. My son will be here shortly. Have a wash. And come back down when the bell rings.

Exit **Blazius**.

Bridaine Might I have a word in your ear, Baron? Your son's tutor stinks of drink.

Baron That is surely not possible!

Bridaine I've never in my life been more certain of anything. When he spoke to me just now, his mouth was very close to my face. The lurid stench was terrifying.

Baron Enough of this! I tell you that what you are insinuating is quite impossible.

Enter **Sister Pluche**.

Baron Ah! Sister Pluche! There you are! And that means, doesn't it, that my niece can't be far away.

Pluche She is following on my footsteps, Baron. I merely came on ahead.

Baron Reverend Bridaine, my very dear friend, may I introduce Sister Pluche who is the governess of my niece. Last night at precisely seven o'clock in the evening my niece was eighteen years of age. She is arriving fresh from the finest convent in France. Sister Pluche, may I introduce the Reverend Bridaine, the parish priest and my very dear friend.

Pluche (*curtsying*) The finest convent in France, yes, Baron, but may I add, in which she is the finest Christian.

Baron Now, Pluche, perhaps you would like to pop up to your room to put your dress in order. I trust my niece will soon be here. And be ready in time for dinner.

Exit **Sister Pluche.**

Bridaine Now this respectable lady gives the impression of being full of unction.

Baron Full of unction and compunction, Bridaine. Her virtue is an unassailable citadel.

Bridaine But the tutor is a boozer. I'm sure of it!

Baron I am afraid, Reverend Bridaine, that there are moments in life when I am forced to ask myself: is this man really my friend? Can it be your role in life to contradict everything I say? Not, I would beg you, not another word on the subject. Now I have devised the following plan. I intend to marry my son and my niece. They are a well-matched couple. Their education has so far cost me six thousand écus.

Bridaine Cousins . . . Hum . . . They will need a dispensation.

Baron Aha. But I have it, Bridaine. The dispensation is on my desk in my office. Oh, my dear friend, my heart is filled with such joy! You know, I know you know, the extent to which I abhor solitude. However, the position that I occupy in society – the important function I exercise – requires of me to remain locked away in this castle for three months during the winter and for three months during the summer. Now, it is impossible to see to the Affairs of Man in general and to the affairs of one's servants in particular without having to give the frequent order: Don't let anyone in! The quality of meditation required of a statesman is both austere and demanding. Since the king appointed me Inspector and Controller of Taxes, I have been prey to bouts of darkness and melancholy. Thus what joy it is for me to temper this solitude with the presence of my two children.

Bridaine   And where is the marriage service to be conducted? In Paris? Or here?

Baron   Aha. I can see you coming, Bridaine! I was sure you were going to pop the question! Now, my dear friend, what would you say if I was to tell you that these very hands, no don't look at your fingernails in such a pitiful way, were to be the hands destined to bestow their solemn blessing on this union which is the fulfilment of my most heartfelt dreams?

Bridaine   I could say nothing. My gratitude would render me speechless.

Baron   Look out of this window. Look at my people thronging around the gates of the castle. My two children are arriving both at the same time. Things could not happen in a more propitious way. And everything has been staged so as to leave nothing to chance! My niece is to enter through this door here. My son is to enter through that door there. I am so looking forward to seeing how they will greet each other. And I am so much looking forward to hearing what they have to say to each other. Six thousand écus is quite a sum I can tell you, and not to be thrown out of the window! These two young people have, moreover, loved each other ever since they were little children together. – Bridaine, wait. I have a bright idea!

Bridaine   Tell me.

Baron   In the course of the dinner, and casually as it were without any fuss, if you see what I'm getting at, my dear friend, in the midst of toasts and things . . . you do speak Latin, Bridaine?

Bridaine   *Ita aedepol*, indeed I do, Baron.

Baron   Well, listen, this is what I would like, I would like you – discreetly as I said – but in front of his cousin because she'd be so impressed – I would like you to converse with him in Latin! No, just a minute, not during the dinner perhaps, because that might be a little on the boring side, because I for one wouldn't understand a word of what was going on – but over the pudding – if you see what I mean?

Bridaine If you don't understand, Baron, then your niece is probably in the same boat.

Baron So much the better, Bridaine. So much the better. How do you expect a woman to admire what she understands! Bridaine. Bridaine. Where have you been, Bridaine! My dear chap. Come, come!

Bridaine I don't know much about women. But I don't understand how you can admire what you don't understand.

Baron Aha. But I do know about women, Bridaine. I know a great deal about these charming, mysterious creatures. And I can assure you that they love to be dazzled, and the more you dazzle them the more they love it and the more they ask for more.

Enter **Perdican** *from one side and* **Camille** *from the other.*

Baron Good day to you, my children; good day, my dear Camille; good day, my dear Perdican! Come. Kiss me. And then kiss each other.

Perdican Good day, dear Father! Good day, my beloved sister! What happiness! I am so happy!

Camille Good day, Father! Good day, cousin!

Perdican How you have grown, Camille! You are as pretty as a summer's day!

Baron When did you leave Paris, Perdican?

Perdican Wednesday, I think. No, Tuesday. How you have changed, Camille. You have changed into a woman. I suppose that means I must have changed into a man. And yet it seems only yesterday that you were no higher than this!

Baron You must be tired. You've had a long journey. The weather is very warm.

Perdican Tired? No. Good God, no! Look, Father! Look at Camille! Look how beautiful she has become!

Baron Well, Camille. Aren't you going too kiss your cousin?

Camille Forgive me. I can't.

Baron He paid you a compliment. A compliment deserves a kiss. You kiss her then, Perdican.

Perdican If my cousin steps back when I offer my hand then I must reply in turn 'Forgive me. Nor can I.' Love can steal a kiss. But friendship never steals.

Camille Neither love nor friendship should accept that which they cannot return.

Baron (*to* **Bridaine**) Oh dear. Not getting off to a very good start, what do you think, Bridaine?

Bridaine (*to the* **Baron**) An excess of modesty often causes problems at the beginning. But marriage tends to get all that sorted out pretty quickly.

Baron (*to* **Bridaine**) But I'm shocked. Indeed I'm a little wounded. I didn't like that reply at all. Did you hear what she said?! She said: 'I'm sorry I can't.' And did you see what she did? She made as if to cross herself. A word in your ear. I have to say that I find all this extremely vexing. I've been so looking forward to this moment for such a long time, and now it's all spoilt. I am angry. I am piqued. I mean . . . Hell! . . . This is a very bad show!

Bridaine Now they've turned their backs on each other. Say a few words to them.

Baron Well now . . . Er . . . Children. Er . . . A penny for your thoughts. What are you doing, Camille? Having a good look at that tapestry, are you?

Camille (*looking at a portrait*) It is a very beautiful portrait, Uncle. If I remember rightly she was a great aunt.

Baron That is correct, my child. Yes. She was in fact your great-great-grandmother. Or rather to be more precise the sister of your great-great-grandfather. Because this dear lady never participated, other that is, of course, than by means of prayer, in the enlargement of the family. She was a saint.

Camille A saint. Saintly great-aunt Isabelle. How beautiful she looks in her nun's costume.

Baron And you, Perdican? A penny for yours. What are you doing in front of this flower pot?

Perdican What an attractive flower, Father. It's a heliotrope.

Baron Attractive. Are you taking the mickey? It's no bigger than a fly.

Perdican This little flower no bigger than a fly has its own particular worth.

Bridaine The learned doctor, of course, doubtless, knows what he is talking about. Perhaps we might also ask him what sex the flower is? To which species it belongs? What are its component parts? Where it gets its sap and its colour from? He will, I am sure, delight us with a detailed exposé starting with the roots and rising to the bloom.

Perdican I don't know anything about it at all, Reverend Bridaine. I just think it smells nice. That's all.

Scene Three

In front of the castle.

Enter **Chorus**.

Chorus Now this is what I call entertainment! I am very curious to know what's going on. Let's try and imagine what's happening inside the castle. At this very moment two very big eaters sit face to face across the table. Now I don't know whether you've noticed but, whenever two men who are in all things equal, that is in this case, equally fat, and equally stupid, and who share the same vices and the same passions, whenever two such forces collide, either they are going to love each other or hate each other. In the present instance, given the law that like repels like, and that the tall and dry prefer the small and plump, the fair the dark and the vice the versa, I foresee a bitter, secret struggle between the priest and the tutor. They are both shameless. They both have guts as big as barrels. They are both gourmets. But they are both greedy. They care for the quality of the supper perhaps, but just as much for the quantity of the quality. So what's going to happen if the fish dish happens to be a small fish dish? A carp's tongue is hardly a delicacy that you can cut into two and carps are never double tongued. And then again, they both talk non-stop. I suppose, if the worse comes to the worst, they'll both speak at the same time and that way they won't have to listen to each other. Bridaine has already tried to catch out Perdican with the odd learned question, and this was decidedly not to the liking of his tutor. Only Blazius has the right to test his pupil. Each one is as stupid as the other. Priests they are, both of them. One will be waxing pompous about his parish, while the other preens himself like a peacock about his pupil. Blazius confesses the son, Bridaine the father. I can just see them now, leaning on the table, with red faces, bulging eyeballs, their jowls shaking with hatred. They eye each other up and down, and hostilities begin with slight skirmishes. But it will soon be open war. The exchanges, at first priggish and pedantic, become sharper and sharper, and to make matters even worse Pluche is huffing and puffing between the two drunkards, giving little knocks with her sharp elbows.

But dinner is over. The castle gates are opening. Let us stand back and observe the guests from a respectable distance.

Exit **Chorus**. *Enter the* **Baron** *and* **Sister Pluche**.

Baron   Venerable Sister Pluche! I am deeply grieved.

Pluche   Can this be true, Baron?

Baron   Yes, Pluche. It can be. I had been looking forward to this for a long long time – I had even written, jotted down on my jotting pad that I always have about me, I had written that this was to be the happiest of moments – yes, dear Pluche, that this was perhaps to be the happiest day of my life. – You are, I trust, aware of the fact that I intended to marry my son and my niece. Everything was settled, everything was agreed, everything was fine and dandy, I'd even spoken to Bridaine and then – I perceive or I believe I perceive that when my children speak to each other they are cool and cold. In fact, they don't even say anything to each other!

Pluche   Here they are coming now, Baron. Are they aware of your designs?

Baron   I did mention it to each of them. But I think it would be advantageous, seeing that at last they are both at least in each other's company, to sit down in the propitious shade of this tree and to leave them alone for a moment.

The **Baron** *and* **Sister Pluche** *move back. Enter* **Camille** *and* **Perdican**.

Perdican   You are aware, Camille, that it was inelegant to refuse to grant me a kiss?

Camille   That's the way I am. I can do nothing about it.

Perdican   Will you take my arm? We could walk down to the village.

Camille   No, thank you. I'm feeling tired.

Perdican Wouldn't you like to see our meadow again? Don't you remember? We used to go out in the boat. Come with me. We could go down to the mill. You steer. I'll row.

Camille That's the last thing I'd like to do.

Perdican You break my heart, Camille. Surely you remember things!? Your heart must beat faster when you remember that we were children together, when you think of the past, which was so sweet, so good, so innocent, so wonderful. Don't you want to see the path we used to take to go to the farm?

Camille Not tonight.

Perdican Not tonight! Then, when, pray? Our whole life is here.

Camille I'm no longer young enough to play with my dolls. But I'm not old enough for . . . nostalgia.

Perdican Say that again, please.

Camille I said, childhood memories are not my cup of tea.

Perdican They don't interest you!

Camille That's right. They don't interest me.

Perdican Poor child. I pity you. Sincerely I do.

They each go their own way.

Baron (*returning with* **Pluche**) You see! You see what it's like. Now you've heard it for yourself, excellent Pluche. I was expecting the sweetest of harmonies. In its place we have this! It's like being at a concert where the violin plays *Mélodie d'amour* and the flute plays *Frère Jacques*. Ah, I assure you! It's just such a din that resounds in my heart.

Pluche You're right. But I cannot in any way find anything to reproach in the behaviour of my ward. To my way of thinking, there is nothing more reprehensible than boat trips.

Baron   Are you being serious?

Pluche   Baron, I can assure you. A self-respecting girl will never ever hazard her virtue on lakes.

Baron   But, please, remember, Pluche, that her cousin is supposed to be marrying her, and given that etc . . .

Pluche   It is highly improper to hold a young man's helm and distinctly dangerous to allow one's feet to quit the *terra firma*.

Baron   But may I repeat . . . I did say . . .

Pluche   I stick to my guns.

Baron   Are you out of your tiny mind, Pluche? In truth you are pushing me to . . . There are expressions I would refrain from . . . Which I find repugnant, but . . . I must say that what you say does make me want to say . . . If, that is, I wasn't exerting the utmost . . . discipline in order to refrain from . . . I would . . . You are a stupid cow, woman! I am most disappointed in you!

Exit.

Scene Four

A village square.

Chorus, Perdican.

Perdican   Good day, my friends. Do you recognize me?

Chorus   Sir! You do look like a child that once we loved dearly.

Perdican   Wasn't it you who carried me on your back across the stream that flows through your meadow? You, who used to bounce me on your knees, who used to lift me up onto the back of your plough horse. And in the evening when you were all eating supper at the farm, who would all squeeze up to make a place for me.

Chorus Indeed we do remember, sir. You were the finest little rascal there ever was.

Perdican Then why don't you take me in your arms, rather than treating me like a stranger?

Chorus Bless you, sir. It's as if you were our own child. We long to take you in our arms. But we're old. And you've grown into a man.

Perdican It is true. I haven't seen you for ten years. And it is as if all under the sun has changed in a day. I've grown a few feet up towards the heavens. And you've bent a few inches back down towards the grave. You are grey. You are slow. You can't stoop to pick me up any more. It is now for me to father you, as you were once fathers to me.

Chorus The day of your homecoming is a day even happier than the day you were born. It is even sweeter to meet up again with one you have once loved than it is to kiss a new-born child.

Perdican So this is my valley! These are my walnut trees. The green path, the small fountain. These are all mine. This is where I spent long days still full of the pleasure of life. This is the mysterious dream world of my childhood. My homeland. Homeland. The word is difficult to understand. Is man made for just one corner of the garden? Is it there that he is supposed to build his home and to live out his days?

Chorus We hear you have become a scholar, sir.

Perdican I've heard the same thing. Knowledge is good and fine. But these trees and these fields teach us a clearer and more beautiful lesson. They teach us to forget what we know.

Chorus A lot of things have happened since you left. A lot of young girls have married. A lot of young men have left for the army.

Perdican You must tell me everything. I was expecting things to change. But to be honest I don't want to know about change. Not just yet. Was the wash-house really as small as that? I used to think it was huge. I left home with my head full of oceans and forests, and I come back to find a puddle and a blade of grass. – Who is that girl singing there behind the trees?

Chorus That's Rosette. She's your cousin Camille's foster-sister.

Perdican (*stepping forward*) Rosette! Come here quickly!

Rosette (*entering*) Yes, my Lord.

Perdican Bad girl. You could see me from there but you didn't come! Give me that hand, yes that one, and give me your cheek so that I can kiss you.

Rosette Yes, sir.

Perdican Are you married, my sweet? I heard that you were.

Rosette Oh, no.

Perdican And why not? There's not a prettier girl in the whole village. Rest assured, we'll marry you, my child!

Chorus My Lord. She wishes to die a virgin.

Perdican Can that be true, Rosette?

Rosette Oh, no.

Perdican Your sister Camille has arrived. Have you seen her yet?

Rosette She has yet to come this way.

Perdican Quickly. Go and put on your new dress. Come and have supper at the castle.

Scene Five

A hall.

Enter the **Baron** *and* **Blazius**.

Blazius Pssssttt. Baron. A word in your ear. The parish priest is a drunkard!

Baron Come come, Dr Blazius! Surely that can't be the case.

Blazius I'm certain of it – at dinner he drank three bottles of wine.

Baron That is, yes, a little excessive.

Blazius And when he got up from table he walked in the flower-beds.

Baron In the flower-beds?! – That is really most surprising! – How strange! – To drink three bottles of wine at dinner and then to walk in the flower-beds. Such behaviour is a little difficult to understand. – Why didn't he walk on the path?

Blazius Because he was walking sideways.

Baron (*aside*) I'm beginning to see what Bridaine meant this morning. This Dr Blazius smells quite repulsively of Dr Drink.

Blazius What is more, he ate an enormous amount. And his speech was slurred.

Baron That is true, yes. I noticed it myself.

Blazius And when he spoke in Latin he got it all wrong. The syntax was all over the place. Baron, this man is depraved.

Baron (*aside*) Ugh! The smell this man exudes is almost unbearable. – I would like you to know, sir, that I have other, more important preoccupations, and that it is not for me to bother myself with what people eat and drink. That is a job for the butler.

Blazius Please God that I should not displease you, Baron. Your wine is delicious.

Baron My cellars do, yes, contain some excellent bottles.

Bridaine (*entering*) Baron! Baron! Your son is on the village square in the company of a lot of local no-goods.

Baron Now that can't be true.

Bridaine I saw him with my own eyes. He was on his hands and knees looking for stones to play ducks and drakes.

Baron Ducks and drakes! – My head spins. These notions are most distressing. – What you tell me, Bridaine, has neither head nor tail. Doctors of the University don't play ducks and drakes!

Bridaine Then come and look out of the window, Baron. You can see it for yourself.

Baron (*aside*) Oh, Lord! Blazius was right. Bridaine is walking sideways.

Bridaine Look, Baron. Just look. Down there by the wash-house. He's got his arm round a wench!

Baron A wench? Can it be, surely not, that my son has returned home merely to debauch my vassals? He has his arm around a wench and all the village around him!! I am beside myself.

Bridaine This calls for vengeance!

Baron All is lost! – All is irredeemably lost! – Even I am lost! Bridaine walks sideways. Blazius stinks of drink. And my son seduces all the village wenches as he plays ducks and drakes!

Exit.

Act Two

Scene One

A garden.

Enter **Blazius** *and* **Perdican**.

Blazius Sir. Your father is in a state of deep despair.

Perdican And why should that be?

Blazius You are surely aware that he had planned a marriage between yourself and your cousin Camille?

Perdican And what of it? – I can think of nothing more pleasant.

Blazius But the Baron did believe that he remarked that your temperaments were ill matched.

HHPerdican That is most unfortunate. There's nothing I can do to change mine.

Blazius Does that mean that the marriage will never take place?

Perdican I have already told you. I can think of nothing more pleasant than to marry Camille. Go and find the Baron and tell him just that.

Blazius I withdraw, sir. Here is your cousin who is coming this way. (*Exits.*)

Enter **Camille**.

Perdican Up already, cousin? I still stand by what I told you yesterday. You are as pretty as a flower.

Camille I would prefer more serious talk, Perdican. It is your father's intention to marry us. I don't know what you think about the idea. But I feel I must warn you that, as far as I'm concerned, I, at least, have made up my mind.

Perdican Then it's just too bad for me if you don't like me.

Camille I don't dislike you more than I dislike anyone else. I don't want to get married. That's all. There's no reason for your pride to be offended.

Perdican Pride is a feeling foreign to me. I know neither the pain nor the pleasure it can afford.

Camille I returned to the castle simply to receive the inheritance which was due to me from my mother. That done, I shall go back to the convent.

Perdican You are frank in your dealings, Camille. Let's shake hands. And be good friends.

Camille I don't want to be touched.

Perdican (*taking her hand*) Please, Camille. Just give me your hand. Please. Why are you so frightened of me? You don't want people to marry us. So let's not get married. Surely that doesn't mean we have to hate each other? Are we not like brother and sister? When your mother in her will ordered that this marriage should take place, did she not wish quite simply that our friendship should last forever. That was surely all she wanted. What's all this business about marriage? Here's your hand. Here's my hand. In order to be united until the day of our death do we need a priest? We only need God.

Camille I am relieved that my refusal leaves you quite indifferent.

Perdican You're wrong. It doesn't leave me indifferent, Camille. Your love would have lent me life. But your friendship is consolation for the loss of your love. Don't depart from the castle tomorrow. Yesterday you refused to walk in the garden with me because I threatened to be a husband you didn't want. Stay a few days more. Let me hope that the days we spent together in the past have not vanished forever from your heart.

Camille I have to go.

Perdican Why?

Camille That's my secret.

Perdican So you love someone else?

Camille No. But I want to go.

Perdican You want to go forever?

Camille Yes. Forever.

Perdican Ah well. Goodbye then . . . I would have liked to sit under the chestnut tree in the small wood and while away the time speaking of this and that. But if you don't like the idea, we'll speak no more of it. Farewell, my child.

Exit.

Camille (*to* **Sister Pluche,** *who enters*) Pluche, is everything ready? Can we leave tomorrow? Has my guardian finished doing his accounts?

Pluche Of course we can leave, my dearest dove. And with no regrets. Yesterday the Baron called me a cow and all I ask is that we leave as fast as we possibly can!

Camille Take this. It is a handwritten note. I want you to give it to Perdican on my behalf before dinner.

Pluche Heaven protect us! Surely my eyes deceive me!! You are not, surely not, writing letters to a man?!

Camille Am I not supposed to marry him? Am I not permitted to write a note to my fiancé?

Pluche But my Lord Perdican has only just left! Why in Heaven's name do you have to write him a letter? And listen to her! Her fiancé! Could it be that you are forgetting Jesus?!

Camille Do what I tell you. And see that all is ready for our departure.

Exeunt.

Scene Two

The dining room. The table is being laid.

Enter **Bridaine**.

Bridaine There's no doubt about it. They're going to do it again. They are going to give him the place of honour. This dining chair, which was once my own, on which I have for so long sat on the Baron's right, has fallen into the clutches of the tutor! Oh I am surely the most unfortunate of men! Because of this stupid ass, because of this shameless drunk, I have been exiled to the far end of the table. And what does that mean? That means that the butler will pour the first glass of malmsey into his glass, and when the dishes do eventually come down to my end what will be on them? Lukewarm left-overs. Oh yes! All the choicest morsels will have already been snatched. When what's left of the partridge gets down to me it will no longer be lying on a bed of carrot and cabbage, oh no. Oh holy Catholic Church! That he should yesterday be allotted to this, to my place, yes, that is conceivable. He had just arrived. And it was the first time, at least for a long time, that he had sat at the Baron's table. Lord Jesus! You should have seen the man stuff his face! When the dish at last gets round to me, what will be on it? Nothing but bones and drumsticks! This is an insult I cannot take! Adieu, dear chair. Never again shall I surrender to your arms, besotted with succulence. Adieu, wax sealed bottles; adieu, aroma of exquisitely cooked venison. Adieu, blissful table; adieu, noble dining room. I have said my last grace. I am going to return to my parish. Never again shall I be seen mingling with the guests. I have at least this in common with the mighty Caesar. I prefer to be number

one in the village than to sit at the far end of the table in
Rome!

Exit.

Scene Three

A field in front of a cottage.

Enter **Perdican** *and* **Rosette**.

Perdican Your mother's not at home. Why don't you
come for a walk, Rosette.

Rosette You never stop giving me kisses. Do you
honestly think they're good for me?

Perdican And what ill could they do you? If your mother
was here I wouldn't stop kissing you. Are you not
Camille's sister? So am I not your brother, just as I am a
brother to her?

Rosette Words are words. Kisses are kisses. I'm not a
clever person. I understand that as soon as I try and say
something. Elegant ladies, they know what they're about.
They know what it means if you kiss their right hand
rather than their left hand. Their fathers kiss them on the
forehead. Their brothers kiss them on the cheek. Their
lovers kiss them on the lips. It's different with me.
Everyone kisses me on both cheeks. It upsets me.

Perdican How pretty you are, my child.

Rosette But don't let all that upset you. You look so sad
this morning. Is it because your marriage is not to be?

Perdican The peasants from the village remember how
once they loved me. The dogs in the farmyards and the
trees in the wood remember. But not Camille. Camille has
lost her memory. And when are you to marry, Rosette?

Rosette I'd prefer not to talk of that, if you don't mind.
We could talk of these flowers growing here, of your
horses, of what I'm wearing on my head.

Perdican We shall speak of whatever you wish, Rosette, of whatever passes through your lips without altering that heavenly smile that I respect more than my life.

Kisses her.

Rosette Maybe you respect my smile. But you don't respect my lips. At least that's what it seems to me. But what's this?! Can this be a drop of rain on my hand? The sky is cloudless.

Perdican Forgive me.

Rosette What have I done to make you cry?

Exeunt.

Scene Four

Inside the castle.

Enter **Blazius** *and the* **Baron**.

Blazius Baron, I have something very strange to tell you. Just a moment ago I was in the pantry, I mean, excuse me, in the gallery – I mean what would a man like me be doing in the pantry?! – I was, therefore, as I was saying in the gallery. I had unexpectedly stumbled on a bottle . . . a bottle I mean . . . a carafe of water – I mean what would a bottle be doing in the gallery? – Therefore, as I was saying, I was just having a little glass of wine . . . I mean water as it were to pass the time of day and in so doing I found myself looking out of the window between two vases which seemed to me to be of a modern style although they were imitations of the Etruscan.

Baron Blazius! You have adopted the most extraordinary way of expressing yourself. I can't make head or tail of what you're saying.

Blazius I beg of you, Baron. Just a moment. Listen. I beseech you. I was, as I was saying, looking out of the window. – Please, in Heaven's name, don't lose patience with me, the honour of your family is at stake.

Baron The honour of my family?! Curiouser and curiouser. The honour of my family indeed! May I take this opportunity of informing you, Dr Blazius, that my family is comprised of thirty-seven males and almost as many females, equally distributed between Paris and the provinces.

Blazius Allow me, I beg you, to continue. Thus as I was idly sipping my glass of wine . . . water to titillate a tardy digestion, I saw Sister Pluche run past under the window. And she was out of breath!

Baron Why should she be out of breath, Blazius? This is most unusual.

Blazius And running alongside her, her features red with anger, was your niece, Camille.

Baron Who was the red one? Camille or Pluche?

Blazius Your niece, Baron.

Baron My niece red with anger! Now that is unheard of!! Ah. But. How do you know, Blazius, that the redness was caused by anger? There are thousands of reasons for being red. She . . . for instance . . . had perhaps been chasing butterflies in the flower garden.

Blazius I know little about redness in young girls. Your interpretation is possible. But as she ran she was at the same time shouting: 'Go on! Find him! Do what I have told you! You are an idiot! Do what I say!' And she was giving Sister Pluche little blows on the elbow with the sharp end of her fan, these blows causing Sister Pluche to execute little jumps in the clover!

Baron Jumping in the clover! What next!? And what reply did the governess give, confronted with what I think can only be qualified as this extravagant behaviour on the part of my niece?

Blazius The governess replied in the following fashion: 'I don't want to go! And I didn't find him. He's making love to the village girls. He's courting goose girls. I'm too old to be a go-between, too old to carry billets-doux. Thank God my hands are still pure!' – And as she spoke she took a piece of paper neatly folded into four and she screwed it up.

Baron I am at a loss to comprehend! There is a dense fog in my mind. Why, now why, should Sister Pluche screw up a neatly folded paper as she jumped up and down in the clover?! No. I can't bring myself to believe these monstrous accusations!!

Blazius But, Baron, can't you see? What this all means is crystal clear!!

Baron To be perfectly frank, my friend, no, I can't see. Such behaviour is yes . . . disorderly, but it is as much without reason as it is without excuse!

Blazius This all means that your niece is writing letters to someone in secret!!

Baron I beg your pardon!! Remember of whom you are speaking, Blazius! Weigh your words.

Blazius I would willingly weigh them in the self-same scales that are going to weigh my soul at the Last Judgement. There's nothing untrue in what I've told you. Your niece is writing secret letters!

Baron Think again, my man. This is not possible!

Blazius Then what was the letter she gave to her governess? Why would she be running after her shouting: 'Find him!' Eh? And what was Pluche sulking for?

Baron And . . . to whom might this . . . secret letter have been addressed?

Blazius Aha. Aha. There's the problem, Baron. There's the rub. *Hic jacet lepus.* To whom, indeed, was the secret letter addressed? Could it have been to a young man who makes love to goose girls? Now. A young man who publicly courts a goose girl is liable to be suspected of being no better than a goose boy himself. But. It is unthinkable that your niece, given the education she has received, should be such a goose as to fall for such a young man. So. And this is my conclusion, saving your grace, I don't understand a word of what is going on either.

Baron Oh heaven! This morning my niece declared that she didn't want to marry her cousin Perdican! Could it be that she, too, has fallen for some goose boy?! Let us both go for a moment into the quiet of my study. I have in the last twenty-four hours encountered such turbulence that I find it almost impossible to put my mind in order.

Exeunt.

Scene Five

A fountain in the small wood.

Enter **Perdican** *reading a letter.*

Perdican 'Meet me at midday by the small fountain in the wood.' Now what can this mean? On one hand she says, 'Forgive me. I can't.' She is cruel, proud, heartless, and then . . . this! A rendezvous. If she had just wanted to talk about legacies and wills she would hardly have chosen to meet me at a fountain in a wood. It couldn't be, could it, that there is something coquettish about this note?! This morning when I was walking with Rosette I did think I heard rustling in the brush behind us. At the time I took it to be the quiet pad of a doe. Surely this can't all be part of a plan?

Enter **Camille**.

Camille Good day, cousin. This morning when you left me I thought I noticed, do correct me if I'm wrong, that you were in some way unhappy. You had taken my hand when I didn't want you to. I've now come to ask you to give me yours. This morning I refused you a kiss. Not now. (*She kisses him.*) This morning you also said that you very much wanted us to be friends and to talk as friends. So. Let's sit down here. Let's talk. (*Sitting down.*)

Perdican Was I dreaming this morning? Or am I dreaming now?

Camille You are doubtless perplexed because you have just received a letter from me. Please, don't be. My moods change rapidly. This morning you said something very just. You said: 'As we must say farewell to each other, let us part on good terms.' You don't yet know why we have to say farewell, and I have come here to tell you . . . I am going to be a nun.

Perdican Can this be true? Is it really you, Camille, sitting at the well surrounded by the wild daisies? Just like it used to be!

Camille Yes, Perdican. I am Camille. I have come back to taste life as it used to be. But just for one last quarter of an hour. I must have given you the impression that I was brusque and offhand. That is simply because I have turned my back on the world. But, before taking this final step, I would like to know your opinion. Do you think I'm doing a wise thing in becoming a nun?

Perdican I'm hardly the person to ask. I'd never be a monk!

Camille We have lived apart for the past ten years and in that time you have begun your apprenticeship of life. I know the kind of person you are. I know that, with your intelligence and your sensitivity, you must have learnt a lot in little time. Tell me this. Have you had a lot of affairs?

Perdican What an odd question.

Camille   I would ask you to reply. Without false modesty. And without conceit.

Perdican   Yes. I've had affairs.

Camille   And these women. Did you love them?

Perdican   Deeply.

Camille   And where are they now? Have you any idea?

Perdican   These are very strange questions. What in God's name do you want me to say? I mean. I'm not their brother, am I? Nor their husband. So. Doubtless they've gone where they judged it fit to go.

Camille   There must have been one that you preferred more than the others. How long did you love the one you loved the most?

Perdican   You are a very peculiar girl. What do you want to do? Confess me?

Camille   I simply ask that you do me the honour of replying to my questions with sincerity. You are not a libertine. And I believe that when you love, you must know how to love with integrity. Your qualities have doubtless caused others to love you. And I don't believe that you are the kind of person who would allow himself to be guided by whim. Therefore, please, give me a straight reply.

Perdican   To be honest, I can't remember.

Camille   Have you ever known a man who has only ever loved one woman?

Perdican   Such a man must exist.

Camille   Have you ever been friends with such a man? If so, I'd like to know his name.

Perdican   I can't think of one offhand. But, yes, I do believe that there are men who are capable of loving only once.

Camille A man who is true to himself, how many times can he fall in love?

Perdican What do you want me to do? Get on my knees and pray for forgiveness? Or would you prefer to throw the prayer book at me!?

Camille I am simply seeking enlightenment. I just want to know if I'm doing the right thing in taking the veil. If I was to marry you, then you would have to answer all these questions. You'd have to bare your heart to me, wouldn't you? I respect you, Perdican, and I do believe, because of your education and your character, that you are better than most men. I am distressed that your memory is so bad and that you can't find an answer to my questions. Perhaps if I knew you better, I could be bolder.

Perdican What do you want, Camille? Tell me. And I'll tell you.

Camille I want you to answer the first question I asked you. Am I doing the right thing in going back to the convent?

Perdican No.

Camille Would I do better to marry you?

Perdican Yes.

Camille If the parish priest took a glass of water, blew on it and said: 'The glass of water is now a glass of wine', would you believe him?

Perdican No.

Camille If the same priest blew on you and then turned to me and said: 'Hey presto. He'll love you for the rest of your life', should I believe him?

Perdican Yes. And no.

Camille On the day when I discover that you no longer love me, what would be your advice?

Perdican Take a lover.

Camille And what shall I do when my lover no longer loves me?

Perdican You'll find another one.

Camille And how long does this all go on for?

Perdican Until your hair turns grey. And mine white.

Camille Perdican, do you know what it means to lead a cloistered life? Have you ever spent a day, one whole day sitting on a bench in a nunnery?

Perdican I have. Yes.

Camille I have a friend, no longer a novice like me, who is only just thirty. When she was fifteen she had an income of five hundred thousand pounds. She is the most noble and the most beautiful creature ever to walk God's earth. She was once a peeress of the government and was married to one of the most distinguished men of France. In her character, none of the most noble qualities of mankind had been left undeveloped. She had grown like a young tree nourished by a very special sap. Each bud gave forth a branch. Each branch bore a fruit. Never had love and happiness crowned a more beautiful brow. Her husband was unfaithful to her. She fell for another man. She is dying of despair.

Perdican So?

Camille We share the same cell in the cloister. We have spent whole nights going over her misfortune. And her misfortune has almost become my own. Don't you think that is strange? I don't quite know how it happened. When she spoke of her marriage, when she described the heady joy of the early days, of the peace that ensued, and when she described how all this happiness had flown away . . . When she told me what it was like, of the evenings they spent, together, she sitting by the fire, he with his back turned to her looking out of the window. Not speaking. Their love had tired. All efforts to rekindle the fire merely roused flames of anger. Some dark stranger had slipped between them and had come to inhabit their suffering. When she spoke, I felt as if it was me speaking. When she said: 'Then, at that moment, I was happy', my heart beat fast. When she said: 'Then, at that moment, I cried', tears streamed from my eyes. But there is something you will find even more difficult to believe. I ended up by creating a whole imaginary world for myself. And that lasted four whole years. There'd be no point in trying to explain to you all the soul-searching and introspection that led to this strange state. But what I do want to tell you, the most curious part of this whole thing, is that when I imagined the stories of Louise, and when I lived these stories in my dreams, all the men looked like you.

Perdican   They all looked like me!

Camille   Yes. Of course, they did. What else do you expect? You were the only man I had ever known. And in truth I had loved you, Perdican.

Perdican   How old are you, Camille?

Camille   Eighteen.

Perdican   Carry on. Please. I am listening.

Camille   There are two hundred nuns in our convent. Of that number, a small proportion will never know what life is. And the others are waiting for death. There are those who, like me today, left the convent full of virginal hope. And who returned soon after, aged and despairing. Every day a nun dies in the dormitory. And every day another nun comes to take her place on the horsehair mattress. People from the outside who visit our order admire the calm and the routine. They look closely at the impeccable whiteness of our veil, but they never ask why we always wear them to cover our eyes. What is your opinion of these women, Perdican? Is what they're doing right? Or is it wrong?

Perdican   Search me.

Camille Amongst the sisters there are those who have told me I should remain a virgin. I am pleased to have the opportunity of asking you. What do you think? Do you think such women would have done better to take a lover? And that this is what they should tell me to do?

Perdican Search me.

Camille You gave your word you would reply.

Perdican Yes. But these are not your questions. So I am freed from my promise.

Camille That may be the case. There is possibly something ridiculous in everything I say. Maybe I am just reciting parrot fashion lessons I haven't understood. There is a picture on the wall of the gallery of the castle. It depicts a monk bent over his missal. But in the distance you can just about make out an inn in an Italian landscape, and in front of the inn there's a man dancing. A goatherd. Which of these two men do you most respect?

Perdican Neither. And both. They are both human. One reads and the other dances. What else can you say? Yes. You're right to become a nun.

Camille Just now you said I wasn't.

Perdican Did I? I suppose that's possible.

Camille So you advise me to take the veil?

Perdican So you don't believe in anything?

Camille Look at me, Perdican. Do you really think that someone who believes in nothing can really exist?

Perdican (*standing up*) There's one standing right in front of you. I don't believe in life after death. – Listen, my dear sweet sister, the nuns have fed you their experience of life, but theirs will not be yours. You won't die without having loved.

Camille I want to love. But I don't want to suffer. I want a love that will never end. I want to make a pledge that can never be broken. Look. Here is my lover. (*She shows him her crucifix.*)

Perdican   He's the one lover you can have at the same time as someone else.

Camille   That's not the way I see it. This love is all-exclusive. Don't smile, Perdican. I haven't seen you for the last ten years and tomorrow I shall be leaving. In another ten years' time, if we should meet, we'll talk again. It's just that I didn't want to live on in your memory as someone who was as cold as a statue, because there are those who are as I am merely because they are insensitive. Listen. Return to live the life you have been living and as long as you can still love as people do in the world, then do it. And forget your sister Camille. But if ever you are betrayed, or if ever you catch yourself betraying someone, if the angel of hope deserts you and you are alone with the emptiness that fills your heart, think of me. Who is praying for you.

Perdican   You are a very proud person, Camille. Tread carefully.

Camille   Why?

Perdican   You are eighteen. And you don't believe in love!

Camille   And you? Do you? You who are talking to me now. Look at you. Bending in front of me on knees worn thin on the mats of mistresses whose name you can't even remember. Oh yes, you may have cried tears of joy and tears of despair. But you know full well that the water of the spring is more fresh and more constant than your tears, and that it will always be there to soothe your red swollen eyes. You are just playing your part. You're doing what young men do. You give a worldly smile when we talk of abandoned women. You who have lived and loved, you can't imagine it is still possible to die for love. What kind of place is this world we live in? It seems to me that you wholeheartedly despise those women who take you as you are, who dispose of the preceding lover just so as to entice you into their arms, your own mouth still warm with another's kisses. Just now I asked you if you had ever loved. And you replied as if you were a traveller who'd been asked if he'd ever been to Italy or Germany, and who'd reply: 'Oh, yes. I've been there', and then who'd suddenly be taken with a desire to . . . go to . . . Switzerland, or somewhere else, to the first . . . country that came to mind. What is this love? Is it like money? Because it seems to pass so readily from hand to hand until the day you die. No. I'm wrong. Money is not the right word. Because a coin, even the thinnest gold coin, however much it goes from palm to palm, still conserves the one effigy it has always carried. And is therefore of more worth than you.

Perdican   You are so beautiful, Camille, when there's fire in your eyes.

Camille   Yes. I am beautiful. I know it. Flatterers can teach me nothing. The cold nun who will cut my hair will blanch and hesitate to mutilate. But this hair will never be cut to be made into bracelets and chains to be flaunted in boudoirs by lovers. When the knife does come to cut, I shall never before have parted with a lock. And I want it cut in one piece. The hair I give the priest, who will bless me as he puts on my finger the ring binding me to my celestial husband, will be as long as a mantle.

Perdican   You are indeed full of anger.

Camille   I was wrong to speak. I am spilling out my life. Oh, Perdican! Don't mock me. All this is so sad, I could die.

Perdican   Poor child. I let you speak on and on. But I want to reply. Just a word. You spoke of a nun who seems to have had a dark influence on you. You told me that she had been deceived, that she in turn had been unfaithful, and that she is now in despair. Do you think that if her husband or lover returned to stretch out a hand through

the bars of the parlour, do you think she in turn would
not stretch out and take the hand?

Camille What are you trying to tell me? Perhaps I haven't
understood.

Perdican If her husband or her lover came back and
offered her the chance of suffering again, do you think
she'd say no?

Camille I think she would.

Perdican There are two hundred women in your
nunnery. Most of them carry wounds, deep in their heart.
And they have stained your virgin's mind with the blood
of their pain. They've lived, haven't they. Oh yes!
They've been through it. And they have told you with
horror of the road they took. And you have crossed
yourself before their scars, as if these were the wounds of
the body of Jesus. And then they all moved up and made a
place for you in their dark procession. From then on,
whenever you see a man pass, you are filled with holy fear
and you press yourself tight in against their fleshless
bodies for protection. But are you so certain that if the
man who passes by were the man who had deceived them,
the one for whom they cry and suffer, the one they curse
as they pray to God, are you really so certain that when
they see him again, that they're not going to break their
chains and run back to embrace their miserable past, to
thrust their breasts up against the knife that once cut into
them? Oh, my child! Do you know what they dream of,
these women who tell you not to dream? Have you heard
the name they whisper when their sob makes the host
tremble in the priest's fingers? These women who perch
next to you with their nodding heads and who pour into
your ear their dank withered bile, these women who sound
the bell of despair in the ruins of your youth, who freeze
your red blood with the chill of the tomb, do you know
who they are, these women?

Camille You are making me frightened. You are also
angry.

Perdican Poor girl, do you know what they are, these nuns? They who tell you that a man's love can never be anything but a lie. Don't they know that there is something worse, which is the lie of divine love? Don't they know that they're guilty of whispering women's words in a virgin's ear. Oh, they've taught you so well! I knew it, I felt it when you stopped to admire the painting of that old aunt of ours. And you wanted to leave without even shaking my hand. You didn't want to see these woods again. You didn't want to see this poor little fountain which now looks at us, crying its tears. You said no to the happy days of your childhood and the plaster death-mask the nuns put on your cheeks even turned away from a brotherly kiss. But then suddenly your heart beat. Your heart forgot its lesson because hearts can't read lessons. And you came back to sit here. On the grass with me. So, Camille. These women have said their say. They have put you well and truly on the straight and narrow. They may have robbed me of the only happiness I would ever have known. But tell them this from Perdican. Heaven is not for them.

Camille Nor for me. Is that what you mean?

Perdican Farewell, Camille. Go back to your nunnery. And when they tell you even more frightening stories, of the kind that have already poisoned your mind, tell them this. They're right. All men are liars. They are unfaithful, false, glib, hypocritical, proud, cowardly, despicable and sensual. All women are treacherous, deceitful, vain, nosy and depraved. The world is a bottomless pit, a sewer in which twisted, shiny seals crawl and writhe on mountains of slime. But there is in this world one thing which is both holy and sublime. That is the union of two of these beings, however imperfect, however appalling. When you are in love, you often get things wrong, you are often hurt, often unhappy. But you love. And when you finally arrive on the brink of your tomb, you can turn around and look back and you can say, 'Yes. I have suffered. Often. I have got things wrong. Often. But I have loved. And it is

I who have lived my life. Not some artificial being, not
some puppet fashioned out of boredom and pride.'

Exit.

Act Three

Scene One

In front of the castle.

Enter the **Baron** *and* **Blazius**.

Baron You are, Dr Blazius, and this quite apart from your drunkenness, a complete and utter good-for-nothing. You have been seen by my servants tip-toeing into the pantry. But, but when you are accused of stealing my wine, what do you do? You seek to justify yourself in the most despicable of fashions by accusing my daughter of carrying on a secret correspondence.

Blazius But, my Lord, sir, would you please remember . . .

Baron Out of my sight, Father. May I never see the likes of you again. Your behaviour is utterly unreasonable and the gravity, of which my person is the very incarnation, excludes all possibility of pardon.

Exit, followed by **Blazius**. *Enter* **Perdican**.

Perdican I would very much like to know whether or not I am in love. On the one hand, her way of asking questions is decidedly forward for a girl of eighteen. On the other hand, the ideas which those nuns have implanted in her mind would be difficult to weed out. To make matters worse she is leaving this very day! To hell with it. I love her. For sure. And who knows? Perhaps she was just repeating to me a lesson she'd learned off by heart. But it is, by the same token, equally clear that she is not in the least interested in me. On the other hand, however beautiful she may be, she's also far too bigoted and aggressive. Listening to myself, I'd say I didn't love her after all. It's true that she is pretty . . . But why can't I get that conversation we had yesterday out of my mind? To tell the truth, I spent the whole night talking gibberish to myself. – Where was I going? – Oh yes. To the village.

Exit.

Scene Two

A path.

Enter **Bridaine**.

Bridaine What would they be doing now? Oh no . . . it's midday! Alas! – They're about to sit down to eat. And what's on the menu today? What isn't, you might just as well ask! I saw the cook walking through the village with a huge turkey under her arm. And her assistant came along behind her, with the muscatel grapes in one basket and the truffles in the other.

Enter **Blazius**.

Blazius Oh, ignominy! Oh, unexpected disgrace! Expelled from the castle! Hence, QED, dismissed from the dining table. Never again shall I drink the wine in the pantry . . .

Bridaine Never again shall I see the vapour rising from the steaming victuals. Never again shall I warm my delicious, replete stomach in front of the noble fire.

Blazius A curse on the curiosity that led me to eavesdrop on the conversation between Pluche and her niece! Why, oh why, did I go and tell the Baron everything I had overheard?

Bridaine Why was I so proud? They were so good to me! I should still be there at my rightful place at the noble table. What does it matter if you are sitting on the right or on the left?!

Blazius Alas! It must be said, when I committed this act of gross folly, I was a little tipsy.

Bridaine Alas! When I made this dreadful blunder, I was a little merry.

Blazius But . . . Do my eyes deceive me? The curate! In person.

Bridaine If it isn't the tutor! In person.

Blazius Good day, Reverend Bridaine. And what would you be doing here?

Bridaine I was just off to table. Will you not accompany me?

Blazius Not today, Reverend Bridaine. Alas, the Baron has banned me from the banquet! Intercede on my behalf, I beg of you. I falsely accused his niece, Camille, of writing secret letters to someone . . . but God will be my witness, I saw, well at least I think I saw, Sister Pluche jumping in the clover. I am a lost man, dear Reverend. Finished!

Bridaine What is this all about?

Blazius I am telling you nothing but the simple truth. I am in the deepest bad odour. Because I purloined a bottle.

Bridaine I can't make head or tail of all this? Purloined bottles? Secret letters? Jumping in the clover?

Blazius All that I ask is that you say a word in my favour. I am an honest man, most Reverend Bridaine. Oh, most worthy Bridaine. I would be ever in your debt.

Bridaine (*aside*) Oh, gracious fortune, is this a dream?! I shall once again be sitting on you oh, happy chair!

Blazius I would be so acutely grateful if you would listen to my story and then give me your absolution, my dearest Reverend, my dearest friend and priest.

Bridaine That I cannot, sir. The clock has struck twelve and I must off to dine. If the Baron is displeased with you that is none of my doing. And it is not for me to intervene on the part of a drunkard. (*Aside.*) Quick. Off to the beautiful wrought iron gate. And you my beloved girth, swell, swell in anticipation.

He runs off.

Blazius (*alone*) Oh, blasted Pluche. You shall pay for this! It is you who are the cause of all this woe, you are the cause of my ruin, shameless woman, base harlot, pimpess, vile madam. I lay my disgrace at your feet. Oh, Holy University of Paris. To be accused of being a drunkard! A sot. I am lost, I am washed up! Unless . . . I can get my hands on a letter which would prove to the Baron that his niece was writing them after all. And this morning I did see her pen in hand at her desk . . . One moment. Take it easy. What have we here?

Sister Pluche *hurries by carrying a letter.*

Blazius Pluche, give me that letter.

Pluche What do you mean!? This letter was written by my mistress and I am off to post it in the village.

Blazius Hand it over. Or I'll kill you.

Pluche Kill me! Oh! Jesus and Mary! Oh! Virgins and martyrs! Kill me!

Blazius Yes, kill you to death, Pluche. Give me that missive.

They fight. Enter **Perdican**.

Perdican Now what's this? What are you doing, Blazius? Why are you attacking this woman?

Pluche Give me my letter back. He's stolen it from me, my Lord! I demand justice!

Blazius She's a go-between, my Lord. This is no ordinary letter. This is a love letter!

Pluche This letter, my Lord, is written by Camille, your fiancée.

Blazius It's a love letter written to a goose boy, that's what it is!

Pluche You're a liar, you dirty abbot!!

Perdican Give me the letter. I can't make head or tail of what you're talking about. But, because I am, as you say, Camille's fiancé, I grant myself the right to read it. (*He reads.*) 'To Sister Louise.' (*Stops.*) Her friend at the convent. (*Aside.*) What is this odd curiosity that has suddenly taken hold of me? My heart is beating fast. I don't understand these feelings. Please, leave me, Sister Pluche. You are a very worthy woman and the Reverend Blazius is an idiot. Go to dinner. I'll take the letter to the post.

Blazius *and* **Pluche** *leave.*

Perdican (*alone*) It is wrong to open a letter addressed to someone else. I know that. And I'm not going to open it. What can Camille be writing in a letter to Sister Louise? Could it be that I am in love? Has this strange girl some power over me? I hold this envelope in my hand. It's got three simple words written on it. And my hand shakes! How odd! During his scrap with Sister Pluche, Blazius must somehow have broken the seal. Unsealing would be a crime . . . but unfolding . . . Anyway . . . What difference does it make? (*He opens the letter and reads it.*)

> 'My dearest, I am leaving today. Everything has gone as I predicted it would. It is very sad. This young man will henceforth walk abroad with the pain of a dagger in his heart. I did everything in my power to make myself unattractive. God, I trust, will forgive me both for having refused and for having caused so much despair in consequence. Alas, my dearest, what else could I do? Pray for me. We shall be together at last tomorrow, and for always. I send you my most heartfelt greetings. Camille.'

It's not possible! Camille wrote this?! And she's speaking about me! Me? In despair at her refusal?! Good God, if that were true everyone would be able to see it! What shame is there in loving? She did all she could to make herself unattractive, she says, and I am going about with a knife through my heart! What can be the point of making up this kind of story? Can it, could it be that the thought that struck me last night is indeed true? What are women? This poor little Camille, who may be truly pious, who may sincerely surrender herself to God, has nonetheless decided and decreed that she was going to drive me to despair! This was the plan hatched by these two bosom friends even before she left the convent to come back home. A plot! 'I'm going to see my cousin again. They're going to want me to marry him. I'm going to say no and the cousin is going to be heartbroken.' This is so exciting. A young girl sacrifices to God the happiness of a young man! No, Camille. You've got it wrong. I am not in love with you. I have no dagger in my heart. And I am going to prove it to you. When you leave, you are going to leave with the knowledge that I love someone else. Here! My man!

Enter a **Peasant**.

Perdican Go to the castle. Go to the kitchens and tell them to deliver this note to Mademoiselle Camille.

He writes it.

Peasant Yes, sir.

Exit.

Perdican And now for the other. I'm in despair! Rosette! Rosette!

He knocks at the door.

Rosette (*opening the door*) Oh. It's you, sir. Come in if you want. My mother's at home.

Perdican Put your prettiest bonnet on, Rosette. You're coming with me!

Rosette Where to, sir?

Perdican You'll see. You can ask your mother's permission if you want. But don't be long.

Rosette Yes, sir.

She goes back into the house.

Perdican I have written to Camille proposing another rendezvous. I'm sure she'll come. But, by God, when she does come she won't find what she expects to find. I am going to make love to Rosette. And before her very eyes. That's what she's going to find.

Scene Three

In the small wood.

Enter **Camille** *and the* **Peasant**.

Peasant Miss . . . I was on my way to the castle to deliver this letter. Do you think I should give it to you now, or shall I take it to the kitchens like Mr Perdican said I was to?

Camille Give it to me.

Peasant But if you'd prefer me to take it to the castle, then there's no point in me losing time dallying, is there?

Camille I said, 'Give it to me.'

Peasant As you like, Miss.

He gives her the letter.

Camille And take this. For your trouble.

Peasant God bless you. I should go now, shouldn't I?

Camille Do as you like.

Peasant I'm off. I'm off.

Exit.

Camille (*reading*) Perdican begs me to come and say farewell before I leave. At the small fountain in the wood where I asked him to meet me yesterday. What can he have to say to me? But here is the fountain. My feet have brought me here without me realizing. Should I or shouldn't I see him a second time? Ah! (*She hides behind a tree.*) Here is Perdican. He's coming along the path with my foster-sister, Rosette. I suppose they are going to take leave of each other here. I'm pleased that he hasn't seen that I was the first to arrive.

Enter **Perdican** *and* **Rosette**. *They sit down.*

Camille (*hidden, aside*) But what are they doing? What does this mean? He asks her to sit down beside him. Can it be that he has arranged a rendezvous with me only to spend his time talking to someone else? I'll be most interested to hear what he has to say to her.

Perdican (*in a voice loud enough for* **Camille** *to hear what he is saying*) I love you, Rosette. You alone in the world have not forgotten the wonderful days of our childhood. You alone can remember this world which sadly is no more. I want you to share my new life. Give me your heart, dear child. And accept this, a token of our love.

He puts a golden chain around her neck.

Rosette You are giving me your gold chain?

Perdican Now I want you to look carefully at this ring. Come closer to the fountain. Look at the still spring water. Can you see our reflection as we lean close into each other? Can you see your beautiful eyes looking into mine? Can you see your hand in mine? Now watch all that disappear. (*He throws the ring in the water.*) Look at the water. See. We've gone. But the image will return. The troubled water will become calm again. The surface is still trembling. Big black circles open and move over it. Be patient. We shall reappear. Already I can see your arms in mine. If we wait another minute there will no longer be even the shade of a ripple on your pretty face. See. That was a ring Camille gave me.

Camille (*aside*) He threw my ring in the water.

Perdican Do you know what love is, Rosette?
isten. Ssshhhh. The wind dies down. The morning rain rolls like polished pearls down the drying leaves as the sun warms them and brings them to life. I swear by the light of the sky, I swear by the sun which begins to shine, that I love you. You do want me, don't you, Rosette? Your youth is still intact, isn't it, Rosette? You have not been infected by bad blood. Yours is still ruby red. You have no desire to be a nun, have you, Rosette? No. You long to be young, to be beautiful, to be in the arms of a young man. O, Rosette. Rosette. Do you know what love is?

Rosette Alas, sir, you are so clever, I can only love you in my own way.

Perdican In your own way. That is enough for me. And you will love me better, however clever I may be, and however simple you may be, than I would ever have been loved by those pale effigies manufactured in convents by nuns, who have their head where their heart should be and who only open their cloister doors to poison life with the dank, rancid odour of their cells. You know nothing, Rosette. You wouldn't know how to read the prayer your mother teaches you just as her mother taught her. You don't even understand the sense of the words you repeat off by heart when you kneel at the foot of your bed. All you know is that you are praying. God asks no more of you.

Rosette You speak to me in such a way, sir.

Perdican You don't know how to read. But you know what the woods say. You understand the fields, the warm waters of the rivers, these lush harvest fields, the world of nature is so fresh and so wonderful. We are, all of us, linked in brotherhood, and in me you see a brother amongst brothers. Stand, Rosette. You shall be my wife and we shall grow like a tree planted here, full of the sap, full of the vital juice of the world.

Exit with **Rosette**.

Scene Four

Enter **Chorus**.

Chorus Something strange indeed is happening at the castle. Camille has said no to Perdican. She won't marry him. She is today supposed to return to the convent where she came from. But I've heard that her noble cousin has turned to Rosette for consolation. Alas! The poor innocent girl doesn't know the danger she is running if she begins to listen to the love talk of such a gallant.

Pluche (*entering*) Fast. Pleb! Quick. Saddle my ass!

Chorus So soon, O venerable sister! Can it be that you will merely pass in our life like some light, fleeting dream? Are you once again to straddle this poor beast who already looks down in the mouth at the thought of having you once again up on his back!

Pluche Mercy! I have no intention of staying here until I die! Serf!

Chorus Then die a long way away, beloved Pluche. Die a lonely death in a festering tomb. We will dutifully pray for your resurrection.

Pluche My mistress is approaching.

Camille *enters*.

Pluche Dear Camille, all is ready for our prompt departure. The Baron has completed his arithmetic and the ass is saddled.

Camille Go to hell. Both of you. You and the ass. I shan't be leaving today.

Exits.

Chorus And what does all this forebode? Sister Pluche is terrified and has gone white as a shroud. Her hair piece tries to stand up on her head, her chest wheezes and whistles and her clenched crabbed fingers seem to get even longer.

Pluche Jesus wept! Camille swore!

Exit.

Scene Five

*Enter the **Baron** and **Bridaine**.*

Bridaine Pssssstttt! My Lord, I just must have a private word in your ear. Your son has been running after a village girl.

Baron Poppycock, my friend.

Bridaine I saw him distinctly and with my own eyes! They were together arm in arm in the heather. He was leaning towards her and whispering in her ear that he promised to marry her.

Baron This is monstrous.

Bridaine And if you want living proof of it: he has given her a present. A very considerable present. That the girl has taken home to show to her mother.

Baron Oh heavens! And when you say considerable, Bridaine. How considerable is considerable?

Bridaine It means that it weighs a considerable amount and will be of considerable importance. He gave her the gold chain he used to wear around his hat.

Baron Step into my study. I no longer know who, what, when or where to believe.

Exeunt.

Scene Six

Camille's *room.*

Enter **Camille** *and* **Pluche.**

Camille Let's get this straight. You say he took my letter.

Pluche He did, my child. And he said that he was going to take it to the post.

Camille Please, be so good, dear Sister Pluche, as to go to the hall and inform Perdican that I am waiting for him here in my room.

Exit **Pluche.**

Camille So he had read my letter. That's for sure. The little scene in the wood was nothing but vengeance. His love for Rosette is nothing more than that! He just wanted to show me that he could love someone else, act the indifferent. To hide his hurt. So could it be that he is in love with me after all? (*She lifts the tapestry.*) Rosette, are you there?

Rosette (*entering*) Yes. May I come in?

Camille Listen, my child. Has Perdican been paying court to you?

Rosette Alas. Yes.

Camille And what do you think of what he told you this morning?

Rosette This morning? This morning, where?

Camille Don't play games, Rosette. – This morning, at the fountain, in the small wood.

Rosette You saw me there?

Camille No, I didn't see you. I'm just guessing, that's all. He told you a lot of wonderful things, didn't he, poor innocent child? I bet he even promised that he would marry you.

Rosette How do you know that?

Camille What does it matter how I know. Do you believe these words and promises, Rosette?

Rosette Why shouldn't I believe them? Why would he deceive me? What would be the point?

Camille Perdican is never going to marry you, my child!

Rosette Alas. I don't know what to think.

Camille Poor girl. You love him. But he will never marry you. And I am about to give you the proof. Stay hidden behind this tapestry curtain. And just listen. That's all you have to do. And then come out when I give you a signal.

Exit **Rosette**.

Camille (*alone*) I thought I was driven by vengeance. But perhaps on second thoughts this is a mercy mission. The poor thing is smitten.

Enter **Perdican**.

Camille Good day, cousin.

Perdican What a stunning dress, Camille! Have you got it in for someone?

Camille For you perhaps. Perhaps I am angry not to have been able to keep the rendezvous you wanted with me. You wished to tell me something?

Perdican (*aside*) This is, upon my life, a very big lie coming from the mouth of so immaculate a lamb! Because I saw her, hiding behind a tree, listening to every word we said. (*Aloud*.) All I had to say was: farewell, Camille. I thought that you were leaving. But I see that your horse is still in the stable. And that is hardly a dress suitable for travelling back to a convent.

Camille I enjoy conversation. I am not even sure that I wasn't taken with the desire to have one last little row with you.

Perdican What's the point of rowing? When we can never kiss and make up. The pleasure of argument is in the making up.

Camille And are you really so certain that I don't want to make up?

Perdican Please. Don't mock. I am not strong enough to reply.

Camille I am even in the mood for someone to make love to me. I don't know why. Maybe it's just because I'm wearing a new dress. I'd like to have a good time. Once you asked me to go down to the village. Let's go. I feel like it. Let's go out in the boat. Let's eat on the grass and idle in the forest. Will there be a moon tonight? That's odd. You're not wearing the ring I gave you.

Perdican I've mislaid it.

Camille That explains why I found it. Here, Perdican. You can put it on again.

Perdican But this is not possible?! Where did you find it?

Camille You're looking at my hands to see if they're wet, aren't you? I'll tell you the truth. I dirtied my convent dress when I was fishing this trinket out of the fountain. That's why I had to change into this one and, I can tell you, I changed my mood with my dress. Put the ring back on.

Perdican You got this ring out of the water?! You, Camille, you leant over! You risked falling in! I must pinch myself to see if I am awake. But no. There you are.

Putting the ring back on my finger. Oh Camille, tell me. Why are you giving it back to me? It is nothing more than the sad reminder of a happiness that once was. Tell me, daring Camille, flirtatious Camille, why are you not leaving? Why are you still here? Why do you change from one hour to the next? You're like the stone in this ring. Your colour changes every time the sun catches you.

Camille Perdican, what do you know of a woman's heart? Are you really so sure of their inconstancy? Does their heart really change that quickly? Is it not just their words that change? There are people who believe that. Often we do play a part. We have to. Often we do tell lies. We have to. You see, Perdican. I'm not hiding anything from you. But are you really so sure that everything is false in a woman? Could it not be that it is only her tongue that is false? Have you really thought about the nature of this . . . creature. She is weak and violent. She is always judged according to the most exacting moral code. She is always bound by the strictest principles. And who knows, maybe if she is forced to cheat, because of the way things are, perhaps this brainless little thing suddenly begins to enjoy it, and begins sometimes to lie, just to pass the time of day. More out of madness than because of any necessity.

Perdican I don't understand a word you are saying. I never lie. I love you, Camille. That's all I know.

Camille You say you love me. And that you never tell lies.

Perdican Never.

Camille Yet here is someone who says that sometimes you do.

She lifts the tapestry curtain. **Rosette** *can be seen behind it. She is on a chair. Lifeless.*

Camille What are you going to tell Rosette, Perdican, when she asks you to explain what you told her? If you never lie, how can you explain that she fainted when she heard you tell me that you loved me. I am going to leave you with her. Try and . . . bring her round.

She goes to leave.

Perdican Just a minute. Camille. Please. Listen to me.

Camille What can you have to say to me? You must talk to Rosette. It's not me who loves you. It wasn't me who went to fish this poor young girl out from the safety of her cottage so that she could serve as a toy, or as bait. It wasn't me who repeated to her those hot and imprudent words that were destined for another. I didn't pretend to throw to the winds the memory of a much cherished friendship. I didn't put my chain around her neck. I didn't say that I would marry her.

Perdican Listen to me. Listen to me.

Camille Just now when I told you that I was unable to keep the appointment at the fountain, you smiled. Didn't you? You were right to. I was there. I did hear everything. But, and God is my witness, I would not want to be the person who spoke as you spoke at the fountain. What are you going to do with Rosette now? Now that she has your kisses burnt onto her lips. What are you going to say when she comes to show you the wound you inflicted? You wanted to take vengeance on me, didn't you? You wanted to punish me for a letter I had written to the convent. You just had to throw something sharp at me, anything that would hurt, and you didn't care if the dart and its poison, on its way to me, had to cut through the body of this child. I had boasted in my letter that I had inspired a feeling of love in you. And that I left you and that you regretted my leaving. Your pride, your noble pride was wounded. Well, Perdican. Learn it from my mouth. It's clear. You love me. Do you understand? But you will marry the other girl. If you don't, you are worthless.

Perdican I am going to marry her.

Camille Excellent!

Perdican And in so doing I shall be doing something better, much better, than if I were to marry you. What's got you so worked up, Camille? Rosette has passed out. That's all. We'll bring her round. That's all. Vinegar under the nose will do it. You wanted to prove to me that at least once in my life I had lied. I'm sure you're right. Only I am far less certain than you as to when I lied. Give me a hand with Rosette, will you?

Exeunt.

Scene Seven

Enter the **Baron** *and* **Camille**.

Baron If that should happen, I'd go quite stark staring mad.

Camille Then do something about it. Use your authority.

Baron I'll go quite round the bend. And I'd refuse to give my blessing. That's what I'd do.

Camille It might be a better idea to have a word with him. Try and make him see reason.

Baron If I did that, the whole business would throw me into such a fit of depression that I'd shut myself away for the whole duration of the carnival and I wouldn't once be seen at court. I mean such a marriage would be . . . wholly disproportionate! It is quite unheard of. To marry one's cousin's foster-sister. That is quite and utterly beyond the pale.

Camille Then call him here. Tell him straight out: 'Sir, I don't like or want this marriage.' Believe me. He's doing it on some crazy impulse. He won't offer any resistance.

Baron I shall be wearing black this winter, you'll see.

Camille In the name of Heaven! Talk to him, won't you? He doesn't know why he's doing what he's doing. But be

quick about it. If he has made up his mind to do
something, he'll do it.

Baron I am going to lock myself away in a room and
surrender to my grief. If he wants to see me, tell him that
I've locked myself away in a room in order to surrender to
grief occasioned by the fact that he is marrying a girl who
does not belong to a noble family.

Exit.

Camille Is there no one in this place with any courage?
When you look around, when you need help . . . There's
no one. You are horribly alone.

Enter **Perdican**.

Camille Well, cousin? Have you fixed the date?

Perdican We shall marry as quickly as possible. I've
already spoken to the notary, to the priest and to the
village.

Camille So you really mean to marry Rosette?

Perdican Of course, I do.

Camille And what will your father say?

Perdican He can say whatever he likes. I like the idea of
marrying Rosette. It was your idea, it was a good one and
I'm going to stick to it. Thank you. Is it really necessary
to go through the old arguments about the disparity
between her station and my station? She is young. She is
pretty. She is in love with me. That's more than enough to
make for happiness. Maybe she's clever, maybe she's
witless, I could do much worse . . . People will get cross.
Wring hands. Shed tears. Shout. I couldn't give a damn.

Camille But no one's saying that there's anything odd in
all this. You are doing the right thing. Only one thing irks
me personally: people will say you turned to her because
you'd been turned down elsewhere.

Perdican Quite honestly I don't believe that that irks you in the least.

Camille I promise you. It really does trouble me. People don't have a good opinion of a young man if they think that he is weak enough to do things out of spite.

Perdican Then you'll just have to be troubled, won't you? Because I told you: I don't care.

Camille But you don't know what you're doing! This girl is nothing.

Perdican Then she'll soon be something, won't she? Because she'll soon be my wife.

Camille You'll be tired of her even before the notary has had time to get into his new suit and shoes and get on up here. You'll be sick at the wedding banquet and, like in Arab tales, at the ball you'll have her hands and feet cut off because she smells of stewed lamb.

Perdican I don't think I will. You've got me wrong. When a woman is sweet, sensitive, fresh, good, and beautiful, that is quite enough for me. I am not in the least concerned whether or not she has mastered Latin.

Camille Then what was the point of you learning it. How much did it cost, your education? Three thousand écus? What a waste!

Perdican In that I agree with you. They would have done better to distribute the money among the poor and needy.

Camille But that's precisely what you are about to do now. At least, that is, amongst the poor and the simple-minded.

Perdican Blessed are the poor for theirs is the Kingdom of Heaven and so it shall be mine as well.

Camille How long is this joke going to last?

Perdican What joke?

Camille Your marriage with Rosette.

Perdican Not long. Man is ephemeral. It is God's will. It can only last thirty or forty years at the most.

Camille What a novel experience it will be, to dance at your wedding.

Perdican Listen, Camille. Stop being clever and witty. It's pointless.

Camille Is it? I like it. I'm not going to stop.

Perdican In that case I am going to stop being here. I think I've had enough.

Camille Perhaps you are going to run back to your intended?

Perdican I am. Yes. I am going to see her in person. Now.

Camille Then give me your arm. I'm coming too.

Enter **Rosette**.

Perdican There you are my child! Come. I want to present you to my father.

Rosette (*on her knees*) Sir, I have come to beg this favour of you. Everybody I spoke to in the village this morning told me that you loved your cousin, and that you've been paying court to me simply because it was a game for both of you. People laugh when I go by and I'd never find a husband hereabouts now because I've become the laughing stock. Allow me to return the necklace you gave me this morning and to go back to my mother, and to live alone in peace.

Camille You are a sensible girl, Rosette. You have a good heart. Keep the necklace. I give it to you. My cousin can have mine in return. As for finding a husband, don't you worry your little head. I'll see to that.

Perdican You're right there. There's nothing easier than that. Come, Rosette. I am going to take you to my father.

Camille But why? What's the point?

Perdican   You're right again. He's not in a mood to see us now. Let him get over the first shock. Come. We'll go down to the village. I find it most amusing that people say I don't love you, when we are about to be married. I think we can put a stop to the gossip.

Exit with **Rosette**.

Camille   What is happening to me? He leads her away on his arm. He looks so calm. This is so strange. I feel giddy. Could it be that he is actually gong to marry her for real? Pluche! Sister Pluche! Can one get no service in this place?

Enter a **Servant**.

Camille   Go quickly! Run and catch up with Lord Perdican and tell him to come back up here. I've got something to tell him.

Exit the **Servant**.

Camille   But what is happening? I can't stand anymore, my legs won't support me.

Perdican *returns*.

Perdican   You called for me, Camille?

Camille   No, – no.

Perdican   You look so white. What did you want to tell me? You did call me back to tell me something, didn't you?

Camille   No. No. – Oh, Lord God!

Exits.

Scene Eight

An oratory.

Enter **Camille**. *She throws herself at the foot of the altar.*

Camille Oh, Lord, why hast Thou forsaken me? Only You know that when I came to this place I had sworn to remain faithful to You. When I refused to become the bride of another I did think I was speaking honestly before You and before my conscience. Only You know this, my Lord. Why, then, do You want me no more? Why do You make everything lie, even truth itself? Why am I so weak? I am a poor forsaken wretch. Oh, woe! I can't even pray any more!

Enter **Perdican**.

Perdican Pride, that most dangerous of counsellors, why have you come between this girl and me? Look at her. Look. Pale as death. Terrified. Lying on the flagstones pressing her cheek and her heart into the cold floor. She could have loved me. We were born to love one another. What were you doing on our lips, pride, when our hearts were poised to join?

Camille Who has followed me? Who is speaking out loud in the vault? Perdican! Is that you?

Perdican We have taken leave of our senses! We love each other, Camille. What is this dream we are living? What vain words, what black fancies have blown between us like a bad wind? Which one of us wanted to deceive the other? You or me? Alas, the life we live is no more than a painful, arduous dream. Why should we try and make it even worse? Oh Lord, happiness is a rare pearl indeed in the oceans in which you have cast us. But you heaved this priceless jewel from the depths of the bottomless pit in your celestial net, and you made us a present of it. But we, spoilt children that we are, turn the pearl into a dangerous toy. Between us, leading from one to the other, there used to be a path, and on the gentle green slope of the path there were bushes and flowers and the path led up to a peaceful welcoming horizon. But vanity, anger and idle words came to pit this path with stones, to make the heavenly road, which leads to your embrace, broken and unpassable. We had to do wrong. Because we are human and that's what human's do. We have taken leave of our senses. We love each other.

He takes her in his arms.

Camille   Yes, Perdican. We do love each other. Let me feel your heart against mine. God, who looks down upon us, will not take offence. God wants Camille to love Perdican. For the last fifteen years He has wanted it.

Perdican   Dearest Camille. At last you are mine.

They kiss. There is a cry from behind the altar.

Camille   That was the voice of my foster-sister!

Perdican   What can she be doing here? I left her on the stairs when you sent for me. She must have followed me here without me seeing!

Camille   The cry came from along this gallery. Follow me.

Perdican   I am suddenly gripped by an awful premonition. It is as if my hands were covered in blood.

Camille   The poor girl must have spied on us. She must have fainted again. We must help her. Quickly! This is all so cruel!

Perdican   No. I will not come with you. I am seized by a deathly cold. It's as if I can't move. Go, Camille. Please, go. Please, bring her round.

Exit **Camille**.

Perdican   I beg of you, oh God. Do not make a murderer of me. You see what is happening. We are just two children. We don't know what we are doing. We have been playing at life and death. But our hearts are pure. Please, God, do not kill Rosette. God of justice, I beg of you. I will find her a husband. I shall repair my fault. She is young. She will be rich. She will be happy. Please, God.

Don't do it. Please. It's not too late. You can still smile down on four of your children. Camille. Tell me.

Camille *returns.*

Camille She is dead. Adieu, Perdican!

Caprice

Un Caprice (15 June 1837)

translated by DONALD WATSON

Characters

Monsieur de Chavigny
Mathilde, *his wife*
Madame de Léry
Servant

Setting: Mathilde's bedroom.

This translation was performed at the Yvonne Arnaud
Theatre, Guildford, in June 1968, in a double bill with
Eugène Ionesco's *Frenzy for Two* (*Délire à deux*) under the
title *Teacups and Handgrenades*.

Scene One

Mathilde, *alone at her needlework.*

Mathilde One more stitch, and I have finished.

She rings. Enter a **Servant.**

Mathilde Have they sent from Janisset yet?

Servant No, Madame. Not yet.

Mathilde It's disgraceful. Go back to the shop again. And hurry!

Exit the **Servant.**

Mathilde I should have taken the first tassels I saw. It is eight o'clock. He must be dressing now. I am sure he will be here before it's all ready. And that will make another day gone. (*She gets up.*) To be making a purse in secret for one's husband would appear to some excessively romantic. After a whole year of marriage! What, for example, would Madame de Léry say? And what will he think? He may laugh at all the mystery, but not at the gift. Why all this mystery, in fact? I do not know. But I doubt I could have worked so wholeheartedly in front of him. It would have looked as if I were saying: 'You see how much I think of you?' Like a sort of reproach. Whereas to show him my handiwork complete will make him see for himself that he has been in my thoughts.

Servant (*returning*) This has just arrived from the jeweller's for Madame.

He gives **Mathilde** *a small packet.*

Mathilde At last! (*She sits down again.*) Let me know before Monsieur de Chavigny comes.

Exit the **Servant.**

Mathilde   Now, my dear little purse, we can add a few finishing touches. Let us see how pretty you look with these tassels. Not bad. What sort of reception will you have now? Will you reveal the pleasure you gave me, the care I took to make you presentable? No one is expecting you, Mademoiselle. So you are not meant to be seen until you are looking your best. You're trying so hard, shall I give you a kiss? (*She kisses her purse, and then pauses.*) Poor little thing! You are not worth much. You would not even fetch two louis d'or. Why does it make me feel sad for us to be parted? When I began you, did I not mean to finish you as soon as possible? Oh dear! I was in better spirits when I started than now, when you're nearly finished. Yet that was only two weeks ago. Can it really be just two weeks? It cannot be more. And how much has happened in two weeks! Shall we be too late, my pet? . . . But why have ideas like that? Someone is coming, I think. Here he is. He still loves me.

Servant (*appearing*)   Monsieur le Comte has arrived, Madame.

Mathilde   Oh! Good heavens! I have only put one tassel on, and forgotten the other! How stupid I am! Now I still cannot give it to him today! Ask him to wait a moment, a minute, in the drawing-room. Quick! Before he arrives . . .

Servant   He is here, Madame.

Exit. **Mathilde** *hides the purse.*

Scene Two

Mathilde, Chavigny.

Chavigny   Good evening, *ma chère*. Am I disturbing you? (*Sitting down.*)

Mathilde   Disturbing me, Henri, what a question!

Chavigny You look upset, preoccupied. I always forget, when I enter your room, that I am your husband. I am far too eager to come in.

Mathilde There is a touch of malice in what you say, but as there is also a touch of affection, I shall kiss you all the same. (*She kisses him.*) So who do you take yourself for, Monsieur, when you forget that you are my husband?

Chavigny Your lover, my sweet. Am I mistaken?

Mathilde Lover and friend, you are not mistaken. (*Aside.*) I am tempted to give him the purse just as it is.

Chavigny What is this dress you are wearing? Are you not going out?

Mathilde No, I wanted . . . I was hoping, perhaps . . .

Chavigny You were hoping? . . . What is it then?

Mathilde You are going to the ball? You look magnificent.

Chavigny Not really. I do not know if it is my fault or my tailor's, but I don't cut the same figure I used to in uniform.

Mathilde You are a faithless man. You do not think of me, when you gaze at your reflection in that mirror.

Chavigny Pshaw! Who else would I think of? Do you imagine I go to the ball in order to dance? I swear to you it is nothing but a chore. Why I drag myself off there, I really wonder!

Mathilde Well, why not stay here? Please do. We shall be alone, and I will tell you . . .

Chavigny I think your clock must be fast. It cannot be so late as that.

Mathilde It is scarcely time yet to go to a ball, whatever the clock may say. It is not long since we left the dining-room.

Chavigny I have told them to harness the horses. I have a call to make.

Mathilde Oh! That's different. I . . . I didn't know . . . I thought . . .

Chavigny Well?

Mathilde I had imagined . . . after what you said . . . But the clock is quite right. It is only just eight. Allow me a few moments. I have a little surprise.

Chavigny (*rising*) You know, my dear, that I leave you quite free to go out whenever you wish. You will agree it is only fair to reciprocate. What surprise have you thought up for me?

Mathilde Nothing. I didn't use that word, did I?

Chavigny I must have made a mistake then. I thought I heard it. Have you those Strauss waltzes to hand? You might lend them to me, if you are not using them.

Mathilde They are over there. Would you like them now?

Chavigny Why, yes, if you really don't mind. Someone has asked me for them, for a day or two. I shall not deprive you of them for long.

Mathilde Are they for Madame de Blainville?

Chavigny (*taking the waltzes*) I beg pardon? Did you mention Madame de Blainville?

Mathilde Did I? Oh no! I never mentioned her.

Chavigny This time I heard you perfectly well. (*He sits down.*) What were you saying about Madame de Blainville?

Mathilde I thought my waltzes might be for her.

Chavigny And why should you think that?

Mathilde Why, because . . . because she likes them.

Chavigny Yes, and so do I. So do you, I believe. There is one especially. Now how does it go? I have forgotten it . . . Might I hear it again?

Mathilde I'm not sure if I can remember it.

She sits at the piano and plays.

Chavigny That's the very one! It is charming, divine! And you play it like an angel, or rather like a true devotee of the waltz.

Mathilde As well as she does, Henri?

Chavigny Who is 'she'? Madame de Blainville? She seems to be quite an obsession.

Mathilde Oh no! Not really! If I were a man, I would not have my head turned by her.

Chavigny And you would be right, Madame. A man should never have his head turned, by a woman or by a waltz.

Mathilde Do you expect to be gambling this evening, dear?

Chavigny Why, sweetheart, what an idea! A gambler never has expectations.

Mathilde Have you any gold coins in your pockets?

Chavigny I may have. Are you wanting some?

Mathilde I! Good Lord no! What should *I* need them for?

Chavigny You might. Even if I am too eager in opening the door of your room, at least I don't open your bureau. Perhaps that too is a mistake.

Mathilde You are lying, Monsieur. Just a short time ago I noticed that you had opened it. And when you left, you left me richer than you should.

Chavigny Not so, my dear, so long as the poor are with us. I know what use you make of your riches, and I beg you to allow me to perform an act of charity, through you.

Mathilde *Cher* Henri! How good and generous you are! Tell me something. Do you remember the day you had a small debt to pay, when you complained that you had no purse?

Chavigny When was that? Oh yes, that's right! It's a fact that, when one goes out, it is madness to put one's trust in pockets, which don't hold a thing . . .

Mathilde Would you like a red purse embroidered in black?

Chavigny No. I dislike red. Good Lord, you remind me that I have a purse here, a brand new one. A present I received only yesterday. What do you think of this? (*He pulls a purse from his pocket.*) It is in good taste, is it not?

Mathilde Let me see. Will you show me?

Chavigny Here.

He gives it to her. She looks at it, then returns it to him.

Mathilde It's very pretty. What colour is it?

Chavigny (*laughing*) What colour? That's a fine question, I must say!

Mathilde I'm sorry . . . What I meant was . . . Who gave it to you?

Chavigny Oh! This is too amusing for words! Your mind does wander! I swear you are quite adorable!

Servant (*announcing*) Madame de Léry!

Mathilde I told them I wished to see no one.

Chavigny No, no! Let her come in. Why not receive your guests?

Mathilde Very well! But this purse, Monsieur, may one know the name of the donor?

Scene Three

Mathilde, Chavigny, Mme de Léry *in a ball dress.*

Chavigny Come in, Madame. Please do come in! You could not have arrived at a better moment. Mathilde has just made such a prize remark, it is worth its weight in gold. Just imagine, I showed her this purse . . .

Mme de Léry Why, it's rather nice! Let me see!

Chavigny I showed her this purse. She looks at it, feels it, turns it about. Then when she gave it back, do you know what she said? She asked me what colour it was!

Mme de Léry Well . . . it's blue.

Chavigny Yes, it's blue all right . . . no doubt about that . . . and that is just what is so amusing . . . How can anyone ask such a question?

Mme de Léry I see. *Bonsoir, chère* Mathilde. You are coming to the embassy tonight?

Mathilde No. I think I'll stay in.

Chavigny But you don't find my story funny?

Mme de Léry Yes, I do. But who is it made that purse? Ah! Now I recognize it. It was Madame de Blainville! Really, I can't tempt you away?

Chavigny (*quickly*) Do you mind telling me how you knew?

Mme de Léry Because it is blue. I have seen it lying about for ages. It was seven years in the making. And you can guess how often in that time it has changed destination. At least three of my acquaintances expected to claim ownership. You have a real treasure there, Monsieur de Chavigny. Quite an inheritance.

Chavigny Anyone would think there was only one purse in the world.

Mme de Léry No, but there is only one blue one. As for me, I find blue quite odious. It doesn't *say* a thing, it's a stupid colour. I cannot be mistaken about something like this. Seeing it once is enough. As much as I adore lilac, I detest blue.

Mathilde It's the colour of constancy.

Mme de Léry Pah! It's a hairdresser's colour! I only dropped in *en passant*. As you see, I'm in full rig. You have to arrive so early at a function like this, or you break your neck in the crush. Why aren't you coming? I would not miss it for the world.

Mathilde I did not think of it, and now it is too late.

Mme de Léry Forget about that, you have plenty of time. Now look, *ma chère*; I shall ring the bell and you shall ask for a gown. We will turn Monsieur de Chavigny out, together with his little . . . what-not. I shall arrange your hair, pop two little flowers on top and sweep you off in my carriage. Come along, the whole matter's settled!

Mathilde Not tonight. I'm determined to stay here.

Mme de Léry Determined? Are you so positive? Then you, Monsieur de Chavigny, shall bring Mathilde.

Chavigny (*curtly*) I never interfere in other people's affairs.

Mme de Léry Ah-ha! Now I see! You like blue, of course! Well now, you know what I shall do? Give me some tea, and I will stay here.

Mathilde Ernestine, you are so kind! But no! I cannot keep the queen of the ball away. Go and dance a waltz or two and, if you still wish, come back here at eleven. We can have a little chat, alone by the fire, as Monsieur de Chavigny is going to abandon us.

Chavigny Am I? I am not at all sure whether I shall go out or not.

Mme de Léry Very well. It's all agreed. I shall leave you. By the way, have you heard of my misfortune? I have been robbed, as well and truly robbed as if I'd fallen among thieves in the forest.

Mathilde Robbed! What on earth do you mean?

Mme de Léry Four gowns, *ma chère*, four darling little creations from London, lost in the customs. If you had only seen them! It's enough to make you weep. One was turquoise, another was puce. There will never be their like again.

Mathilde But that's tragic, Ernestine! I presume they were confiscated?

Mme de Léry Confiscated? No. If that had been all, I should have howled so loud they would have given them back. Screamed blue murder! Now I shall be naked throughout the summer. You have no idea how they cut them to pieces, sticking their probe all through my trunk. The holes are as big as my finger. And that is what they brought me, yesterday, for breakfast.

Chavigny I don't suppose there was, by chance, a blue one?

Mme de Léry No, Monsieur, not a remnant. *Au revoir*, my love. I shall only put in a very brief appearance. I believe I have scored up to a dozen colds this winter. Now I shall catch the thirteenth, and as soon as that's done, I shall race back and recline on your lovely chaise-longue. Then we can talk clothes, can't we, and the customs? No, I feel melancholic, we'll indulge our emotions. Oh well, no matter! *Bonsoir*, Monsieur Indigo . . . If you show me out, I swear I shall never set foot inside this house again.

Scene Four

Chavigny, Mathilde.

Chavigny What a madcap that woman is! You know how to choose your friends.

Mathilde It was you who wished her to come up.

Chavigny I am willing to wager you believe it was Madame de Blainville who made my purse.

Mathilde No, I don't, as you deny it.

Chavigny I am sure you believe it.

Mathilde And why are you so sure?

Chavigny Because I know what you're like. Madame de Léry is an oracle for you. Even if it is a nonsensical idea.

Mathilde A fine compliment! Though I hardly deserve it.

Chavigny Oh, you do, you know! But I'd far rather you were frank about it, than conceal your feelings.

Mathilde If I do not believe it, I cannot pretend to, in order to appear to be sincere.

Chavigny I tell you, you do believe it. It is written all over your face.

Mathilde If I must say so, to satisfy you: all right, then, I do believe it.

Chavigny You do believe it? And suppose it were true, what harm would there be?

Mathilde None at all. And that's why I fail to see why you should deny it.

Chavigny I don't deny it. It was she who made it. – (*Rising.*) Goodbye for now. I may come back later to take tea with your friend.

Mathilde Henri, don't leave me like this!

Chavigny What do you mean: *like this*? Have we
quarrelled? So far as I can see it is all perfectly simple.
Someone makes a purse for me. I put it to good use. You
ask me who and I tell you. Nothing looks less like a
quarrel to me.

Mathilde And if I asked you for that purse, would you
make me a present of it?

Chavigny Perhaps. What would you do with it?

Mathilde That doesn't matter. I am asking you for it.

Chavigny Not to carry it with you, I presume? I should
like to know what you would do with it.

Mathilde Use it.

Chavigny Is this a joke? You would use a purse made by
Madame de Blainville?

Mathilde And why not? You do.

Chavigny A fine reason. I am not a woman.

Mathilde Well, if I do not make use of it, I shall throw it
in the fire.

Chavigny Ah-ha! Now you really are sincere. Very well, I
too will be sincere. And with your permission, I shall keep
it.

Mathilde You are perfectly free to do so, of course. But I
confess I suffer cruelly to think that when you display it to
all and sundry, everyone will know who made it.

Chavigny Display it! Anyone would think it was a
trophy!

Mathilde Listen to me! Please listen! And leave your
hand in mine. (*She kisses him.*) Henri, do you love me?
Answer me.

Chavigny I love you and I am listening.

Mathilde I promise you I am not jealous. But if you give me that purse without rancour, I shall thank you from the bottom of my heart. What I am proposing is a small exchange, and I believe, at any rate I hope, you will find you are not the loser.

Chavigny Let us see this exchange of yours. What is it?

Mathilde I will tell you, if you wish. But if you give me your purse first, and take me at my word, you will make me happy indeed.

Chavigny I give nothing away on the strength of a word.

Mathilde Oh, please, Henri, I beg you!

Chavigny No.

Mathilde Very well! I shall ask you on my knees.

Chavigny Stand up, Mathilde! It is my turn to beg you to get off your knees. You know I dislike this kind of behaviour. I cannot bear to see people abase themselves, particularly in a case like this. It is childish of you to be so insistent. If in all seriousness you demanded this purse of me, I would throw it in the fire myself, and I would expect nothing in exchange. Come, stand up! Let us say no more about it. *Au revoir*. Till later this evening. I shall be back.

Exit.

Scene Five

Mathilde, *alone*.

Mathilde Well, if it cannot be that one, this is the one I shall burn. (*She goes to her desk and takes out the purse she has made.*) Poor little purse! Just now I touched you with my lips. Remember what I whispered? We were too late, you see. He does not want you. And now he does not want me either. (*She moves to the fireplace.*) How foolish we are

to live on dreams. They never come true. What is that
fatal charm which makes us cherish our illusions? Why
does it give such pleasure to nurse an idle fancy, and then
in secret try and bring it to fruition? What good does it
do? It only leads to tears. Fate is too capricious. What
more does it want of us? How many prayers, how much
cautious preparation, before it fulfils the meanest of our
hopes? You were right, Monsieur le Comte, to say I was
childish to be so insistent. But how I enjoyed insisting!
And what of you? Proud or inconstant as you are, it would
have cost so little to pander to my childish whim. Oh no!
He no longer loves me, loves me no more. It is you he
loves, Madame de Blainville! (*She weeps.*) Now . . . not
another thought! I will throw this . . . plaything into the
fire. It was not ready in time. Yet even if he had received
it tonight, he would surely have lost it tomorrow! Yes, of
course he would! He would have left my purse lying
around on some table, among his old junk, Heaven knows
where, while that other purse would never leave his side! I
can see him now, at his gambling, proudly take it from his
pocket and cast it down on the green baize, with the gold
coins jingling inside. And now I *am* jealous: what more
does an unhappy wife need to make her husband hate her!
(*She is about to throw the purse on the fire, then she stops.*)
But what have you done? Why destroy you? I made you
with my own hands, an unlucky token of my love. It is no
fault of yours. You were waiting and hoping too. That
cruel scene between us did not turn you pale. Your colour
is bright as ever. I feel quite fond of you. Two whole
weeks of my life are caught up in your fine threads. No!
Oh no! These hands that made you will not murder you. I
want to save you and complete my work on you. Like a
relic close o my heart you will make me happy and sad.
Reminding me of my love for him, of his neglect and his
caprices. And who knows but he might come back again,
to seek you out in your secret hiding-place?

She sits down and sews on the missing tassel.

Scene Six

Mathilde, Mme de Léry.

Mme de Léry (*from off-stage*) Not a soul about! What does this mean? Here they keep open house indeed, you walk straight in. (*She opens the door and cries out, laughing.*) Madame de Léry! (*She comes in,* **Mathilde** *rises to her feet.*) Back again, my dear! Not a servant in sight. I've searched high and low. Oh, I am ready to drop!

She sits down.

Mathilde Why don't you take off your furs?

Mme de Léry In a moment. I'm frozen. Do you like this sort of . . . weasel? They say it's sable from Ethiopia, or some such place, but Monsieur de Léry brought it back for me from Holland. Frankly, I think it's hideous. I shall wear it three times, for courtesy's sake, then pop goes the weasel, I pass it to Ursula.

Mathilde No maid could wear that.

Mme de Léry True enough. I'll have a little rug made out of it.

Mathilde Well now, was it a lovely ball?

Mme de Léry Ah! *Mon Dieu!* That ball! I never reached it. You would never credit what happened to me.

Mathilde So you didn't go after all?

Mme de Léry Oh, but I did! I went all right, but I never got as far as the entrance. You'll die laughing. Imagine a queue . . . an endless tail of carriages . . . (*She bursts out laughing.*) Does that sort of thing frighten you?

Mathilde Yes, I can't bear it. A street choked with vehicles.

Mme de Léry It's desolating, when one's alone. Cry as I would to the coachman to keep us moving, it was all in vain. He never budged an inch. I was in such a fury, I felt inclined to climb up there and take his place. And I guarantee I would have cut through that tail! But one feels so helpless, in all one's finery, staring out of a rain-splashed window. For, to cap it all, it was pouring in torrents. So I spent an entertaining half-hour watching the people paddling past. Then I told him to turn back. And that was my ball . . . This fire is quite reviving me, I feel almost alive again!

Mme de Léry *removes her furs.* **Mathilde** *rings and a* **Servant** *enters.*

Mathilde Bring the tea.

Exit the **Servant**.

Mme de Léry So Monsieur de Chavigny did go out?

Mathilde Yes. I think he is going to the ball, and he is more persevering than you.

Mme de Léry Just between ourselves, I think he is none too fond of me.

Mathilde You are wrong, I assure you. He has told me a hundred times that in his eyes you are one of the handsomest women in Paris.

Mme de Léry Really? Very courteous of him. But I merit the compliment, for I think him a handsome man. Will you lend me a pin?

Mathilde You have some there, just beside you.

Mme de Léry That Palmire woman makes you such gowns, you feel you have no shoulders at all. At every moment one expects the whole affair to slide off. Is it she who made you those sleeves?

Mathilde Yes.

Mme de Léry Pretty, very fine, very pretty. Close-fitting sleeves, there is really nothing like them. But it took me a long time to see it. Still, I feel one should not be too plump to wear them. Or else one resembles a grasshopper, all body, with arms jutting out like sticks.

Mathilde I like the comparison.

*A **Servant** brings the tea.*

Mme de Léry Is it not so? Think of Mademoiselle Saint-Ange. Yet it doesn't do to be too thin either, or nothing is left of you at all. Everyone acclaims the Marquise d'Ermont, but I find she looks like a gallows. I grant you her beautiful face. A madonna's, but stuck on top of a pole.

Mathilde (*laughing*) How would you like your tea, *ma chère*?

Mme de Léry Hot water, with a touch of tea, just clouded with milk.

Mathilde (*pouring the tea*) Are you going to Madame d'Egly's tomorrow? I can collect you, if you wish.

Mme de Léry Oh! Madame d'Egly! There's another! With her frizzy hair and her skinny legs, she reminds me of one of those brooms for swishing away the spiders. (*She drinks.*) But I shall certainly go tomorrow. Oh no! I'm prevented! I am going to the concert.

Mathilde It's true, she is rather quaint.

Mme de Léry Look at me, please.

Mathilde Why?

Mme de Léry Look me straight in the face.

Mathilde Can you see something strange about me?

Mme de Léry Yes, your eyes are certainly red. You have just been crying, that is clear as daylight. What on earth is wrong, my dear Mathilde?

Mathilde Nothing. I promise you. What do you think could be wrong?

Mme de Léry I have no idea, but you have just been crying. I feel I am *de trop*, so I shall leave you.

Mathilde No, please don't! I beg you to stay.

Mme de Léry You really mean it? I will stay, if you wish. But you must tell me what is troubling you. (**Mathilde** *shakes her head.*) No? Then I shall leave you. Understand? If I can't be of use, willy-nilly, my presence only makes things worse.

Mathilde Stay with me. I value your company. Your sense of humour diverts me. And if it were true that I had cares on my mind, your high spirits would chase them away.

Mme de Léry You know how much I like you. It may be that you think me frivolous. But no one is more serious than I about serious matters. I cannot understand how people play with the feelings of others. That is why I appear to have none. I know what suffering means. I was very young when I was taught that lesson. I know what it means to open one's heart, to confide in someone. If you can, speak out: I am not prompted by mere curiosity.

Mathilde I believe you to be good, and above all most sincere: forgive me if I decline your offer.

Mme de Léry Ah, *mon Dieu*! I have it! The blue purse! I made a terrible blunder when I mentioned Madame de Blainville. It crossed my mind as I was leaving you. Is Monsieur de Chavigny really seeking her favours?

Mathilde *rises, unable to reply, turns away and dabs her eyes with her handkerchief.*

Mme de Léry Impossible!

A long silence. **Mathilde** *moves around for a while, then goes to sit down at the opposite end of the room.* **Mme de Léry** *seems deep in thought. She rises and goes up to* **Mathilde**, *who stretches her hand out to her.*

Mme de Léry You know, my sweet, what the dentists say: when they hurt you, shout! Now I tell you, weep. Weep, Mathilde! Whether it be for joy or sorrow, it is always comforting to shed tears.

Mathilde Oh heavens!

Mme de Léry Such a thing is quite incredible! How could anyone love Madame de Blainville! A coquette with no wit and no beauty. She cannot hold a candle to you. No one would leave an angel for a witch.

Mathilde (*sobbing*) I am sure he loves her, quite quite sure.

Mme de Léry No, my pet, that cannot be. It's a caprice, a passing fancy. I know Monsieur de Chavigny better than he thinks. He's a wicked man, but not a bad one. He must have been moved by a sudden impulse. Have you ever wept in front of him?

Mathilde Oh no! Never!

Mme de Léry Bravo! I suspect he would not be exactly displeased to see you in tears.

Mathilde Not displeased? Pleased to see me cry?

Mme de Léry But of course! Yes, indeed! Yesterday I reached the age of twenty-five, but I have learnt a few things in my life. How did all this come about?

Mathilde I . . . I don't know . . .

Mme de Léry Come on, tell me. You are not afraid of me? I shall put your mind at rest at once. If you would have me commit my secrets to you, I will prove to you that I trust you, and oblige you to trust in me. If that will assist you, I will do so. What shall I tell you about myself?

Mathilde You are my dearest friend. I will tell you all, and trust in you completely. It's a storm in a teacup, but my head is full of silly notions, which lead me astray. I had made a little purse for Monsieur de Chavigny, in secret, and I wished to give it to him today. For the last two weeks I have hardly seen him. He spends his days at Madame de Blainville's. This little gift was a means of gently reproaching him for his absence, to remind him that he was neglecting me. But just as I was about to give him my purse, he produced the other one.

Mme de Léry In all this there is nothing to weep for.

Mathilde Oh yes! There is plenty to weep for! For I did a wild and stupid thing: I asked him for the other purse.

Mme de Léry Oh dear! That was undiplomatic.

Mathilde Yes, Ernestine, it was. And he refused . . . So then I . . . Oh no! I am so ashamed . . .

Mme de Léry And then?

Mathilde And then . . . I asked him for it on my knees. I wanted him to make this little sacrifice for me, and I would have given him my purse in exchange for his. I begged him . . . I pleaded with him . . .

Mme de Léry And, needless to say, he did nothing of the sort. Poor little lamb, he's unworthy of you.

Mathilde Oh no! Despite everything, I'll not believe that!

Mme de Léry You're quite right. I expressed myself badly. He is worthy of you, and he loves you. But he is a man, so he has his pride. What a shame! And where is this purse of yours?

Mathilde This is it, here, on the table.

Mme de Léry (*picking up the purse*) This one? Well, I must say, it is ten times as pretty as his! To start with, it is not blue! And it really is charming. Lend it to me. I will discover a way to make him find it to his taste.

Mathilde Try, and you make my life worth living.

Mme de Léry To have come to this, after one year of marriage! It is fantastic! There must be witchcraft in it.

That Blainville woman, I detest her from top to toe, with her indigo blue! The circles round her eyes are so huge they reach down to her chin! Mathilde, will you try a little experiment? It will cost us nothing. Will your husband be back this evening?

Mathilde I don't really know, but he said he would.

Mme de Léry How were you, when he left?

Mathilde Oh! I was very upset. And he was very severe.

Mme de Léry He will come. Have you the courage? When an idea enters my mind, I warn you, I must grasp it at once. But I know myself. I shall win.

Mathilde Give the orders then. I obey.

Mme de Léry Slip into your dressing-room, quickly put your cloak on and jump into my carriage. I do not intend to send you to the ball, but when you return you must look as though you had been there. You can have yourself driven wherever you like, to the Invalides, or the Bastille . . . it may not be vastly entertaining, but you will be just as well off there as here, unable to sleep. You agree? Now take your purse and wrap it up in this paper. I shall write the address. Good. Now that's done. Halt the carriage at the corner of the street. Then tell my groom to bring the little packet here, give it to the first servant he sees and then depart at once without further explanation.

Mathilde Tell me at least what you are trying to do.

Mme de Léry What I am trying to do, my child, is impossible to tell. And I shall discover if it is possible to do. Now, once and for all, do you trust me?

Mathilde I would let you do anything in the world, for love of him.

Mme de Léry Off with you, then! There's a carriage.

Mathilde Here he is. I can hear his voice in the courtyard.

Mme de Léry Hurry! Is there a back staircase through there?

Mathilde Yes, luckily. But my hair is not dressed for the ball. How could anyone believe that I had been?

Mme de Léry (*taking the garland from her own head and giving it to* **Mathilde**) Here! You can arrange all that *en route*!

Exit **Mathilde**.

Scene Seven

Mme de Léry, *alone*.

Mme de Léry On her knees! A girl like that on her knees! And that Monsieur still denies her! A girl of twenty, lovely as a rose and faithful as a spaniel! Poor child! Asking as a favour that he should deign to accept a purse made by her in exchange for a gift from Madame de Blainville! What sinks of iniquity the hearts of men must be! Upon my honour! A woman is worth ten times a man. (*She sits down, and picks a magazine up from the table. A moment later, there is a knock on the door.*) Come in.

Scene Eight

Mme de Léry, **Chavigny**.

Mme de Léry (*reading, absent-mindedly*) *Bonsoir*, Comte, would you like some tea?

Chavigny You are most kind, but I never take it.

He sits down and looks around him.

Mme de Léry Was it amusing, the ball?

Chavigny How do you mean? Were you not there?

Mme de Léry That is a question that is hardly gallant: no, I was not there. But I did send Mathilde, whom you seem to be seeking with those wandering glances.

Chavigny You are joking, if I'm not mistaken?

Mme de Léry What was that? I beg your pardon. I am reading an article in this magazine which interests me greatly.

A silence. **Chavigny** *anxiously stands up and paces about.*

Chavigny Is it really true that Mathilde is at the ball?

Mme de Léry Why, yes, of course. You can see I am waiting for her.

Chavigny That's odd. When you suggested it, she did not wish to go.

Mme de Léry She changed her mind, apparently.

Chavigny Why did she not go with you?

Mme de Léry Because I abandoned the idea.

Chavigny She went without a carriage then?

Mme de Léry No, I loaned her mine. Have you read this, Monsieur de Chavigny?

Chavigny What is it?

Mme de Léry *La Revue des Deux Mondes*: a delightful article by Madame George Sand. About orang-outangs.

Chavigny About . . . ?

Mme de Léry Orang-outangs. Oh no! I mistake. Her article is not on orang-outangs. It's on the Venus of Milo. How amusing!

Chavigny I simply cannot understand this idea of going to the ball without informing me. I could at least have accompanied her home.

Mme de Léry Do you like the novels of George Sand?

Chavigny No, I do not. But if she was there, how did I not see her?

Mme de Léry Who? Madame Sand? She was on that table. In the magazine.

Chavigny Are you making sport of me, Madame?

Mme de Léry Perhaps. It depends what you really mean.

Chavigny I am talking about my wife.

Mme de Léry Did you entrust her into my keeping?

Chavigny You are right. I am quite ridiculous. I shall go and fetch her at once.

Mme de Léry If you do, you will get caught in that awful queue of vehicles.

Chavigny That's true. I might just as well wait. So I shall wait.

He goes to the fireplace and sits down.

Mme de Léry (*putting down her magazine*) Do you know, Monsieur de Chavigny, that you really astonish me? I was convinced you followed the fashion and left Mathilde free to go wherever she liked.

Chavigny Of course. You have proof of that.

Mme de Léry Not exactly. You look furious.

Chavigny I do? Good heavens, not in the slightest!

Mme de Léry You can hardly keep still on your chair. I believed you to be a very different sort of man, I confess. And, in all seriousness, I would not have loaned my carriage to Mathilde, had I known how matters really stood.

Chavigny But I assure you I see nothing to complain of. And I thank you for what you did.

Mme de Léry Oh, no! You are not thanking me at all! I assure you that you are angry. To be perfectly honest, if she did go, I believe it was partly in order to join you.

Chavigny I like that! Then why did she not come with me?

Mme de Léry Why, yes, that is precisely what I told her. But it is so like us! We women, now we won't, and then we will! Are you sure you will not take tea?

Chavigny No. It upsets me.

Mme de Léry Well, perhaps you will give me some?

Chavigny I beg pardon, Madame?

Mme de Léry Give me some. (**Chavigny** *stands up and pours out a cup, which he offers to* **Mme de Léry**.) That's fine. Put it there. Have we a government this evening?

Chavigny I have no idea.

Mme de Léry Strange lodging-houses these governments are. With people parading in and out like puppets, without rhyme or reason.

Chavigny Why don't you drink your tea? It is half cold already.

Mme de Léry You did not add any sugar. One lump please.

Chavigny As you wish.

Mme de Léry No, two.

Chavigny It will be undrinkable.

Mme de Léry Fine. And now a drop more milk.

Chavigny Does that satisfy you?

Mme de Léry A dash of hot water. Have you done that? Pass me the cup.

Chavigny (*offering her the cup*) Here it is. But it will be undrinkable.

Mme de Léry You think so? Are you quite sure?

Chavigny There is not the slightest doubt.

Mme de Léry And why will it be undrinkable?

Chavigny Because it is cold, and too sweet.

Mme de Léry Very well, then! If it's undrinkable, throw it away! (**Chavigny** *is standing, holding the cup.* **Mme de Léry** *looks at him and laughs.*) *Mon Dieu*! How funny you are! I have never seen so sulky a look.

Chavigny (*out of patience, empties the cup into the fire, then paces up and down, and says moodily*) It's quite true! I really am a fool.

Mme de Léry I have never seen you jealous until now. But you are. Quite an Othello.

Chavigny Not in the very least. I cannot stand embarrassment at any price. Or those who embarrass others. Why should I be jealous?

Mme de Léry Vanity. Like all husbands.

Chavigny Pooh! Woman's talk! 'Vanity makes a man jealous', they say. A platitude, as trite as 'your humble servant'. The world is very severe on us poor maligned husbands.

Mme de Léry Not so severe as on us poor maligned wives.

Chavigny Lord, yes, far more! Everything is relative. Can women be permitted to lead the same sort of life as we do? That's obviously absurd. There are a thousand things of great import to them, which matter precious little to men.

Mme de Léry Yes, a passing fancy, for example.

Chavigny Why not, indeed? Yes, a caprice. A little adventure. There's no doubt but that a man may have them, and that a woman . . .

Mme de Léry Has one from time to time. Do you really believe that a skirt is some sort of charm, which protects her from . . . passing fancies?

Chavigny It is an obstacle, which should keep them at bay.

Mme de Léry Unless it be a veil, which conceals them. I hear footsteps. Mathilde has returned..

Chavigny No, that cannot be. It is not yet midnight.

Enter a **Servant** *who hands a small packet to* **Monsieur de Chavigny**.

Chavigny What is it? What do you want?

Servant This packet has just been delivered for Monsieur le Comte.

Exit. **Chavigny** *undoes the packet, which contains* **Mathilde**'s *purse.*

Mme de Léry Yet another present for you! At this hour, it's almost alarming!

Chavigny What the devil does this mean! Hey! François! Hey there! Who was it brought this packet?

Servant (*returning*) Monsieur?

Chavigny Who was it came with this packet?

Servant Monsieur, the porter just brought it up.

Chavigny There was nothing with it? No letter?

Servant No, Monsieur.

Chavigny Was it delivered to the porter some while ago?

Servant No, Monsieur. He had only just received it.

Chavigny Who brought it?

Servant He doesn't know, Monsieur.

Chavigny He doesn't know! Are you out of your mind? Was it a man or a woman?

Servant It was a servant. In livery. But not one he knew.

Chavigny Is he still below, this servant?

Servant No, Monsieur. He left immediately.

Chavigny And he said nothing?

Servant No, Monsieur.

Chavigny Very good.

Exit **Servant**.

Mme de Léry You are well and truly spoilt, Monsieur de Chavigny. If you drop your money, it will not be the fault of the ladies.

Chavigny Hang me if I can make head or tail of it.

Mme de Léry Stop pretending! You're like a child.

Chavigny No, I give you my word that I cannot guess who sent it. There must be some mistake.

Mme de Léry Is there no address on it?

Chavigny Why of course! You are right. That's odd. I recognize the writing.

Mme de Léry May one look?

Chavigny It may be indiscreet of me to show it to you. But whoever it incriminates, it serves them right. Here! I am sure I have seen that writing somewhere before.

Mme de Léry I am quite sure I have.

Chavigny Wait! I have it . . . No, I'm wrong. Would you call this a round or a sloping hand?

Mme de Léry Come, now! It's a thoroughbred English hand. See how delicately those letters are formed! Oh! The lady is surely *comme il faut*.

Chavigny You seem to have recognized it.

Mme de Léry (*feigning confusion*) I do? Not at all.
(**Chavigny** *looks at her in astonishment, then resumes his
perambulation.*) Now, what point had we reached in our
conversation? . . . Ah yes! I believe we were talking
whims and fancies. This little red billet-doux arrived in
the nick of time.

Chavigny Admit that you are in the secret.

Mme de Léry Some people are quite hopeless. If I had
been you, I would have guessed by now.

Chavigny Why not be frank! Tell me who it is.

Mme de Léry I am almost persuaded it is . . . Madame
de Blainville.

Chavigny You are pitiless, Madame. Do you realize we
might come to cross swords with each other?

Mme de Léry Not yet, I hope. Let us remain at cross
purposes.

Chavigny You do not wish to help me solve the mystery?

Mme de Léry A waste of time! Forget it. It seems this is
not your métier. It would be more polite, if you reflected
on it at leisure.

Chavigny Is there any more tea? I feel like taking some.

Mme de Léry I will give you a cup. So don't say I'm not
kind to you.

A pause.

Chavigny (*still pacing*) The more I rack my brains, the
less I find.

Mme de Léry Not again? Tell me, is it on purpose that
you speak of nothing but that purse? I shall leave you to
ruminate alone.

Chavigny The truth is I am utterly bewildered.

Mme de Léry I tell you it is Madame de Blainville. She
had second thoughts about the colour of her purse, and
she has sent you this one in atonement. Or better still, to

put you to the test and see which one you use, this one or hers.

Chavigny   I shall use this one, of course. It is the only way to find out who has made it.

Mme de Léry   I don't follow. It is all too deep for me.

Chavigny   I am assuming that the person who has sent it might see me using it tomorrow. Surely then I would know for certain who it is?

Mme de Léry (*bursts out laughing*)   Oh no! It's too much! I can't keep it up!

Chavigny   Could it, by any chance, be you?

A pause.

Mme de Léry   Here is your tea, made with my own fair hand. And it will be better than the cup you concocted for me just now. But stop staring at me! What do you take me for? An anonymous letter?

Chavigny   It is you, you are playing some little game. There's a plot afoot.

Mme de Léry   A plot that's been carefully hatched.

Chavigny   Then admit you are part of it.

Mme de Léry   No.

Chavigny   I beg of you.

Mme de Léry   The answer's still no.

Chavigny   I'm pleading with you.

Mme de Léry   Ask me on your knees, and I will tell you.

Chavigny   On my knees?

Mme de Léry   Yes, on your knees.

Chavigny   Whatever you like.

Mme de Léry   Come along, then!

Chavigny   You really mean it?

He kneels, laughing, in front of **Mme de Léry.**

Mme de Léry (*drily*) I like you in that posture. It suits you to perfection. But you had better stand up, or I shall feel too sorry for you.

Chavigny (*standing up*) So, you won't tell, will you?

Mme de Léry Do you have your blue purse on you?

Chavigny I don't know, I think so.

Mme de Léry I think so, too. Give it to me, and I will say who made the other.

Chavigny You do know, then?

Mme de Léry Yes, I know.

Chavigny It is a woman?

Mme de Léry Who else, were it not a man, and I hardly see . . .

Chavigny A handsome woman, I mean?

Mme de Léry A woman who, in your eyes, passes for one of the handsomest women in Paris.

Chavigny Blonde or brunette?

Mme de Léry Blue.

Chavigny What is the first letter of her name?

Mme de Léry My bargain does not tempt you? It's a fair exchange. Madame de Blainville's purse.

Chavigny Is she short or tall?

Mme de Léry Give me that purse.

Chavigny Just tell me if she has a well-turned ankle.

Mme de Léry Your money-bag or your life!

Chavigny If I give you the purse, you will tell me her name?

Mme de Léry Yes.

Chavigny (*taking out the blue purse*) Cross your heart!

Mme de Léry Cross my heart!

Chavigny (*appears to hesitate,* **Mme de Léry** *holds out her hand. He watches her attentively. Suddenly he sits down beside her, and says gaily*) Let us talk passing fancies. So you admit that a woman may have them?

Mme de Léry You don't still doubt it, do you?

Chavigny Not exactly. But it sometimes happens that a married man has two modes of expression, and even, one might say, two modes of behaviour.

Mme de Léry Yes, but what about our bargain? Has it evaporated? I thought it had been agreed.

Chavigny A married man remains no less a man. The wedding service does not change his nature, though at times it may oblige him to make the speeches suited to the role he has to play. In this world all we need to know, when folk address us, is whether they are speaking to the real man or the fiction we personify.

Mme de Léry I see. It's up to us to choose. But how do people know which is which?

Chavigny I do not think the intelligent find it hard. They can soon tell.

Mme de Léry So you no longer wish to solve the riddle of the name? Come on, now, give me that purse.

Chavigny An intelligent woman, for example – such women know many things – would, I think, never mistake the true character of her acquaintances. She would tell at a glance.

Mme de Léry So you really intend to keep that purse?

Chavigny You seem most anxious about it. An intelligent woman should know, should she not, Madame, how to recognize the husband, and therefore how to distinguish the man? But how have you arranged your hair? You were wearing flowers before.

Mme de Léry Yes. They began to trouble me, so I removed them. *Mon Dieu!* My hair needs tidying. (*She rises and tidies her hair in front of the mirror.*)

Chavigny I have never seen a neater waist than yours. An intelligent woman like you . . .

Mme de Léry An intelligent woman like me can easily go to the devil when she has to deal with an intelligent man like you.

Chavigny Never mind. I am a pretty decent sort of devil.

Mme de Léry Not for me. At least, not as I see it.

Chavigny Someone, it seems, is spoiling my chances.

Mme de Léry And what exactly does that signify?

Chavigny It signifies that, if I fail to please you, someone else prevents my pleasing you more.

Mme de Léry Modest and polite. But you are wrong. There is no one to please me and no one I wish to please.

Chavigny At your age and with eyes like yours, that is beyond belief.

Mme de Léry It is, however, the truth. And nothing but the truth.

Chavigny If I were to credit that, I would not hold my fellow men in very high esteem.

Mme de Léry I can make you believe it easily enough. I am proud and wish to remain mistress of myself.

Chavigny So proud you cannot take a servant?

Mme de Léry Psh! Master or servant, you are tyrants all of you.

Chavigny (*rising*) That is true enough. And on this point I confess I have always loathed the conduct of men. God knows where this passion for domination comes from, but it only serves to make them thoroughly detested.

Mme de Léry Is that your sincere opinion?

Chavigny Most sincere. I cannot conceive how, when we have triumphed in the evening, we think we can assume the right to abuse our power next day.

Mme de Léry Yet that is the first chapter in the history of mankind.

Chavigny Yes. And if men were more reasonable, women would be less prudent.

Mme de Léry Possibly. Liaisons today are like marriages. And a wedding day calls for a moment's reflection.

Chavigny How very right you are. But tell me: why should it be like this? Why so little honesty and so much play-acting? If a handsome woman puts her trust in a man of honour, why should she not grant him her favours? Are all the men in this world fools?

Mme de Léry That is a leading question.

Chavigny Let me suppose that one man can by chance be found, who does not behave like these other fools. And let me suppose that an occasion offers for being frank, without danger, reservations or fear of indiscretion. (*He takes her hand in his.*) Let us suppose the lady is addressed as follows. We are alone, you are young and beautiful, and the esteem I have for you is as great as your qualities of heart and mind deserve. A hundred obstacles divide us, a hundred cares await us if tomorrow we attempt to meet again. In your pride you reject all domination, in your prudence you accept no bonds, none of this you have to fear from me. You are not asked for protestations, promises or sacrifice, merely for a smile from those rose-red lips, and a glance from those lovely eyes. Smile – while that door is closed: there on the threshold waits your freedom, restored when you leave this room. What lies within your grasp is not pleasure without love, but love without pain and bitterness. A caprice, a passing fancy, as that is the subject of our discourse: not the blind fancy of the senses, but a fancy of the heart, born in a flash of time, yet dwelling in the mind for all eternity.

Mme de Léry Did you speak of play-acting? If the right occasion arose, I think you could give a highly disturbing performance! Before replying to that little speech of yours, I have some inclination to indulge a fancy myself. This would seem to be the moment, when you have just been pleading the cause of passing fancies. Have you a pack of cards?

Chavigny Yes, in the drawer of that table. What do you wish to do?

Mme de Léry I have my own caprice. You can hardly deny me, lest you contradict yourself. Pass it to me. (*She takes a card from the pack.*) Red or black?

Chavigny Will you tell me what the stakes are?

Mme de Léry No stakes. A forfeit.

Chavigny Right . . . I call red.

Mme de Léry The knave of spades. You lose. Give me the blue purse.

Chavigny With all my heart. But I keep the red one. And though red was the colour that made me lose, never shall I blame this purse. For I know as well as you do whose is the hand that made it.

Mme de Léry Is it a small hand, or a large one?

Chavigny It is charming and soft as silk.

Mme de Léry Will you allow it to dispose of a slight twinge of jealousy?

She throws the blue purse on the fire.

Chavigny Ernestine, I adore you!

Mme de Léry (*watches the purse burn, then she goes up to* **Chavigny** *and says tenderly*) So you no longer love Madame de Blainville?

Chavigny   *Grand Dieu!* I have never loved her!

Mme de Léry   Neither have I, Monsieur de Chavigny.

Chavigny   But who could have told you I was ever thinking of her? That is not the woman I would turn to for even one brief moment of bliss. She is not the woman who can grant me that.

Mme de Léry   Neither am I, Monsieur de Chavigny. You have just made me a small sacrifice. It was most chivalrous of you. But I have no desire to deceive you. The red purse is not of my making.

Chavigny   It's not true! Who did make it then?

Mme de Léry   A fairer hand than mine. Do me the favour to reflect an instant, and solve this puzzle for me. Like a true Frenchman you have just made me a delightful proposition. You have knelt before me, on both your knees, and note that there is no carpet. I have asked you for your blue purse, and you gave me permission to consign it to the flames. Who then am I, pray tell me, that I should deserve all this? What do you find in me that is so remarkable? I am young and not bad-looking, it is true, and no doubt I have a well-turned ankle. But that after all is not so very rare. Once we have proved to each other that I am a coquette and you a man of spirit, simply because it is midnight and we are *tête-à-tête*, what a fine exploit that will make to write up in our Memoirs! Yet that is all it is, isn't it? And what you accord me with a laugh, without trace of a regret, this trivial sacrifice you make for a still more trivial caprice, is one you refuse to the only woman who loves you, the only woman you love!

The sound of a carriage is heard.

Chavigny   But who, Madame, can have told you all this?

Mme de Léry Speak softly, Monsieur! Here she is. Arriving in the same carriage that must take me home. I have no time to point the moral for you. You are an honest man at heart, and your heart will teach it you. If you notice that your Mathilde's eyes are red, wipe away her tears with this little purse. They are already well-acquainted. Your good and faithful little wife spent two weeks making it. Adieu. Today you may resent my conduct, but tomorrow you may feel more friendly towards me. And, believe me, friendship is worth more than a caprice. But if you simply must have an adventure, why, here's Mathilde: you can award yourself an enchanting one tonight. I hope it will help you to forget this other one, which no one in the world, not even Mathilde herself, will ever hear of.

Mathilde *comes in.* **Mme de Léry** *goes to greet her and kisses her.* **Monsieur de Chavigny** *looks at them, approaches and takes from his wife's head* **Mme de Léry**'s *spray of flowers, which he returns to her, saying:*

Chavigny Forgive me, Madame, but she shall hear of it. And I shall never forget that if there's beauty in wisdom, there's wisdom in beauty too.

Printed in the United States
69281LVS00001B/20